Performance-Based Management for Police Organizations

Paul E. O'Connell
Iona College

Frank Straub
Commissioner of Public Safety, City of White Plains, NY

WAVELAND PRESS, INC.

Long Grove, Illinois

The views and opinions expressed are those of the authors, and do not necessarily represent those of the City of White Plains, or any other party.

For information about this book, contact:
Waveland Press, Inc.
4180 IL Route 83, Suite 101
Long Grove, IL 60047-9580
(847) 634-0081
info@waveland.com
www.waveland.com

CONTENTS

PREFACE

In 1985, New York Mets manager Davey Johnson shocked the baseball world by moving a personal computer into his team's clubhouse for the purpose of informing his on-the-field decisions. The press mocked this use of technology, as did his peers who felt that intuition and years of experience were the only true means of achieving success. Baseball had a long history of strong personalities and a strong culture that was reluctant to accept innovation, particularly if it involved reliance on something other than a manager's personal expertise and instinct. Forget the technology; let the better man win. This attitude changed abruptly in 1986 when Davey Johnson's team won the World Series. Today, baseball managers at every level, across the world, utilize computer-generated, real-time data not only to plan but also to direct the players while they are actually playing the game.

During this same period, personal computers made their way into police stations across the United States—sometimes as a result of a planned technological advance, other times solely due to the desire of forward-thinking administrators. Rather than placing the data in some remotely located storage facility, it was now housed in the field commands where it was easily accessible. Just like in baseball, some "old-time" police managers still lament about the changing world. Most police administrators, however, recognize that this new technology is an asset that will support police operations while facilitating an entirely new way of looking at this thing we call "policing." This book is about that change in thinking, a dramatic shift in approach that has transformed U.S. policing.

The role of the police is not simple, nor is it static. Progressive police departments continuously refine their missions making themselves into more complex and sophisticated organizations dedicated to community service, public safety, crime prevention and law enforcement. Following the terrorist attacks on September 11, 2001, police leaders shifted considerable resources to counterterrorism and intelligence operations in order to prevent future attacks. The devastation wrought by hurricane Katrina challenged police officials to rethink their homeland security programs and to build the capacity to anticipate and respond to natural as well as man-made disasters. A recent resurgence of violent crime has police officials questioning how to address multiple complex tasks, anticipate new challenges, and continue to deliver high quality police services.

As the police role expands and becomes more complex it becomes critically important that police leaders make decisions as systematically as possible—weighing alternative strategies, assembling information on the advantages and disadvantages of each decision, and estimating the costs and benefits of their actions. Police leaders must develop a corporate strategy that helps them think about how their environment is likely to change, how they can exploit opportunities and respond to challenges, and what investments undertaken now will strengthen their positions in the future. Police leaders must become entrepreneurs, leaders willing to take on risk to create new organizations that exploit innovative processes and technology in order to generate value for their communities.

To effect change, police leaders must clearly define their goals and objectives. They need to ensure that progress on those goals and objectives is measured, and they need to frame everything they do in terms of that mission and those results. On the day New York City Mayor Rudolph Giuliani announced that Bill Bratton would be his police commissioner, Bratton made this promise: "We will fight for every house in this city. We will fight for every street. We will fight for every borough. And we will win" (Bratton, 1998, p. xi). Having declared that the New York City Police Department would reduce crime and restore order, Bratton built a leadership team that shared his vision and commitment. He gave the department's operating units (precinct commanders) the responsibility of developing and implementing strategies to target illegal guns, drug activity, youth and domestic violence, and quality of life crimes. Bratton guided the department's crime control strategies and monitored their results using computerized crime statistics and crime maps during intensive management meetings (Compstat).

Bratton's remarkable success in reducing crime and reengineering the NYPD have been repeated by him in Los Angeles and by other police leaders who have embraced performance-based management in communities such as Lowell, Massachusetts; Providence, Rhode Island; and White Plains, New York. The use of performance-based management systems has helped police leaders and other public officials build agile organizations that anticipate challenges, build capacity, and consistently deliver high quality police services.

At an education summit in 1988, remarks by Louis V. Gerstner, Jr. (then president of American Express, later chief executive officer of IBM) included what he dubbed the Noah Principle: "No more prizes for predicting rain. Prizes only for building the arks." This epigrammatic expression has been repeated often to illustrate the necessity to devise a workable strategy plus measures of success for every vision. Gerstner is also credited with the phrase "people respect what you inspect." We believe that, as the police role becomes more complex and sophisticated, performance-based management systems will be critical to building organizations that are capable of building arks.

INTRODUCTION

Over the past fifteen years, many different initiatives have been undertaken in the United States at the federal, state, and local levels to ensure that public service agencies and their personnel are effective and accountable in fulfilling the needs of the general public. The movement, known today as "performance-based management," first developed in the federal system but has now spread to virtually every level and corner of public service. The U. S. Government Performance and Results Act (GPRA) of 1993 made funding for federal agencies contingent on the development of strategic plans that included clear and measurable outcomes and the collection and use of performance data to justify budget allocations (Simeone, Carnevale, & Millar, 2005). Today, state and local police officials face similar challenges to those faced by federal administrators several years ago (Moynihan, 2006; Melkers & Willoughby, 2005).

In its most common usage, performance-based management includes concepts such as performance monitoring, performance measurement, strategic planning, and total quality management (TQM) (Simeone et al., 2005). Police managers today must not only understand the demands associated with this perspective on public management but also must continually meet those demands. Specifically, they must be able to identify exactly what their programs or services are intended to accomplish and then demonstrate their relative success in achieving those goals. This applies to all police agencies, not simply the nation's largest departments.

This text is designed to provide practitioners and students of police management with a clear and understandable resource that explains both the purpose and practice of performance-based policing. It will examine modern management techniques currently employed by many of this

1

nation's most forward-thinking and effective police agencies. It will explain and analyze these techniques and practices, place them in historical context, and provide the reader with a workable blueprint for incorporating these techniques into the day-to-day operations of a police organization of virtually any size. It will provide the reader with a firsthand account of how these changes were successfully incorporated into the management structure of a public safety department in a typical U.S. city (White Plains, New York). It will also highlight the various challenges that are likely to be encountered by any agency or official seeking to adopt these techniques and practices.

Some readers might mistakenly conclude that the term *performance-based management* (hereafter we will use the acronym PBM) refers only to the process of measuring outputs for the purpose of performing audits and inspections. The term, as it is used in this text, refers to the process of using accurate, real-time data as a basis for operational and long-range strategic decision making. In other words, rather than using data for retrospective analysis and record keeping, managers are using it to "steer the ship." Data are being used not only to record where crime is occurring but also to predict where it will occur and to measure the relative effectiveness of the police response (see, e.g., Gendar & Katz, 2005). PBM systems can be used by police managers to communicate "what works and what doesn't, speeding both the uptake of effective practices and the discard of ineffective ones" (Metzenbaum, 2006, p. 8).

The distinguishing characteristic of this process is a "system of use." In other words, this new type of performance measurement system must include and be driven by an effective mechanism for management. Measurement or reporting alone is simply not sufficient.

> Success in setting and attaining appropriate performance goals depends upon structures and processes designed to involve unions and empower front line staff, as well as supervisors and middle managers, in ways that utilize their knowledge, problem-solving abilities and desire to excel in serving the public. Implementing such a model involves the transformation of a performance measures *reporting* system into a comprehensive performance *management* system with alignment between the goals and the performance of the organization. (Plant, Agocs, Brunet-Jailly, & Douglas, 2005, p. 6; emphasis added)

This text describes a system of use that has been successful in a variety of public service settings (O'Connell, 2001b). It is, for all intents and purposes, essentially the same as the PBM system used by numerous successful private corporations to "encourage personal accountability, give employees a deeper understanding of business performance and foster collaboration by putting people on the same page when making decisions" (Charan, 2006, p. 61). In addition to managing performance, such a system also has value in terms of knowledge management and increased organizational learning. Police organizations should have no difficulty developing and using such a system, provided it is properly designed and understood.

PBM systems can certainly be useful in terms of performing an economic analysis of police operations. The purpose of such measurement is not, however, solely for the purpose of cutting costs. Rather, the purpose is to record and be able to demonstrate relative effectiveness, to avoid making anecdotal, qualitative assessments of organizational performance based solely on opinion (Drake & Simper, 2004). Police managers are expected to demonstrate organizational "success," and the adage "you can't manage what you don't measure" offers sage advice.

Adoption of this method of management entails a fundamental change in behavior and the necessity for enhanced technological capabilities. It requires that the organization make "a commitment to quantitative, fact-based analysis" (Davenport, 2006, p. 100). Some agencies are simply not willing to make this commitment. Rather, they are content to maintain the operational status quo and to address issues by reacting only as the need arises. This approach is, unfortunately, consistent with the traditional hierarchical and bureaucratic form of policing that developed from the paramilitary model. Such organizations fail to recognize the ongoing dynamics of change and do a disservice to their agency, its personnel, and the public they serve. Annette Davies and Robyn Thomas (2003) recommend a "move from a largely hierarchical, formalized [management] approach with an emphasis on mistake avoidance, caution and systematic rule application to one where the values of innovation, enterprise, management and problem solving are paramount" (p. 682).

Simply stated, modern policing entails getting the information you need when you need it and using it to inform management and operations. Real-time feedback fosters real-time decisions that enable the organization to maximize effectiveness, minimize mistakes, and make "on the fly" adjustments (such as resource allocation, training, etc.) as necessary. A PBM system can help an organization discover hidden patterns and relationships among data, increase overall effectiveness, capitalize on unexpected opportunities, and transform itself from a merely capable organization into a highly effective one (Meyerson, 2001).

Every law enforcement agency has its own unique culture, history, and set of organizational challenges. Nevertheless, they all function in accordance with certain fundamental principles. Much can be gained from a thoughtful review of performance-enhancing business practices and the experiences of successful police organizations.

This text is intended to serve as a resource. It is designed to provide the reader with a deeper understanding of this model of police management and an insight into how organizational learning can be harnessed to enhance both productivity and accountability.

ORGANIZATIONAL STRUCTURE IN POLICE ORGANIZATIONS
TRADITIONAL RESISTANCE TO CHANGE

There is a vast body of literature that exists on the topic of police management and the traditional resistance that police organizations have toward change. This chapter will streamline that information, present it in a clear, direct, and understandable manner, and provide a context for the state of policing in the United States prior to the dramatic reforms of the early 1990s.

The Trouble with Bureaucracies

Any examination of the topic of police administration and management necessarily entails a brief discussion of the nature and purpose of bureaucracies. Indeed, the police organization, due to its paramilitary nature, is often cited as the quintessential example of a modern bureaucracy.

The bureaucratic model, originally described by Max Weber, incorporates the concepts of hierarchy, span of control, "precision, speed, unambiguity, knowledge of files, continuity, discretion, strict subordination, reduction of friction and of material and personal costs" (Presthus, 1965, p. 5). Weber spells out in considerable detail a "highly rational structure" with numerous advantages that make it, in his view, technically superior to any other form of organization (Etzioni, 1964, p. 53). For many decades, Weber's model has been extremely useful for public administrators and students of large organizations. However, many of his most basic concepts have been challenged for failing to incorporate the more emotional and psychological dimensions of human work organizations. In other words, Weber's model is often viewed as being too impersonal. "Organizations are, after all, made up of people" (Perrow, 1970, p. 2).

Others agree that Weber's model is far from perfect. "Weber's analysis provides a good beginning, but it has serious limitations. . . . Weber deals almost exclusively with the formal, manifest functions of bureaucracy and gives little attention to their unanticipated consequences, both functional and dysfunctional" (Presthus, 1965, p. 6). Many specific dysfunctions that are associated with the model have been well documented in academic literature. Individuals (i.e., citizens) who are subjected to large, impersonal governmental agencies begin to feel disenfranchised and become disillusioned with bureaucratic processes.

> These individuals have rejected the image of public bureaucracy as an effective, equitable, and responsive problem-solving mechanism. In long-range terms, the application of the rigid, impersonal side of the bureaucracy has resulted in a steady compilation of perceived losses by an expanding segment of the body politic; such losses can never be offset by any subsequent incremental gains as long as the allocation and control processes are maintained within the same structural framework. (Gawthrop, 1971, p. 89)

Critics fault the bureaucratic model for its inability to provide for the emotional welfare of employees. Louis Gawthrop (1971) uses the term "synergy" to describe the process of interpersonal relationships whereby an individual, in pursuit of his/her own self-interests, enhances the self-interests of others. He suggests that bureaucracies stifle the development of synergy, and he identifies the suppressive nature of the traditional hierarchical model as the primary factor inhibiting the development of a psychologically healthy individual (p. 103). Other criticisms have pulled no punches.

> Bureaucracies have been described as systems designed by a genius to be run by idiots. . . . In the soul of the bureaucratic machine there lurks a control freak. (Osborne & Plastrik, 1997, p. 17)

Barry Bozeman (2000) details particular problems associated with "red tape," which he describes as "rules, regulations, and procedures that remain in force and entail a compliance burden for the organization but have no efficacy for the rules' functional object" (p. 283). He suggests that there are two distinct manifestations of red tape: rules that are "born bad" (i.e., red tape from their very inception) and rules that have "gone bad" over time. Red tape is identified as a significant barrier to innovation and responsiveness, particularly in the field of policing.

Charles Perrow (1972) contends that the criticisms of bureaucracy generally fall into two categories: (1) Bureaucracies are inflexible, inefficient, uncreative, and unresponsive in times of rapid change; and (2) bureaucracies stifle the spontaneity, freedom, and self-realization of their employees. He also suggests that "the sins generally attributed to bureaucracy are either not sins at all or are consequences of the failure to bureaucratize sufficiently" (p. 6). Perrow does identify several "bureaupathologies" and explains that the bureaucratic model generally fails "when rapid changes in some of the organizational tasks are required" (p. 7). He contends that bureaucracies are established to deal primarily with stable and routine tasks; the division of labor is established accordingly. Once unforeseen events occur, the preexisting structures fail to react quickly enough: "Where the environment changes too rapidly to be controlled or compensated for, and where tasks are too ill-defined or too variable to permit maximum specialization, a high degree of bureaucracy or structure is not possible" (Perrow, 1970, pp. 178–179).

David Osborne and Peter Plastrik (1997) note: "Bureaucracies often have multiple, sometimes conflicting, missions; few face direct competition or experience the consequences of poor or mediocre performance; in fact, few actually measure their performance; and fewer still are accountable to their customers" (p. 12). This is particularly problematic in the field of policing, where rapid change, lack of competition, and a vague organizational mission often lead to mediocrity.

Change is inevitable, rapid, dramatic, and unpredictable. Many institutions, not just police organizations, have developed and organized around a core presumption of the status quo. This presumption is often unstated but is nonetheless quite real. Many organizations apparently believe that they can define and control their own realities. Unfortunately, this is impossible in a rapidly changing world.

> The information revolution, the globalization of economies, the proliferation of events that undermine all our certainties, the collapse of the grand ideologies, the arrival of the CNN society which transforms us into an immense, planetary village—all these shocks have overturned the rules of the game and suddenly turned yesterday's organizations into antiques. (Serieyx, 1993, pp. 14–15).

Change is often resisted not only by organizations but also by the people working within them. Perrow (1972) notes "certain tendencies among workers towards conservatism and self-protective behavior" (p. 39; see also R. Kuhn, 1993; Medina, 1982; Osborne & Plastrik, 1997.). The inherent nature of a bureaucracy alters the personalities of those working within the organization. As a general rule, risk taking and creativity are not encouraged within bureaucracies. Once fully established, the social structure of bureaucracy is very difficult to dislodge. This entrenchment does not bode well for would-be police reformers.

Despite the foregoing criticisms, a growing body of research and literature has developed with regard to the more positive efforts of large bureaucratic organizations to engage in planned change (i.e., to substantially adapt or innovate). Recent literature suggests that decentralized decision making can increase the effectiveness of bureaucratic organizations, such as police departments, that face constantly changing circumstances. A decentralized organization can

> take . . . advantage of the knowledge of its workers, enabling it to adjust quickly to local circumstances. It is most effective when circumstances vary in different areas of organizational responsibility and over time, as is the case in most urban police departments. (Maltz, Gordon, & Friedman, p. 144)

Many scholars agree that bureaucracies can, and often do, change and adapt. Perrow (1970) explains that bureaucratization is not a dichotomous variable but is actually a continuum or scale.

> Actually, of course, the terms bureaucratic and non-bureaucratic are only crude extremes. Not only might there be many shades of gray between the two, but . . . there may be alternative forms which are not even on that continuum or line running from bureaucracy to non-bureaucracy. More important . . . is the possibility of using both types of structure in the same organization. (p. 68)

Therefore, organizations may become more or less bureaucratic over time, depending on their goals, functions, etc. Perrow's concept of a "mixed model" raises several obvious problems related to coordination, but it has the potential to inform administrators and students of organizations of the possibilities of successful planned change efforts within large bureaucratic organizations. Perrow (1972) speaks of the continued "viability of the bureaucratic model" and suggests that it will "remain the dominant mode of organization" (p. 171).

> Every organization of any significant size is bureaucraticized to some degree or, to put it differently, exhibits more or less stable patterns of behavior based upon a structure of roles and specialized tasks. Bureaucracy, in this sense, is another word for structure. (Perrow, 1970, p. 50)

This should come as good news to police administrators since, for a variety of reasons such as civil service laws and the rank structure, police organizations will always be bureaucracies. Police organizations can become modified bureaucracies though and thereby deal more effectively with change.

Perrow (1970) argues that bureaucracies can indeed change, improve quality, and learn to react quickly and effectively to a changing environment. He explains that, "Many [positive] . . . changes can be readily incorporated into the bureaucratic organization—such an organization is not inflexible . . . a bureaucracy can accommodate much superficial change without altering its structure" (pp. 60, 64). In sum, he claims that the skeletal framework of bureaucracy can continue to exist within a modern organization, provided internal processes are developed to plan for, and react to, unforeseen events and circumstances.

Others agree that the bureaucratic model will continue to exist, provided internal mechanisms exist that allow these organizations to detect changes in their environments and to react accordingly.

> Some arguments for continued forms of bureaucracy in the public sector exist, primarily in response to appropriate needs for control and efficiency. However, . . . organizations are moving toward forms of flatter hierarchies, decentralized decision making, permeable boundaries, empowerment, self-organizing units, and so forth. (Battalino, Beutler, & Shani, 1996, p. 26)

As Perrow (1970) notes, "The solution is not to do away with rules and specialists and routinization and mechanization. The answer is to continuously make these tendencies serve the ends you value most" (p. 59).

Perhaps the most provocative argument for the continued viability of the bureaucratic model relates to the possibility of incorporating more responsive management processes directly into the preexisting bureaucratic structure. In other words, the bureaucratic model should be revised but not completely rejected. Gervace Bushe and Abraham Shani (1988) theorize that organizational change interventions based on a "sociotechnological-systems-theory-based-design" can be used to operate parallel to formal structure and permit the advantages of learning-, values-, and/or process-based change while retaining the original form. Parallel structures also "permit change at different rates, allowing for evaluative and corrective components" (Battalino et al., 1996, p. 26).

In sum, it is possible to make necessary alterations, yet maintain the traditional structure of many bureaucratic organizations. Such alterations, however, necessarily have a significant impact on individuals working within these organizations. Reform efforts of this type typically encounter resistance from an entrenched bureaucratic culture—one that colors the worldview of its members and develops naturally.

> No one set out intentionally to create a bureaucratic culture; it grew up because people experienced bureaucratic government realities. These experiences produced a set of unspoken, often unconscious emotional commitments, expectations, fears, hopes and dreams. Together, these experiences and emotional commitments shaped a set of ideas, assumptions, and attitudes—mental models of reality. (Osborne & Plastrik, 1997, p. 268)

In order to effect significant change in the operating procedures of a traditionally bureaucratic organization, it is necessary to address and to change the existing organizational culture.

Osborne and Plastrik (1997) offer the following advice and present seven "guidelines for leading paradigm shifts."

> To change a culture, you have to change people's paradigms. You will need to change . . . the [following] assumptions: That rank rules; that risk is to be avoided at all costs; that every mistake will be punished;

that decisions must be kicked upstairs. This is extremely difficult, because people cling ferociously to their paradigms. (p. 265)

1. Introduce anomalies and help people perceive them
2. Provide a clearly defined new paradigm
3. Build faith in the new paradigm
4. Help people let go of their old paradigm
5. Give people time in the neutral zone
6. Give people touchstones
7. Provide a safety net. (p. 267)

In addition to organizational culture, other factors may serve as impediments to change, including organizational design and external factors, such as regulatory, political, or social factors (R. Kuhn, 1993; T. Kuhn, 1996). One of the most significant barriers to organizational change is the fact that top-level administrators are often political appointees. Tenured civil servants, who make up the bulk of police personnel, often resist change initiatives and might believe that they can simply give "lip service" to incoming change agents and simply "wait them out" until the next administration arrives in office (often with an entirely new agenda).

These impediments are not insurmountable. A well-designed and executed program of change should be able to shift organizational focus and create innovative mechanisms that will allow a traditional bureaucratic organization to anticipate and react to changing conditions (both internal and external to the organization) As Robert Kuhn (1993) notes: "Large organizations are traditionally non-innovative. Yet there is nothing in largeness that prohibits creativity and innovation. It is possible to balance both creativity and productivity in a large organization" (p. 111).

Police Management

An abundant body of literature exists about the management and operation of police organizations. Much of it focuses on the unique mission and methods of police organizations and efforts undertaken to enhance efficiency and the overall quality of performance.

Maurice Punch (1983) identified a number of internal and external constraints that hinder police organizations. Indeed, he suggested that the "greatest guarantee of civil rights is the inefficiency and creative incompetence of the police organization" (p. xii). He described a deeply entrenched informal culture that exists among police officers and limits productivity. He referred to this innate propensity for the avoidance of work as "easing behavior."

> Police organizations all too frequently reflect the classic deficiencies of public, "not for profit" bureaucracies in the sense of producing leaders

with low managerial competence, lacking vision and administrative skills, largely incapable of formulating and implementing policies, and addicted to formal rules and procedures. (p. xiv)

The need for accurate assessments of police performance does exist. Punch, (1983) identified crime control as the core measure of analysis: the preeminent purpose of the police is to enhance public safety—crime control is what police themselves say they do. While police do engage in other activities, it is not unfair to ask for evidence that the crime-control responsibility is being met. "Failing to evaluate the crime-related results of police action is like not determining whether schools teach children to read" (p. 22).

Police organizations have traditionally "grown like an elemental force of nature, according to half understood forces, rather than as a rationally planned instrument of social effect" (Punch, 1983, p. 26). Police organizations tend to work to improve efficiency rather than to implement true innovation. A number of structural forces enable this resistance to change: a hierarchical chain of command, a unique police culture, and police unions. "The likelihood of achieving significant change seems remote" (p. 99). Dorothy Guyot (1978) concurs, noting that

> there is an impressive list of management problems which are exacerbated by the prevailing rank structure of police departments. Lack of flexibility and lack of incentives . . . are the problems most frequently recognized by police managers. More subtle problems of insularity, blockage of communication and militarism are rarely addressed. (p. 1)

In the last decade, a few police managers have attempted to chip away at the edge of the granite rank structure of their departments with no marked success. The support for the traditional rank structure is so strong within the police subculture that new departments founded with less hierarchic structure undergo metamorphosis to the traditional form.

Police agencies in the United States intentionally placed decision-making power in the hands of headquarters, in an effort to retain control and to decrease the overall level of community involvement in police operations (Reiss, 1992). This meant that field commanders were rarely free to exercise decision-making authority in "traditional" police agencies (see also Corsianos, 2006).

Nevertheless, there were attempts to change. Hans Toch and J. Douglas Grant (1982) describe various programs associated with the organization development (OD) movement that were designed to enhance U.S. policing in the 1970s. As a result of the President's Commission on Law Enforcement and Criminal Justice (1967), a job enrichment model known as team policing was designed, primarily to instill a sense of "pride and of self-importance in doing police work" (p. 191). It was generally believed that such efforts would result in enhanced productivity (Sherman, Milton, & Kelly, 1973; see also Argyris, 1957; French & Bell, 1990). A similar program was implemented by the NYPD but is generally thought to have had little success (Weisburd, Mastrofski, McNally, Greenspan & Willis, 2003). Other attempts to enhance productivity and increase job satisfaction were stymied by one fundamental factor: the structure of police organizations. In a paper entitled *Bending Granite: Attempts to Change the Rank Structure of American Police Departments,* Guyot (1978) argued that "hierarchical structures are particularly ill-suited to police work" (p. 28). By the early 1980s, it appeared that any effort to improve the quality of U.S. policing would necessarily entail reconsideration of such fundamental issues as, "How should police departments be structured?" and "How should the police go about their business?"

In "Broken Windows," James Q. Wilson and George Kelling (1982) advocated a mission for modern police that focused on community disorder and reconnection with the community. Malcolm Sparrow, Mark Moore, and David Kennedy (1992) describe a subtle but clear shift in management style that swept U.S. policing in the 1980s, as administrators sought a "closer, more productive relationship with the cities they served" (p. 114). They recognized this to be a dramatic shift from operational autonomy to reliance on the community. Such a shift is difficult due to the fact that "police departments are typically rigid bureaucracies, fiercely defensive of the status quo. Their considerable institutional momentum stands as a major barrier to change or development" (p. 121).

Sparrow and his colleagues (1992) championed the movement toward a more open-minded and innovative form of policing. They provided a rather straightforward rationale for their beliefs by identifying

> the long denied but inescapable fact that the centralized style of policing relies on a fictitious and entirely inappropriate picture of the operational realities of police work. Police work is not rote: it is varied, unpredictable and full of surprises that cannot be covered by precise rules. (p. 121)

Herman Goldstein (1990) wrote *Problem-Oriented Policing,* perhaps the single most important work with regard to the changing organizational culture of policing in the 1990s. It championed an entirely new approach, one that recognized the extraordinarily complex nature of policing and the "myriad conflicts and incongruities built into the police function" (p. xii). Goldstein criticized the simplistic concern for operating efficiency (i.e., simply responding to incidents and processing cases more quickly). He advocated a more thoughtful and proactive form of inquiry, one that identified underlying problems and systematically drew connections between them (Eck & Spelman, 1987).

Building on the "Broken Windows" theory of policing and previous literature regarding "community policing" techniques (Skogan & Maxfield, 1981; Skolnick & Bayley, 1986), Goldstein (1990) recognized that "the objective in attempting to bring about change is not simply to improve the police, but rather to solve community problems" (p. 179). To do so, he called for "increased regulation, through statutes and ordinances, of conditions that contribute to problems" and "using civil law to control public nuisances, offensive behavior and conditions contributing to crime" (p. 139). By attacking underlying (i.e., criminogenic) conditions, he believed that police officials could achieve significant and long-lasting reductions in the overall crime rate.

The revolutionary new management style for police administrators included the following proposals.

1. Police leaders must articulate the basic values that influence their management techniques and how they approach the police task.

2. Police managers must have a strong commitment to problem solving as the core of policing.

3. Management must promote fundamental changes in the relationships that exist between leadership and the rank and file in a police agency.

Goldstein (1990) called for a flexible management style that would provide a greater degree of freedom to administrators. His recommendations encompassed the entire police organization. He believed that it was necessary to create an entirely new management structure for police organizations—one that was able to detect and respond to subtle changes in the internal and external work environments.

> A whole new dimension must be added to prior research and planning activities. In a rough equivalent to the private sector, it calls for going beyond operational research concerned with efficient ways to produce a product. It extends to developing the ability to access and control the quality of the product, to engage in market research, and to design new products. A centralized planning and research unit could contribute a great deal by providing training to field personnel (in problem-solving) and by monitoring department-wide problem-solving efforts, alert to additional ways in which it might support these efforts. (p. 162)

By the early 1990s, a number of other leading scholars advocated the adoption of corporate strategies and an entrepreneurial approach in police agencies (see, e.g., Bruns, 1989; Moore & Trojanowicz, 1988).

Planned Change/Strategic Management

Modern police managers would be well-advised to consult and become aware of the growing body of scholarly literature in the field of strategic management and planned change (for both the public and private sectors). In fact, many progressive police agencies currently encourage their managers to pursue advanced degrees (such as MBAs or MPAs) and/or include these topics in executive development, or in-service training programs. Several authors of leading works in the field of management suggest that their recommended techniques and approaches could be as easily applied in the public sector as they could in the private sector (e.g., Robertson & Seneviratne, 1995).

Warren Bennis (1978) described the general need for all organizations to have an orderly response to changing environments. He identified three essential steps in the change process: (1) the act of "unfreezing"; (2) "changing"; and (3) "re-freezing" (p. 98). He believed that management systems generally needed to be far more responsive and that they needed to move from a mechanistic to a more organic approach to changing environmental conditions. This fundamental shift in mindset is necessary "when novelty and unfamiliarity in both market situation and technical information become the accepted order of things" (Burns & Stalker, 1961, p. vii). The key here is that management should recognize that change is inevitable. It is therefore better to plan for it than to hope futilely that it won't occur.

Bennis suggested that successful organizations operate as open systems that engage in mutual goal setting and incorporate "the spirit of inquiry as a model for organization" (as cited in Gluckstein & Packard, 1977, p. 46). He viewed planned change efforts as "the critical link between theory and practice, between knowledge and action" (p. 81).

Building on this concept, Peter Senge (1994) suggests that successful organizations engage in systems thinking—a nonlinear approach that focuses on the connected patterns and mutual influence of apparently isolated events. By recognizing the complexity of issues and patterns of interrelationships, Senge believes organizations can avoid myopic and short-term decision making. Systems thinking enables the organization to alter its structure, utilizing modern information technologies to learn and adapt to changing conditions (Davenport, 1993; Drucker, 1995; Fritz, 1996). Moore (1995) explained that such changes would transform public managers from technicians to strategists and create public value as a result.

During the 1990s, there was new interest in the design and implementation of valid, legitimate, and functional performance measures for the public sector (Kravchuk & Schack, 1996; Wholey & Hatry, 1992). This movement was fueled in large part by the Government Performance and Results Act of 1993 (GPRA) and the publication of *Reinventing Government* (Osborne & Gaebler, 1992) The reinventing government movement (as it became known) developed as the public sector analogue to the corporate "business process engineering" movement, which has been described as "one of the most influential management ideas of the 'nineties'" (Case, 1999).

Two essential concepts associated with reengineering are "benchmarking" and the sharing of internal "best practices." Both relate to goal setting and the ongoing quest for continuous improvement in performance; both recognize that valuable lessons can be learned from other organizations and shared throughout the organization (Coe, 1999). These skills, combined with an entrepreneurial mindset, enable the organization to exploit opportunities for success (Morris & Jones, 1999).

By the early 1990s, reinvention was a trend in government agencies and in the business world. Organizations dramatically altered administrative structures and operational processes in order to enhance efficiency and the overall quality of performance. Police administrators soon found themselves utilizing many of the same strategies that were being used successfully in the public sector and in the corporate world. Gradually, the line between "public" and "corporate" business practices began to blur. Police managers began to avail themselves of skills and technologies employed by business managers. Lee Bolman and Terrence Deal (2003) explain that

> the bulk of work in organization theory has focused almost exclusively on either the private *or* the public sector, but not both. We think this is a mistake. Managers need to understand similarities and differences among all types of organizations. The public and private sectors increasingly inter-penetrate one another. (p. xvii; emphasis in original)

This interpenetration suggests that a thoughtful police administrator can now avail him or herself of additional management tools to enhance the organization's capacity to perform its core business function, crime fighting.

Perhaps the most notable structured change initiative was the reengineering program undertaken by the New York City Police Department during the Giuliani administration (which will be discussed further in chapter 5). The Department of Public Safety in White Plains, New York, was another notable success. The case study below describes that agency's move from a traditional, hierarchical organization to one built on performance-based management, continuous learning, innovation, and improvement.

The City of White Plains, NY, Department of Public Safety

The rivalry between the police and fire services is one of the most "enduring fault-lines in municipal government" (Buntin, 2005, p. 46). For example, New York City's police and fire departments have circled each other for years, competing over the delivery of specialized emergency and rescue services during a variety of incidents. According to Patrick O'Hara (2005), this "cultural divide" is based, in part, on function—police officers fight crime and firefighters fight fires. In addition, disparate salaries plus the competition for limited municipal funds and resources place the departments in direct competition. The system creates "an adversarial position and if you've got a culture that lets it flourish, it continues to go and go" (p. 46).

The 2001 attacks on the World Trade Center and Pentagon caused practitioners, scholars, and policy makers to question whether existing public safety models offered adequate responses to crisis or routine emergencies. For example, Jerome Hauer, former director of the New York City Office of Emergency Management (OEM), argued that the OEM represented the best solution to crisis response and police-fire rivalries. In Phoenix, Arizona, police and fire officials staff a unified Homeland Security Bureau, responding together to emergencies on a daily basis and training and preparing for acts of terrorism or other crises. In Charlotte-Mecklenberg, North Carolina, officials formed "ALERT" (Advanced Local Emergency Response Team), composed of police officers, firefighters, emergency medical personnel, the FBI, the county medical examiner, and the Carolinas Medical Center. In Seattle, Washington, police and fire officials meet quarterly to develop and implement domestic preparedness programs. This case study examines another model of police-fire cooperation and collaboration, the "public safety agency," in which both professions work under a single commissioner. It also explores how the model evolved in the City of White Plains, New York, and the role of PBM in building the department.

Established in 1916, the White Plains Department of Public Safety brought the city's police and fire services together under a single commissioner. However, for decades, both bureaus continued to function autonomously, worked out of their own headquarters, utilized separate communication systems, and defined success individually. The commissioner provided administrative, budgetary, and disciplinary oversight to the organization. The department functioned in this manner until the late 1990s, when several issues emerged that became the catalyst for change.

While other cities hired more police officers and firefighters in response to growth and increased demand for service, police and fire staffing in White Plains remained unchanged despite significant residential and commercial growth (Liebson, 2001). Police manpower issues were further exacerbated as police officers transferred to other departments that offered higher salaries, different work schedules, and better opportunities (Liebson, 1999). Firefighters attempted to separate the departments and to have their own commissioner appointed, in part because of staff reductions that caused apparatus to be taken out of service, perceived unequal status in the combined department, and accumulating labor-management issues (Liebson, 2002).

In July 2002, Frank Straub (co-author of this text) was appointed as public safety commissioner. At the time, the department's senior managers were unfocused, comfortable with the status quo, resistant to change, and risk adverse. The organization looked inward, and internal communication was vertical. Policies and procedures were highly restrictive, which led to low organizational performance and poor morale. Although police and fire personnel were generally highly qualified and displayed a solid work ethic, they were constrained by the organizational environment. Even as the department was confronted with changing environmental conditions, it hunkered down and persisted in familiar behaviors—behavior consistent with traditional bureaucratic organizations (Wilson, 1989).

To build an effective public safety department, the business practices and the mindset of employees had to change. First, police officers and firefighters had to enjoy equal status. Second, the entire department had to focus on reducing crime and improving safety, as well as enhancing the department's domestic preparedness capabilities. Third, employees at all levels of the department had to be authorized to take risks, decision making had to be pushed down toward the field level, and all personnel needed to be held accountable for achieving results. According to Osborne and Plastrik (1997), culture begins to change when a leader visibly signals a break with the existing culture. In fact, unless leaders proclaim and demonstrate their total, sustained commitment to changing the culture, little is likely to happen.

The night the commissioner was sworn in, he went to the midnight roll call. The next day, he attended police roll calls and visited the city's firehouses. He responded to fires, major accidents, and significant police incidents regardless of the shift or day of the week in order to meet as many employees as possible and to identify the issues and ideas they thought were most important. Personal interactions helped the commissioner develop an understanding of the department as well as the people running it. By actively eliciting operational knowledge from police officers and firefighters, the intellectual foundation for the change effort was established, and the commissioner gained the support he needed for it to succeed (Ostroff, 2006). Personal encounters provided opportunities to tell police officers, firefighters, and civilian employees that the department was going to change. The interactions personalized the message and encouraged and authorized police officers and firefighters to engage in the process (Bossidy & Charan, 2002).

To address the perceived inequity between the police and fire bureaus, two deputy commissioners were hired: a former police commander and a nationally recognized fire and emergency services professional. The commissioner attended and completed the basic firefighter's training program at the county fire center. He moved the offices of both the police and the fire chief to the same floor as his own. Historically, the police chief's office was on the floor below the commissioner, and the fire chief's office was in a firehouse located across town. The message was twofold—both enjoyed equal footing and both were part of an integrated management team.

The commissioner also addressed issues that directly affected rank-and-file police officers and firefighters. Police vehicles were redesigned. The department purchased bicycles and deployed them in the central business district. Police officers were sent for outside training at the Federal Bureau of Investigation's National Academy and the Police Executive Research Forum's Senior Management Institute for Police. Firefighters and police officers were also sent to various federal homeland security training facilities to develop expertise in responding to potential terrorist attacks. When possible, police officers and firefighters trained together in order to build relationships, cultural appreciation, and technical expertise.

Historically, firefighters did not participate in the design of fire apparatus and were critical of the "substandard" vehicles they operated. Working with the union, an apparatus committee was established. The apparatus committee designed two new engines and a technical rescue vehicle. Using private donations, the fire bureau purchased defibrillators and other equipment. A certified first responder (emergency medicine) training program was begun for all members of the fire bureau.

To bolster the department's domestic preparedness capabilities a police emergency service unit and a fire technical rescue unit were created. Clear response protocols were established, and personnel were cross-trained. When appropriate, the units responded together to emergencies. Today, both units are part of the Unified Special Operations Command (USOC), which is led by a police lieutenant and a fire deputy chief. USOC operates out of a former firehouse.

Enthusiastic and talented personnel were identified—police officers and firefighters who had tried at various times in the past to suggest or make changes. As opportunities presented themselves, they were moved into key positions and promoted. For example, a police lieutenant who was a midnight tour commander and recently elected as union vice president was asked to become the commissioner's chief of staff. The lieutenant, now a deputy commissioner, resigned his union position, became the chief of staff, and provided invaluable guidance regarding the inner workings of the department as well as contractual issues. A recently promoted sergeant was tasked with developing a "neighborhood conditions unit" that would provide field training for new police officers and also address citywide crime patterns. Under his leadership, the unit succeeded in both aspects of its mission.

During the first year, the commissioner's efforts focused on breaking down barriers, building trust, identifying key players, and mobilizing support for change. A performance-based management approach was adopted to ensure efficiency and accountability. The system was based on the Compstat system first developed by the New York City Police Department in 1994. The use of Compstat in White Plains is unique in that it includes the participation of both police and fire commanders.

Previously, the department, like many public agencies, gathered information but did not use it to inform strategic planning or daily operations. Shortly after joining the department, the new management team began studying what data was being collected, what data was needed, and how it could be used to inform decision making and operations. Early efforts met with tremendous resistance from managers and the "in-house" IT sergeant who believed the system either would not or could not produce what was needed. Subsequently, a police officer was identified to "mine" data and present it in a timely, accurate, and useable format.

Regardless of the venue in which it is used, the Compstat process has two distinct components—the gathering and analysis of statistical data and the "meeting." The analysis of statistical data informs decision making by operations personnel as well as senior and executive staff. Data analysis provides the basis for the development and implementation of strategies that are consistent with current and emerging issues. Further, by continuously collecting and analyzing information, the commissioner and his staff are able to monitor the progress, success, and/or failure of new initiatives.

The second part of the Compstat process, the meeting, is the most visible component. The meeting requires police and fire commanders to be knowledgeable about critical issues and to accomplish measurable results. Therefore, prior to each weekly meeting a detailed statistical (Compstat) report is distributed to each of the participants and posted on the department's intranet (see appendix). It is important to note that, during the early stages of the White Plains experience, police commanders balked at the suggestion that fire officials would be present during discussions of investigations, crime patterns, and performance issues. However, over time the meetings became the foundation for interbureau problem solving, provided a mechanism for department-wide learning, improved operations, performance, and accountability. Compstat meetings challenged police and fire commanders to think outside the box, to question the status quo, and to participate in the change process. Each participant, regardless of rank, was encouraged to think of new ways of doing business in order to achieve results.

Weekly Compstat meetings also provide an open forum in which to evaluate the success or lack of success regarding initiatives, strategies, and tactics that have been implemented. Discussions are direct and require every participant to be familiar with specific incidents, patterns, and trends and to articulate cogent action plans. Each participant is held accountable for achieving results regardless of the unit or bureau to which he/she is assigned. The message is clear—poor performance must be corrected and good performance will be rewarded. The process is not without its casualties. Veteran police and fire commanders have retired because they were either unable or unwilling to meet the demands of the department's new business model. Other commanders, however, have met the challenge and excelled.

This PBM approach has played a direct role in the department's efforts to reduce crime, fires, and motor vehicle accidents. From 2002 to 2005, Part 1 crimes have decreased by 33%. Within the same reporting period, crimes against persons decreased by 32% and property crimes by 33%. Arrests increased by 69% and traffic enforcement, the issuance of vehicle and traffic summonses, by 81%. The dramatic increase in traffic enforcement led to a 6.4% reduction in motor vehicle accidents despite a significant increase in traffic volume. Similar results were achieved in the fire bureau as increased life safety inspections, public education, and consultations with businesses and homeowners led to a 17% reduction in structure fires. The fire bureau also increased its response to medical emergencies and motor vehicle accidents by 62%.

Statistical data is not the only measure of success. A number of comprehensive "public safety" strategies were developed during or as a result of Compstat meetings. At one early meeting, a police commander described a number of calls that revealed overcrowding and other potentially dangerous housing conditions. The fire chief volunteered to send firefighters to the scene to document the conditions, to summon violators, and to install smoke detectors if appropriate. Police officers are now trained to recognize potential fire violations and firefighters to recognize the signs of gang or other criminal activity and report them to the police. The result was the creation of a safe housing task force comprised of various city agencies that now responds to unsafe housing locations, brings coordinated administrative actions against landlords, and works to resolve life safety issues. During another meeting, police and fire commanders identified a number of quality of life issues that affected the central business district. Subsequently, police and fire personnel met with pub and restaurant owners to develop emergency evacuation plans, discuss underage drinking, designer drugs, and other public safety concerns. By leveraging the resources of the police and fire bureaus, the department has been able to address significant issues (e.g. unsafe housing, bar overcrowding, emergency evacuation) and prevent tragedies that have confronted other communities.

This system is also used to process and monitor internal performance indicators such as overtime, sick time, and employee injuries. Since 2003, fire sick time has been reduced by 38%. By monitoring sick time and employee injuries, administrators can anticipate scheduling and other operational consequences. Managers are held accountable for understanding the fiscal implications of their operations and for deploying their personnel and resources in a cost effective and strategic manner.

These meetings have given executive staff the capacity to remain fully conversant with the specific problems their personnel face. They provide a forum in which police and fire field commanders can openly discuss crime, life safety, and other issues with executives and their peers. At the same time, the meetings provide an opportunity for the department's executives to assess the strengths and weaknesses of individual commanders as well as their ability to develop and implement effective strategies. Firefighters and police officers have gained an appreciation for each others' cultures, abilities, and limitations. Daily interaction, cross-training, and communication have established a public safety department built on mutual respect and equal status.

Performance-based management played an important role in transforming a department organized around separate professions and cultures into one that is organized and managed for results, rewards risk-taking and initiative. In other words, it has created an entirely new culture, derived from the core mission of providing for public safety. It has also provided a catalyst for continuous learning, collaboration and cooperation, and restructuring or reengineering to remove impediments to high performance.

The performance-based management model should continue to play a critical role throughout the coming years as the business model of public safety organizations continues to evolve. Its capacity to address the many challenges associated with a changing work environment (both internal and external to the organization) suggests that it will continue to be a useful tool for many years to come.

A HISTORY OF THE DEVELOPMENT OF CRIME ANALYSIS CAPABILITIES IN AMERICAN POLICE ORGANIZATIONS

In order to understand the philosophy and methods of performance-based police management more thoroughly, it is useful to examine the history of crime analysis and the development of information-based deployment techniques. This historical perspective helps us appreciate how police management techniques have developed over the years (albeit gradually) and how continually evolving information technologies have affected police work. The historical context illustrates how the initial use of computerized data management systems evolved from a more efficient form of record keeping (essentially a computerized file cabinet) into a more proactive tool that could assist the police in forecasting, planning, and deploying resources.

The Development of Crime Analysis Practices in American Police Agencies

Since their inception, police agencies have tracked and analyzed crime.

Every organization whether it is a private corporation or a government agency must operate on the basis of information—accurate, up-to-date

> information that it can get quickly on a need basis for day-to-day man-
> agement and day-to-day operations. It must be in a form that can also
> be used at both the management level and at the planning level. The
> police are no exception. (Reed, 1980, p. 43; citation omitted)

At the beginning of the twentieth century, August Vollmer wrote an
essay entitled "The Police Beat," which included the following assertion.

> On the assumption of regularity of crime and similar occurrences, it is
> possible to tabulate these occurrences by areas within a city and thus
> determine the points which have the greatest danger of such crimes
> and what points have the least danger. (cited in Groff & LaVigne,
> 2001, p. 146)

Vollmer was the first to adapt the English technique of systematic classification of known-offender modus operandi to policing in the United
States. He is also credited with being the "originator of the modern police
records system, beat analysis based upon the examination of recorded
calls for service, and the concept of pin or spot mapping to visually identify areas where crime and service calls are concentrated" (Reinier et al.,
1977, p. 1-2). Pin mapping served as a simple means of illustrating where
the efforts of law enforcement agencies were needed, and whether or not
they were having any measurable effect. Typically, pins representing a
crime were placed on a map to note crime clusters (distinguished, perhaps, by different colored pins), the land use characteristics of the location
(i.e., near a park or school), and so on (Maltz et al., 1991, p.24).

Pin maps, however, have numerous shortcomings. As the characteristics of the crime or the locations multiply, or as crimes proliferate, the density and complexity of the map can become unmanageable. Sometimes,
even if properly prepared and maintained, "the amount of information on
a pin map can be so extensive that it defies easy analysis" (Illinois Criminal
Justice Information Authority, 1987, p. 1). Pin maps also take time to prepare, they are difficult to maintain, labor intensive, and static (i.e., cannot
be queried) (Harries, 1999). As technology evolved, police organizations
began to use other methods of improving their methods of analysis.

O. W. Wilson furthered the development of crime analysis by expanding Vollmer's beat analysis techniques to include hazard formulas or
assignment of weighting factors to various categories of crimes and service
calls. He did this to provide a systematic approach to the allocation of
patrol resources. These efforts gradually led to the development of processes designed to determine how to allocate patrol resources among districts and among beats within districts, when and where to patrol, who the
likely suspects of a crime are, which offenses are likely to be solved, and in
general how to serve and protect the community. Wilson described crime
analysis as a function of a police planning division, "with the purpose of
examining daily reports of serious crime to determine locations, times,
particular characteristics, similarities to other criminal incidents, and vari-

ous other characteristics that might assist in identifying specific suspects or patterns of criminal activity" (cited in Reinier et al., 1977, pp. 1-2, 1-3).

Police departments developed statistical methods to analyze criminal incidents by type, area, and/or time. The purpose was to identify trends and to support long-term police planning and action based on crime analysis (Chang, Simms, Makres, & Bodnar, 1979, p. xix.). The ability to predict the exact time and location of future criminal events for short-range purposes proved to be somewhat more difficult. While the prediction of crime potentials for specific targets was viewed as "the ultimate goal of crime analysis," the achievement of such predictions with any degree of accuracy was thought to be virtually impossible.

The rapid development of computer technology through the 1960s greatly enhanced analysis capabilities and motivated U.S. police departments to explore more advanced investigation and forecasting methods. In 1967, the President's Commission on Law Enforcement and the Administration of Justice noted the labor-intensive nature of police work and urged the use of modern technology to help improve deployment procedures. The report indicated that "criminal justice could benefit dramatically from computer-based information systems" and called for the immediate "development of a network designed specifically for its operation" (Challenge of Crime in a Free Society, 1967, p. 599).

In addition to the development of automated crime files, police departments began developing real-time computer systems to provide rapid feedback to queries on stolen cars, warrants, and gun ownership. In 1964, the St. Louis Police Department became the first to establish on-line information retrieval capabilities, "one of the first police information systems in the world" (Reed, 1980, p. 40). Remote terminals were located in district stations. By channeling field inquiries to analysts at base commands, the department linked patrol officers and information by means of the computer.

Visual investigative analysis (VIA) was developed by members of the Los Angeles Police Department during the mid-1960s. VIA defined activities and graphically linked them in order of occurrence (Morris, 1982). VIA was essentially a flow chart to direct and track all aspects of a criminal investigation. This process utilized computers to document particular steps and enhance information retrieval capabilities. By the early 1970s, the California Department of Justice formed a statewide VIA unit and began to provide VIA services to local law enforcement agencies and district attorney's offices. By the early 1980s the concept had spread throughout law enforcement agencies across the country.

Once police agencies were able to retrieve statistical information rapidly, it was obvious that computers could perform a broader function, and possibly support the patrol function. The executive assistant to O. W. Wilson when he was superintendent of the Chicago Police Department, George Gorgol (1966), noted that the department utilized computer technology for the "gathering and reporting of information which [was] required for the proper evaluation of field work," including the analysis of patrol and detective operations in 1966 (p. 4-3). He described a number of statistical reports that were prepared and distributed semiannually, such as the beat workload report, which was a series of seven computer reports analyzing police service for geographical segments of the city. Beat configurations and patrol patterns were established to conform to the needs identified in these reports.

> I feel that we have only scratched the surface in using the capability of electronic computation. To date, the primary interest of police agencies has been in the relief of manual effort involved in the storage and accessibility of large volumes of records and information. In most cases, we have failed to recognize the real power and analytic capability of the computer in accomplishing technical and scientific analysis. Our mental and physical ability to utilize electronic computation to its capacity has lagged far behind computer development. . . . Computers are capable of analyzing crime patterns and of predicting the most probable location of future crimes . . . we can evaluate the probable results of applying new police practices before they are accepted for operational use. (p. 4-6)

The Chicago Police Department utilized the power of the technology to provide "a thick blanket of patrolmen scientifically employed to area of need" (Cawley, 1966, p. A-9).

The establishment and funding of the Law Enforcement Assistance Administration (LEAA) was critical to the further development and implementation of computerized crime analysis systems in the United States. The LEAA *Crime Analysis Operations Manual* called for a "comprehensive effort to plan and evaluate the delivery of patrol services as efficiently as possible" (Reinier et al., 1977, p. 2-1). The computer was a key component of this type of analysis. LEAA's "insistence on the use of analysis in support and evaluation of its grant aid programs . . . stimulated the now-rapid growth of crime analysis" and furthered the practice of computer analysis (p. 1-3).

During the 1970s, the LEAA also contributed by surveying 3,400 law enforcement agencies throughout the United States and found that very few of the surveyed agencies "could be described as being comprehensive or current, or having an effective operational program [of crime analysis]" (Chang et al., 1979, p. xv). Many of the responding agencies were not utilizing computers to any significant degree at the time of the survey. That is not to say that there had been no progress. By the early 1970s, the Los Angeles Police Department pioneered the use of a system of pattern recognition (Maltz et al., 1991). PATRIC (Pattern Recognition for Investigating Crime) derived its data from offense/incident and field interrogation reports. Through a series of programmed sort routines, a PATRIC analyst would compare new offenses, investigator requests, or arrest descriptions against the information in the computer files for possible matches. PATRIC also utilized a flexible data management system for ad hoc information retrieval (Chang et al., 1979, p. 38).

The LEAA worked to develop crime analysis capabilities on a national scale. In 1973, it compiled a *Police Crime Analysis Unit Handbook* that described how to implement such a unit and the benefits to law enforcement agencies through the operation of crime analysis units. The overall purpose of the LEAA was "to help analyze problems encountered by police departments in their day-to-day operations and to provide assistance to police departments to help them 'modernize' their operations to reduce the rising crime rates" (Reed, 1980, p. 24). Departments were encouraged to utilize computers for deployment purposes, as well as for record keeping and computation purposes. Considerable effort was expended to develop crime analysis systems that could support and ultimately help direct both patrol and specific tactical operations.

LEAA prepared a series of manuals on behalf of the Integrated Criminal Apprehension Program (ICAP). The specific manuals comprising the series were the: (1) Crime Analysis Executive Manual; (2) Crime Analysis Systems Manual; (3) Crime Analysis Operations Manual; and (4) Model Records System Manual and Reporting Guides (pp. iii–iv). The ICAP program helped LEAA support projects in local police departments, establishing a formal crime analysis function to aid patrol supervisors in a more structured method of managing the work of officers on the street.

The Santa Cruz (California) Police Department allocated patrol forces based on POSSE (Police On Spot System of Enforcement), its automated manpower allocation system (Chang et al., 1979). It was designed to provide field commanders with "an information/decision matrix to enable manpower deployment decisions, specifically when and where to deploy available resources" and to "provide a feedback capability for evaluating what effect, if any, these decisions had on calls for service" (p. 122). Watch commanders received the information matrix prior to each 28-day report period. The results compiled from previous scheduling and beat assignments allowed commanders to evaluate the effectiveness of the scheduling. Watch commanders were instructed to work with analysts to develop the "master manpower schedule for the 28 day report period" (p. 123).

The POSSE system generated feedback information for decision makers. There were two feedback reports. The first graphically displayed the percentage of patrolmen available hourly against the actual hourly calls-for-service from the preceding report period. The report was generated for each day of the week. The patrol commander could immediately assess how well he had allocated his personnel and if they were under- or over-staffed on certain shifts. The second feedback report was designed to inform decision makers how well the POSSE system forecasted calls-for-service (Chang et al., 1979). The tactical applications of most of the computerized systems in police agencies were initially limited to recording, monitoring, and controlling cases. The POSSE system was noteworthy for its more generalized application to patrol services.

By the early 1970s, U.S. police departments made extensive use of the analysis of patterns of crime and noncrime calls for service for allocating manpower across shifts and patrol cars across beats. Programs funded by NIJ and other agencies resulted in several patrol car allocation models (PCAM) that focused "on departmental administrative and resource allocation matters—such as drawing beat boundaries for equalizing workloads—rather than on offense patterns for investigating, preventing, or deterring crimes" (Maltz et al., 1991, p. 24 citations omitted). During the 1970s, the Portland, Oregon Police Department utilized a computerized system for tactical resource deployment (Chang et al., 1979, pp. 90–93; Richardson & Stout, 1975). The St. Louis police also developed an automatic means of depicting crime graphically during this period. By using an IBM mainframe computer and SYMAP (a mapping program developed at Harvard), the department developed a system that would eventually spread to police departments throughout the United States (Maltz et al., 1991).

Through the 1970s, crime analysis units proliferated to support the deployment of patrol, investigative, crime prevention, and special tactical units. The basic function of the crime analysis unit was to identify, describe, and disseminate information concerning crime patterns and problems. The patrol supervisor would then use this information in developing a tactical response and coordinating the efforts of his/her personnel with those of other units in the department.

> As the primary user of crime analysis products, the patrol supervisor is the key connecting link back to the crime analysis unit. The patrol supervisor can improve the products of the crime analysis unit by explaining the types of information he requires and the form in which it will be most useful to him. (Reinier et al., 1977, p. 1-13)

At the time, many departments used the information only to support the operations of a special tactical unit targeting a specific crime (i.e., residential burglary), although other departments were beginning to use the information to support more proactive patrol deployment.

As departments began to establish crime analysis units, scholars and police administrators were also questioning the efficacy of the police tactic known as random patrol. This was due largely to the somewhat unexpected results of the Kansas City Preventive Patrol Experiment (Kelling, 1974). The relative effectiveness of this method of enforcement was a distinct question from whether the computer could be of assistance in terms of overall police productivity.

> The recent attention given to patrol has increased an overall understanding of the realities and potential of this vital police function. The detection and deterrent values of random, as distinct from directed, preventive patrol have been recently questioned. Random, non-

directed patrol is now seen as a costly strategy with very little benefit to either the department or the community. As a result, police agencies are focusing closer scrutiny on the large amount of unstructured patrol time purportedly dedicated to preventive patrol. Consistently, departments are having great difficulty in defining how this segment of time is expended and for what purposes. (Reinier et al., 1977, p. 2-2)

Because patrol has the largest portion of department resources and because it contributes by far the most to meeting department objectives, small increases in patrol efficiency and effectiveness promise to provide the most significant operational gains for the police department. (p. 2-2)

The architects of the ICAP program recognized that patrol was both the "chief user and principal supplier of crime analysis information" and envisioned a process whereby crime analysis unit interaction with patrol would be a constant process (Reinier et al., 1977). They directed patrol supervisors to take a key role in the program and to take full advantage of the decision-making latitude "available for initiating or influencing change and innovation. This involves constant recognition of opportunities to improve patrol decision making" (p. 2-8). In order for a crime analysis unit to be effective, it must

establish credibility with all patrol users, especially the patrol supervisor. This is accomplished through the analysis unit's provision of timely and accurate crime bulletins to all patrol users, and through the unit's solicitation of feedback from patrol supervisors and line officers on the crime analysis products. (p. 2-8)

Crime analysis information supported decision making on two levels: strategic (policy-oriented decisions made at the highest command levels of the department) and tactical (action-oriented decisions made close to the service delivery level) (Reinier et al., 1977, p. 1-6). Specific deployment decisions could be made for an entire patrol force, or there could be a more short-term focus, such as the particular location and activity of a special tactical unit. Allocation decisions could similarly be made by "determining the necessity for such a unit, its objectives, its size, and its organizational placement—factors that provide the structural framework for the deployment decisions" (p. 1-7).

Despite the significant progress in tactical applications, the computer was not viewed as a panacea.

During the 1960s and 1970s the police [automated] many of their data management, patrol allocation, and patrol dispatching functions. Large amounts of data are [now] in machine readable form. It would seem that the gloomy crime data picture has improved. This is not entirely true. First, the development of these police systems has been haphazard. This type of development produces different formats for the data over time, different types of data over time, and different data archival techniques over time. This becomes a researcher's nightmare to untangle. (Reed, 1980, p. 3)

Thus, further research and development was required if the police were going to be able to utilize computers for more intelligent and effective deployment strategies. These capabilities gradually came about due, in large part, to the development of mapping science.

The Development of Mapping Science and Real-Time Deployment Capabilities

The discipline known as geography has been defined as "the science of distributions, . . . its basic tool is the map and its prime function is to express facts on maps—in other words the cartographical interpretation of data" (Stamp, 1965, p. 14). Geographers have, for centuries, utilized maps "for the analysis of data in a spatial context" (Carter, 1984, p. 3). The skills and practices associated with geography can be used to add insight to patterns of distribution, gradients, densities, and associations among physical or social phenomena. Social scientists have used geography to study "social patterns, frequency of arrests, population density, resource potential or consumption" (p. 3).

The geographical distribution of disease has been monitored for quite some time.

> It is not surprising that this method of descriptive analysis was first used for communicable diseases in an attempt to identify the sources of infection, and to describe the rate of spread. Mapping of chronic diseases probably started with the recognition that environmental factors play an essential role in their aetiology. (Elliot, Cuzik, & Stern, 1996, p. 235)

Density maps were developed and used by medical practitioners and public health officials to track and perhaps prevent disease, using gradations in color or shading to indicate relative intensities of disease incidence (Stamp, 1965). By the early 1900s, the use of density maps by epidemiologists was quite common. Today, the representation and analysis of maps of disease incidence data is "established as a basic tool in the analysis of regional public health" (Lawson et al., 1999, p. 3).

> One of the earliest examples of the important role of geographical analysis of disease was the analysis of cholera outbreaks in the east end of London by John Snow in 1854. Snow constructed maps of the locations of cholera deaths and noted the particular elevated incidence around the Broad Street water pump, a source of water supply for the local area. (p. xiii)

The major aim in studying geographical variation in disease rates is "to formulate hypotheses about the aetiology of disease by taking into account spatial variation in environmental factors" (Elliot et al., 1996, p. 3). Maps of disease incidence can also be used to assess the need for geographical variation in health resource allocation or could be useful in research studies of the relation of incidence to explanatory variables. Epidemiologists utilize various types of geographical studies.

> The first category includes studies where the aim is simply to describe the distribution of disease with respect to place of occurrence. The results of these studies are often presented in maps. The second category includes ecological studies (sometimes known as geographical correlation studies) in which the aim is to describe the relationship between geographical variation in disease and concomitant variation in degree of exposure to a particular factor (usually an environmental agent or a life-style-related characteristic, such as diet). (p. 4)

> Maps provide the most succinct summary of descriptive geographical data since they display the spatial distribution of the characteristic of interest. On a map, the geographical distribution of disease is readily visible to the eye. (p. 5).

> Statistical tables, while able to present more data than maps, cannot easily convey these spatial patterns and so are a less comprehensible or accessible means of presenting geographical data. Subtle patterns may be missed in tables. . . . [However,] it is difficult to present more than one variable on a single map so that important features of the data (e.g., the number of cases on which a rate is based) may not be portrayed. Ideally, supporting tabular data should be presented alongside the maps. (p. 5)

In 1927 an extensive survey of mental hygiene services in New York City was conducted to determine the adequacy of treatment provided by out-patient clinics throughout the city. The analysis included the following data: the type of patient examined and treated; age, sex, and race; the diagnosis made and the method of examination which led to it; and the treatment given through psychiatric, medical and social procedures (Greene, Pratt, Davies, & Branham, 1929). While the survey did not study all psychiatric cases that were treated in the city, it did examine case records from all major mental hygiene clinics operating within the city at the time (a total of 350 cases). A special examination of geographical distribution was made for these cases and twenty-five (25) cases from each clinic were randomly selected and examined in-depth.

> While twenty-five cases alone hardly give an adequate picture of an individual clinic, yet where supplemented by personal visits and by other reliable data it is not improper to assume that this information when evaluated as a whole indicates rather clearly the types of clinic patients and clinic methods. (p. 19)

Epidemiologists continued to utilize mapping science throughout the twentieth century, often with great success. For example, the incidence of asbestos-related lung cancer among shipyard workers in Georgia was established during this period by "large-scale comparative mapping of the geographical distribution of the disease" (p. xiii). In 1965, the Laboratory for Computer Graphics and Spatial Analysis, Graduate School of Design was established at Harvard University (Carter, 1984).

Mapping science was also critical in defining the nature of the threat of AIDS (Acquired Immune Deficiency Syndrome) to the population of New York City when the epidemic was first publicly recognized in 1981 (see generally Bayer, 1995). Similarly, mapping science has greatly assisted epidemiologists in tracking and responding to the "return" of tuberculosis to certain populations and communities within New York City (p. 147).

Piers Bierne (1993) notes, "concept formation in positivist criminology was closely tied to the movements in public health" (p. 111). Perhaps the most striking similarity is the degree to which the search for a disease "cluster" resembles the attempts to identify and react to crime "hot spots." The term "hot spot" denotes a location where a number of criminal incidents have taken place. The first use of the term in academic literature was by Lawrence Sherman, Patrick Gartin, and Michael Buerger (1989). Since there are both spatial and temporal characteristics to crime, specific areas of crime occurrence can be studied in detail. "When a crime is committed, both the location of the crime and the general time the crime occurred are known" (Reed, 1980, p. 1). Mapping science led to considerable advancements in the field of medicine, and sociologists began to tap the potential of the various techniques for the field of criminology.

The Ecology of Crime and Crime Mapping

Geography is not only a science, it is also an orientation or a perspective. "One must consider geography more as a point of view than as a field dealing with particular types of phenomena" (Taaffe & Gauthier, 1973, p. 6). Criminologists have long been fascinated with the ecology of crime and have sought out specific techniques and methods for the spatial and temporal expression of crime data.

Siméon-Denis Poisson was one of the first to subject geographical and chronological variations in crime and criminal justice to scientific scrutiny (Maltz et al., 1991). In a study of crime in nineteenth-century France, Poisson found a significant difference between the conviction rate in Paris and that in the rest of France. The first use of shaded maps to portray crime rates was produced jointly in Paris by Guerry and Balbi (Bierne, 1993). Guerry's maps included

> the type and the number of crimes (against persons and against property) committed annually in France between 1825 and 1830, with variations in their commission associated with sex, age, and season;

the underlying motive behind capital crimes such as poisoning, murder, and assassination; and the geographical distribution of personal and property crimes. (p. 115)

Guerry's cartography of crime resulted from the positivist belief that "the observation and study of facts are the basis of our knowledge" (Bierne, 1993, p. 115). His maps were based on data from the French national census of 1822 and were utilized to identify correlates of criminality, such as poverty or lack of education. Guerry's maps were also believed to be a more effective means of representing otherwise abstract concepts and phenomena to policy makers and administrators.

Social cartography substantially influenced concept formation in the relatively new field of criminology. According to Keith Harries (1999), "Hundreds of spatially oriented studies of crime and delinquency have been written by sociologists and criminologists since about 1830" (p. 16).

The skills associated with cartography reemerged during the 1930s and 1940s, when the search for the root causes of crime led to the development of "opportunity theories," where "offenders are influenced by situational and environmental features that provide desirable—or undesirable—offending opportunities" (Groff & LaVigne, 2001, p. 258). The most recognized and sustained study of the ecology of crime was conducted by the sociologists of the Chicago School. They detailed variation in delinquency rates among different communities and attributed the differences to poverty, poor housing, etc. Clifford Shaw and Henry McKay are generally credited with producing "the landmark piece of research involving crime mapping in the first half of the twentieth century" (Harries, 1999, p. 16).

A critical component of these studies was the use of shaded density maps of Chicago neighborhoods (see, e.g., Shaw, 1966, pp. 34–44). However, many of these maps depicted the movements of offenders but not necessarily their crimes. If one were to summarize the early research in intraurban crime variation, "one would find that instead of inquiring into the nature of these spatial variations, workers from many different disciplines have been . . . preoccupied with the ecology of so-called delinquent and criminal areas within the cities" (Reed, 1980, p. 11). The mapping skills could have been used in a more tactical fashion to analyze the information that was available at the time, studying and perhaps predicting or preventing crime occurrence. The tactical process "begins with the analysis of patterns, then moves to the processes that have brought these patterns about" (Taaffe & Gauthier, 1973, p. 1).

Thus, despite the fact that criminologists considered environmental issues as possible criminogenic factors, few focused solely on the issue of crime and place. Not until the late 1960s did geographers begin to have an interest in the spatio-temporal structure of crime (Reed, 1980).

Oscar Newman (1972) was a leader in the identification and correction of criminogenic features of the physical environment.

> Physical features that offer better surveillance, delineation between
> public and private space, segmentation of outdoor space into locations
> controlled by smaller groups, and proximity of sites to well-used loca-
> tions, enable stronger resident-based informal control of outdoor,
> near-home spaces. (Taylor & Harrell, 1996)

Studies testing these theories were conducted throughout the 1970s and
1980s (see, e.g., Taylor & Covington, 1988).

The President's Commission on Law Enforcement and Administration
of Justice (Challenge of Crime in a Free Society, 1967) looked at the spatial distribution of reported crime (as evidenced by the Uniform Crime
Reports). The Commission utilized simple density maps that were drawn
to represent the "variation in index offense rates by police district" (pp.
66–67). This technique isolated the prevalence of crime and identified the
concentration of its occurrence in the inner city (Newman, 1972).

Throughout the 1970s and 1980s, an array of scholarly works was
devoted to studying the ecological variation of crime (see generally Figlio,
Hakim, & Rengert, 1986; Harries, 1999; Newman, 1972; Pyle 1974). These
studies described the role that community characteristics play in the generation or prevention of crime. Slowly, researchers began to avail themselves
of available geographic data (primarily made available through the national
census and crime reporting instruments, such as the Uniform Crime Reports
and the National Crime Victimization Survey) and began to create computerized mapping systems to be used by American police departments.

The Geographic Base Files for Law Enforcement project represents one
of the earliest and most ambitious programs for the use of computerized
geographic data by police agencies in the United States (International
Association of Chiefs of Police, 1975). From 1974 to 1978, the International Association of Chiefs of Police (IACP) studied the requirements and
feasibility of implementing GBF in law enforcement agencies. With the
support of the Census Bureau and the Department of Commerce, the
project provided technical assistance in developing computer mapping systems and implementing geocoding (Chang et al., 1979, p. 18).

Initially, it was intended that GBF would be used to assist the dispatching component of police command and control operations. These computerized files would be used to determine which patrol unit was geographically
nearest to the reported incident (International Association of Chiefs of
Police, 1975, p. vii). In its 1973 report entitled, *Police: Command and Control Operations*, the National Advisory Commission on Criminal Justice
Standards and Goals promulgated Standard 23.2, which stated that

> every police agency should acknowledge that the speed with which it
> can communicate with field units is critical: that it affects the success
> of agency efforts to preserve life and property; and that it increases the
> potential for immediate apprehension of criminal suspects. Therefore,
> a rapid and accurate communications capability should be developed.
> (cited in International Association of Chiefs of Police, p. 29)

The creators of the project anticipated additional uses, including a more proactive crime analysis function. Standard 4.2 specifically recommended: "Every police department should improve its crime analysis capability," including detecting crime trends and patterns. (International Association of Chiefs of Police, 1975, p. 39) The Commission also recommended (Standard 4.8) that departments collecting information on

> all incidents considered to be crimes and that these data should be identified according to geographical location and type of location. . . . It is important to know where crimes occur. Data should be available for small geographic areas such as police beats or even by block. Data by precinct or police district is the minimum acceptable for reasonable planning. (p. 39)

GBF projects were established during the 1970s in Dallas, San Francisco, and Kansas City, Missouri, but not in New York.

The defining feature of these early systems was the use of the geocode—a location or geographic reference variable such as a "census tract identifier, police patrol beat, or a unique X/Y coordinate" (Reed, 1980, p. 34). The GBF process was an effective and powerful tool for information management that contributed to the development of several sophisticated computerized crime analysis and deployment systems during the 1970s and 1980s (Chang et al., 1979).

The Kansas City Police Department Resource Allocation System (KCPRAS)

During the 1970s, the Kansas City, Missouri Police Department developed a computerized information system with a particularly expansive scope. It served as both a manpower utilization analysis and a forecasting system. Its most significant feature was the forecasting package. It used a weighted exponential smoothing technique to forecast (1) man-hours of workload and (2) man events (at the option of the user) for a one-week projection period. The forecasting reports would then be expressed by census tracts and blocks or patrol beats, whichever was desired. This information would be displayed on computer-generated maps, which were distributed for further analysis.

Interestingly, the Kansas City system did not forecast crime. It did however forecast the number of calls-for-service and the number of self-initiated activities). It served as an administrative tool that provided information regarding the availability of patrol units, where they were needed, the time of need, and why. The information was used to assist police administrators in defining workload prior to the occurrence of crime by showing the distribution and volume of patrol service requirements with respect to: hour of day, day of week, geographic area, week of year, and class of activity. The system utilized an online census file (developed in 1968) that had street address information. By utilizing geographic-based census files, its developers and users could produce reports on an area as small as one block or much larger areas. If they wanted crime information on a controlled area, they could extract that data by selecting the census tracts and blocks that encompassed the area and view the crime that had occurred there (International Association of Chiefs of Police, 1975, p. 44) The source of data for this system was police dispatch cards; the database had one full year's supply of these patrol dispatch-workload records (Chang et al., 1979, p. 118).

Throughout the 1970s, police departments in other cities began to experiment with similar resource allocation programs. These cities included St. Louis, Boston, Los Angeles, and others. Computer mapping had a number of applications in the field of policing. Information contained in crime reports could be converted into "X/Y" coordinates on a map and a computer could then be used to relate the coordinates of an offense to a given neighborhood, block, patrol beat, or patrol sector. Alternatively, some departments used a system of geocoding based on census tract information (Grassie, Macsas, & Wallace, 1977). This meant that the input data had to include at least the address of the crime location, the date of occurrence, and the crime type. The data typically needed to be captured, coded, and produced in the computer-plotted format at the beginning of each working day (Chang et al., 1979, p. 18).

Real-Time Tactical Deployment (RTD)

Computer mapping played an integral role in the development and application in Dallas, Texas, of an RTD system. RTD was "a three-year effort designed to develop the necessary software system for impact crime problem identification, analysis, and prediction on as near a real-time basis as possible" (International Association of Chiefs of Police, 1975, p. 41). RTD was a computerized system that selected the deployment of tactical units of the police department. The unit of analysis was high crime areas

> detected by comparing the current day's crime count for each adjacency cluster with the corresponding daily count for a selected time cycle. The time cycle selected [would] be some representative time period which [would] yield a good estimate of crime activity in the adjacency cluster. (Grassie, et al., 1977, p. 3-8)

When the daily crime for the adjacency cluster exceeded the expected level of crime by some threshold amount, the adjacency cluster would be considered a "hot" area, and detailed crime occurrence reports would be generated describing activity in the cluster (International Association of Chiefs of Police, 1975, p. 41). RTD provided detailed geographical crime information

> quickly enough to allow tactical assignment areas to be selected daily, if necessary, without the use of spot maps or manually prepared analysis reports. Tactical planners need[ed] only to review the information provided to decide where to make deployments (and where to conclude previous deployments). (Grassie et al., 1977, p. 3-8)

The RTD system was operated by the Dallas Police Department's Crime Analysis Section to identify and analyze concentrated crime areas in the city. They concentrated the use of the system on residential burglaries during the week and on business burglaries during the weekends.

The particular methods and practices associated with RTD are notable due to their uniqueness. Each of the 158 patrol beats in Dallas was evaluated each morning for burglary problems through examination of summary reports provided by the RTD system. The information provided in these reports identified hot areas by evaluating the daily burglary occurrence frequency for beats experiencing an abnormally high number of crimes during a fourteen-day period (Chang et al., 1979, p. 19). The report was output separately in two sort orders, one by number of crimes and one by beat to provide the crime analysts with two independent perspectives of viewing current crime patterns (p. 20). If an increasing trend was indicated (e.g., more burglaries during the last seven days), that area would then be designated "hot" and analyzed further.

For that purpose, detailed reports were provided daily in a format that could be disseminated to tactical and patrol personnel. These reports included a fourteen-day burglary review of each hot area, all suspect descriptions, and all suspect vehicle descriptions for the preceding fourteen days. Other available information included people arrested in hot areas, partial license plate checks against traffic citation and wanted vehicle files, and known offenders living in hot areas. The RTD system provided tactical forces with the information necessary for deployment within three to twenty-four hours of crime problem occurrence (Chang et al., 1979; Reed, 1980).

The RTD system required data entry within 24 hours of reporting a crime. This system included the capability to display the crime occurrence frequency for the geocoded area type (i.e., beat, reporting area) on a daily basis and the ability to automatically generate crime occurrence reports for each patrol area in the city (Chang et al., 1979). The major advantage of the system transfer was shortening the time delay between pattern detection and report dissemination, which could take up to three days if entered manually. The RTD system reduced the three-day time lag to just a few hours.

Through the Dallas Police Department's Direct Entry Field Reporting System, all major offense reports were called in and entered into the computer within two hours of crime occurrence. The RTD reports were batch processed between two and four in the morning and delivered to the Crime Analysis Section by 6:00 AM; this crime information could therefore be as current as only a few hours old. The reports were then separated, analyzed, and distributed by 8:00 AM each morning (Chang et al., 1979).

Although the summary and detail reports were ideally designed for tactical applications, they were also distributed to patrol. The summary reports allowed patrol planners to identify problem areas while the detail reports provided convenient summaries for individual patrol elements. For such purposes, a ten-day summary report of all major crime was provided daily by the RTD system (Chang et al., 1979). Overlooking similar offense crime patterns was one possible problem with a system such as RTD. Since the RTD system eliminated the analyst's dependence on the offense/incident report as a source for geographical data or further analysis information, the analyst may have been tempted to avoid reading daily offense reports altogether. If this were to occur, an important technique of identifying related crimes would be lost (p. 28).

The successful implementation of the Dallas and Kansas City analysis systems influenced the further development of crime geographic information systems (CRGIS). Carl Reed (1980) recognized the vast potential of these systems and explained the positive effect that they could have on U.S. policing techniques.

> The addition of a well conceptualized CRGIS, may solve many of the problems in police information flow while at the same time adding a new dimension to the police decision process that is extremely potent.
>
> Geographically referenced crime data can provide effective information for the decision-maker in many ways such as computer generated maps that depict self-explanatory patterns of crime. Maps of crimes for different time periods can be used effectively to portray changes in crime patterns over time.
>
> CRGIS can give information on crime that can greatly facilitate the timeliness and accuracy of decisions in the police department. (p. 44)

He identified four specific goals for computer-based geographic applications: (1) to make more effective use of individual patrol units; (2) to provide better service; (3) to make best use of the budget dollar; and (4) to provide better information for patrol and for management (p. 73).

The efforts of U.S. police agencies to create more efficient systems of crime analysis advanced as computer technology proliferated. Reed (1980) conducted a survey of 88 police departments in the United States and Canada: "The focus of the survey was on computer applications with special emphasis on geographic applications, such as computerized mapping and geographic base files" (p. 50). He found that 93.9% of the reporting departments utilized computer processing in some aspect of their operations. In 1971, only 38.8% were doing so. According to Harries (1999), crime-mapping applications "took off in the late 1980s and early 1990s as desktop computing became cheaper and software became more accessible and user friendly" (pp. 92–94).

The Chicago Crime-Mapping Project

A sophisticated crime-mapping project was funded by NIJ in November 1986. The project contributed to a philosophical shift toward proactive management.

> Rather than having to rely on central headquarters capabilities and wait for a cumbersome mainframe computer operation to eventually provide the requisite analysis, the district [precinct] commander can now delegate the crime analysis officer to do the work, receive the results that day, and make management decisions as indicated. (Maltz et al., 1991, p. 107)

However, an interesting phenomenon severely limited the overall effectiveness of this project.

> One of the difficulties we had was our naïve assumption that simply providing good intelligence to beat officers would result in their using it effectively. Our interviews with and observations of patrol officers indicated a lack of understanding of what to do with the maps. Many patrol officers were as likely to use the maps as scrap paper as to keep them in their beat books for later referral. The assumption of these beat officers appeared to be that any paperwork that came down from the commander was just additional busywork. (p. 110)

The project was, however, generally viewed as a success. These systems provided the ability to "see only burglaries, only crimes committed after dark, only those committed in September, only those committed by juveniles, or all of these" (Maltz et al., 1991, p. 45). The maps that were generated served as the beat's "institutional memory" (p. 76).

The project's use of computerized mapping "greatly facilitated communication between groups that were not especially known for communicating in the past," such as patrol officers and detectives (Maltz et al., 1991, p. 144). Administrators identified officers who were using the maps and convened a series of meetings, attended by the precinct commander, the crime analysis officer, and representatives of three other specialty units within each command (p. 110). These meetings were not, however, designed to plan tactical operations or to allocate resources. Rather, they were intended to encourage a "frank discussion of the use of the maps, why they were not being used by many officers, and what steps might be taken to encourage their use" (p. 110).

The Illinois Criminal Justice Information Authority (ICJIA) Project

A grant from the U.S. Bureau of Justice Statistics funded another crime analysis project that utilized computer graphics—the Spatial and Temporal Analysis of Crime (STAC). Developed in Illinois during the late 1980s, STAC focused on "the use of maps to locate concentrations of criminal activity in Chicago suburbs, using cluster analysis algorithms" (Maltz et al., 1991, p. 26). It was based on ICJIA's Police Information Management System (PIMS), a centralized system that served a number of suburbs in greater Chicago. The purpose was to develop more efficient ways of analyzing and representing the data traditionally shown on pin maps.

STAC was designed as an exploratory procedure to investigate the feasibility of "detecting patterns of crime in a community, using both geographic and time data" (Illinois Criminal Justice Information Authority, 1987, p. 1). It was not, however, "a mapping package in itself but an analytical package to be used in conjunction with a mapping software" (Craglia, Haining, & Wiles, 2000, p. 712).

STAC's primary function was to "condense large amounts of crime information into a manageable form. The analytical methods could be used in resource allocation, crime analysis, beat definition, and other applications" (Illinois Criminal Justice Information Authority, 1987, p. 1). Thirty months of data were obtained for each crime and town, spanning the period between January 1983 and June 1985. The spatial analysis program examined the geographic distribution of incidents, coding information about crimes that law enforcement officials could use for strategic and tactical crime analysis. Under the system, "areas ranging from a city block to an entire town [could] be examined using the radial search and scanning procedure" (p. 9). The information helped define beat structure and the best times to change shifts. "The hot spot procedure could be used to find the principal centers of crime, and the beats could be defined or redefined to take these centers into account" (p. 1).

STAC suffered from certain technical limitations. Computer technology during this time period simply did not allow for the simultaneous performance of temporal and spatial analysis (i.e., on one map). In other words, STAC did not produce usable crime maps that displayed both the time and location of occurrence for reported crimes. Although this capability was not available to them at the time, STAC's developers understood the utility of such an application and actually predicted a time when it would become generally available.

> One direction for further analysis is the combination of temporal and spatial analysis. This is already possible to a certain extent, since the results of one type of analysis can be used as the data for the other. . . . The ultimate goal of the project is to produce a package of computer programs that applies them simultaneously. (Illinois Criminal Justice Information Authority, 1987, p. 1)

By the mid-1980s, computer technology had advanced considerably. Perhaps the most significant cause of this rapid development was the advent of the microcomputer and its general availability to U.S. police agencies (Harries, 1999; Rich, 1995).

> Now we are witnessing the invasion of the microcomputer. For under $5,000 it is possible to configure a micro with a digitizer, disk, color monitor, and software that can do some of the same things the large turnkey systems can do. . . . True, the resolution is not as high, the processing speeds are much slower and users must train themselves, but such microcomputer systems cost only one-tenth to one-one-hun-

> dredth of what it costs to buy the powerful turnkey system. (Carter,
> 1984, p. 39)

Turnkey systems generally included the delivery of "everything needed to
produce maps," including

> a complete setup of hardware with appropriate peripherals, an inte-
> grated package of software including an operating system and applica-
> tion software, plus training staff and customer engineers to make sure
> the system is used to its full advantage. Such systems are usually con-
> figured to the purchaser's particular needs and desires. Purchases are
> usually made only after the organization carries out analyses of what it
> wants to do and how it is going to finance, maintain, and use it. Initial
> investments of half a million dollars or more for such systems are not
> uncommon. . . . (p. 27)

While the turnkey system represented the ultimate in capability and
convenience, it also represented the ultimate in price. For many police
agencies at the time, it was neither possible nor practical to have large
turnkey systems available for all possible applications. Many agencies
instead relied on mainframe computers with software packages that could
give reasonable service to a great number of users trying to perform a variety of tasks. Cartographic software packages on the mainframes were used
to perform some of the functions that were otherwise available on turnkey
mapping systems.

Reed (1980) cautioned that advances in mapping technology were
not, in and of themselves, a panacea. He suggested that the use of geographically referenced crime data could be hampered by "[the] lack of
crime data in automated form that is collected in a consistent manner over
time and that is accurately and usefully geocoded" (p. 21). Such difficul-
ties would severely limit the potential usefulness of even the most sophisticated crime analysis packages.

Crime analysis could be hampered by an even more fundamental
problem. A threshold question for any agency interested in implementing
such a system is, "How exactly will the crime analysis function affect the
agency's organizational architecture?" John Simmons and Dennis Kenney
(1995) discuss an organizational issue many departments face.

> A fundamental organizational issue in many departments is whether
> to establish a centralized crime analysis unit or have analysts dis-
> persed throughout the agency. The advantage of a centralized unit
> may be in the simplicity of supervising the unit and setting consistent
> priorities and goals. . . . The advantage of decentralizing analysts
> appears to be an increased access to crime data in all areas of the
> department, which permits individuals to customize reports and analy-
> sis strategies to their own needs. Conversely, supervision of the ana-
> lysts is difficult when they are spread out and answer to different
> supervisors, and a coherent approach to analyzing crime data may be
> lost. (p. 4)

They propose that there may be a compromise position that is consistent with a community-policing philosophy. That approach "involves having a centralized analysis staff that essentially decentralizes the information they collate and analyze by routinely sharing it with the individual units" (p. 4).

A key issue is therefore the dissemination and use of the information. Clearly, analysts must provide crime information to field-level and executive staff on a timely and regular basis. The format of such reports

> can be simple, such as a small chart showing the status of crime for the previous week or month, or more complex, involving elaborate maps and statistical analysis indicating possible future trends. As for the content of these reports, they may include comparisons of each geographic area over time, both with itself and with other areas. This information can also be compared with a similar time frame from the previous year. (Reuland, 1995, p. 72)

The crime analysis unit should prepare a daily information bulletin to be distributed to each line officer (Reinier et al., 1977). The patrol supervisor would "find the contents particularly useful as the basis for instructions and discussion during rollcalls" (pp. 3-16, 3-22). Such a report would contain summary information concerning significant events that occurred over the previous 24 hours, thus being the most current information source available to the patrol supervisor and patrol officers. The flow of information would be continuous, rather than a one-time function (i.e., from the crime analysis unit to senior administrators).

The patrol supervisor plays a critical role and must "pass on to his subordinates all of the information he has that can be useful to them" (Reinier et al., 1977, p. 3-44). Interpersonal transfer of information is preferable to a distribution of computer-generated maps or data.

> The patrol supervisor should encourage face-to-face informal contact between the crime analysis unit personnel and all users of analysis information under his supervision. In addition, the patrol supervisor should make every effort to meet with the crime analyst to discuss general problems within his area of responsibility. (p. 3-50)

A well-designed system allows supervisors to select particular problems for further analysis. In essence, there is a feedback loop whereby data prepared by the crime analysis unit would be regularly fed to field units, who in turn would provide them with feedback for further analysis.

Unfortunately, few of the early computerized crime analysis systems effectively used the information that was prepared. Very often, maps or data that were prepared by crime analysts were forwarded only to senior administrators or members of specialized tactical units. "Although a computer-aided approach to crime analysis was promoted as a means of using computers to fight crime, the actual results fell far short of the promises made" (Maltz et al., 1991, p. 25). Apparently, vast amounts of computerized crime data were produced and stored as part of these programs, but the information was not effectively utilized by the field commands. Often, very limited methods existed whereby field personnel could search and retrieve this data. Information retrieval was either limited to a few administratively applicable summary reports (e.g., UCR or other such summary reports) or to requests for special programming that often had to be performed by another city department or agency when time permitted. There was no efficient method for accessing stored crime data for use in analyzing a specific application (Chang et al., 1979).

The Development of Crime Analysis Practices in the NYPD

The NYPD's documented use of crime maps dates back to 1900; it is possible, however, that the practice began well before then (Harries, 1999). Handmade pin maps were used in many police commands within the city, but their use was apparently not institutionalized until the turn of the century. Pin maps then served as the primary means of tracking and analyzing crime. With the advent of the computer, crime analysis methods in New York gradually modernized.

On February 1, 1966, the NYPD hosted a seminar at the New York City Police Academy, at which the department's top administrators met with managers from other police agencies and executives from the UNIVAC Division of Sperry Rand Corporation and the Westinghouse Electric Corporation. The overall purpose of this meeting was to discuss the various benefits and associated challenges of "real-time" computing (NYPD, 1966, p. 1-1). NYPD speakers at the meeting included the police commissioner, the department's chief of planning, and the commanding officer of the statistical and records bureau.

In his opening address, Police Commissioner Vincent L. Broderick provided a particularly detailed explanation of why the seminar was convened.

> There's a very good reason for all of you to be here today. It is not for you to learn how to operate a computer, but it is for you to learn, in a very general way, the computer's capability. How the computer is to be used, then, is something you, as well as the computer experts, will have to work out together. It is merely the law enforcement role to make demands. We have to spell out where the problems are. We have to spell out the areas in which we are losing manpower and in which we are leaking out information, in which we are failing to commit all our resources, because somehow the effort of pulling information together is too burdensome an effort. . . . We are here today, and you particularly, as professional law enforcement commanders in the field, to learn what the capabilities of the computer are, what the potentials of the computer are. Then we expect you to use your imagination to determine just what we should be demanding of the computer, what we should be asking it, how we should be applying it in ways that may never have occurred to [the computer "experts"].
>
> We have, in this room, the greatest collection of imaginative police administrators in the world. I would think that we have in this room, a

group of men who would challenge any organization such as Sperry Rand or IBM, or Westinghouse, to move into areas that have never occurred to them before. I hope that what stems from today's session will stimulate your imagination, individually and collectively. I would hope that after seeing what the computer can do, that you will be continually thinking of how we in police work can use the computer to help us do our job. (NYPD, 1966, p. 2-1)

Deputy Inspector McCabe explained the functions of the computer, and the overall mission of the department's Statistical and Records Bureau (as of 1966).

Source documents are received from various commands. These documents are often manually verified for accuracy of classification and completeness and then coded. The documents are forwarded to the data processing section where the coded information is key-punched, verified and then machine-edited for accuracy. The data is processed. Controls are compiled to guarantee receipt of every document, and as far as is humanly possible, the accuracy of every report we produce. The documents then go to the designated filing section and the machine-produced reports are distributed throughout the department to other agencies or to file for reference. (NYPD, 1966, p. 3-2)

Arrest reports, which were prepared at the field commands, served as source documents. He explained that every item of original information needed to be keypunched before it was entered into the computer system. He cited this as a problematic area.

The machines cannot perform without the operators. Not all operators are equal in production, or equal in accuracy. Yet, the flow of documents never seems to cease. We have, in addition to the key-punch machines, other electric accounting machines which are used to sort, collate, interpret and reproduce punch cards. (NYPD, 1966, p. 3-2)

The department's computer capabilities were described as "moderately fast"—capable of reading 800 cards per minute or punching 250 cards per minute (NYPD, 1966, p. 3-2).

Four reels of tape can store one entire year's worth of UF-61 complaint reports. These reports can be retrieved from the tapes at the rate of 15,000 records per minute. Our printer can print 600 lines per minute. Reports are prepared by the computer for the Federal Bureau of Investigation, [and] the State Department of Corrections (which is the collection agency for crime complaints for New York State). (p. 3-2)

The department's Statistical and Records Bureau utilized this technology to "prepare a post-analysis report, precinct clearance report, a listing of taxi robberies, hourly and tour report, a weapons and location report. All of these reports and others [were] matched with the arrest activity to guarantee accuracy" (NYPD, 1966, p. 3-3). The department assigned approximately ten people from within the Statistical Records Bureau to design the system to prepare monthly reports. Other applications included "arrest summaries, complaint summaries, and certain types of summonses and youth referrals, listings of hack drivers, personnel skills inventories, and fingerprint searches" (Cawley, 1966, p. A-10).

> The reports that come off the machine at month's end include arrest registers, reports again for the Federal Bureau of Investigation and the State Department of Corrections, reports as to age and sex, reports by police department code, day, tour, and hour arrest reports, arresting officer reports, reports for the Youth Division. All of this information is used to answer three basic questions. What has happened? Where has it happened? And who was doing it? (p. 3-3)

McCabe uses the past tense; his explanation refers to retrospective crime analysis, rather than any form of forecasting or predictive modeling. That is not to say, however, that department officials did not envision a proactive system. As McCabe noted at the time, "The system which we visualize for the future will not be geared to monthly reporting but to almost instantaneous response" (NYPD, 1966, p. 3-4).

Indeed, McCabe's comments reveal his department's interest in developing an organization-wide information system that could obtain information from the field, analyze it, then redirect it to the field for appropriate "use."

> Perhaps the best approach to the problem of the department would be the development of a management information system. This has been designed as a total complex in which data are generated, recorded, processed and refined to produce the information needed at all levels of organization for planning, directing, coordinating and controlling an enterprise. (NYPD, 1966, p. 3-4)

> A system which will permit useful information to be gathered and a communication network to disseminate that information man to man is a must. Information received too late for action is virtually useless and only adds to the frustration which we face every day. . . . The creation of purely functional files, the existence of which are unknown or little known and hence unused is a condition which we can no longer tolerate. Redundant record keeping functions must be consolidated. Paper work has to be reduced. We in the department have been forerunners in the use of electronic data processing.
>
> We intend to remain forerunners. In the near future, a system design group will be established within the department. This will be the first step towards the implementation of a law enforcement network second to none. (p. 3-4)

Daniel Cawley (1966) concurred, predicting that a time would come when "the police executive [would] become . . . directly involved in the growing E.D.P. (electronic data processing) field in order to carry out his mandate to provide the greatest possible service and protection at the lowest possible cost" (p. A-1). He envisioned a day when information generated from other public agencies would be made available to the police, in order to support their overall operations.

> It is not in the public interest to deny the police any informational assistance in their search for a murderer, child molester, or rapist, especially since such information is already public property. A home address furnished by the Board of Elections or a physical description of a suspect supplied by the Department of Hospitals could be obtained merely by initiating a computer search of all city agencies' files. It is in these areas, that is, rapid and comprehensive file searches, that computers appear to offer the greatest potential for practical police applications. (p. A-2)

Cawley (1966) proved to be remarkably prescient in his description of a process that closely resembles those of PBM systems developed some thirty years later.

> What comes next? . . . To sum up without being guilty of prophesying, perhaps the following hypothetical narrative best illustrates what future possibilities the computer may hold in store for us. "As Lieutenant Jones began his tour of desk duty in the 11th precinct, he picked up the roll call from the remote printer next to the desk. The computer in Police Headquarters had just finished transmitting the duty assignments to him as it had to the other 100 odd commands in the Department. Since the printer operated at 600 lines per minute, Jones' roll call was finished in ten seconds. The individual roll calls for the entire department were completed during this same ten seconds. Last minute sick reports, post changes, and post assignments were teletyped back to the computer and Jones made corresponding corrections on his copy. . . posts 3, 4, and 9 . . . had recently been assigned a higher hazard rating because of a significant rise in the crime rate. The computer program had calculated that these posts had a high priority and reassigned three officers from the posts with the lowest hazard ratings.
>
> More instructions were being received on the remote printer, such as notifications from operations Bureau on out-of-command assignments, court appearances and a synopsis of crime complaints, arrests, and traffic accidents since the precinct commander's last tour of duty. Captain Smith had just arrived for duty and quickly noted the contents of the last three reports. Using the concise report, he was able to brief the outgoing platoon within moments of his arrival. (p. A-11)

Cawley (1966) recognized that such a system would still need to be closely connected to the field.

> Many persons believe that the old time foot patrolman, with his broad experience and intimate knowledge of persons living or doing business on his post, was the best deterrent to crime. The development of a police computer concept does not necessarily change that image. In many respects, the effectiveness of the foot patrolman will now be enhanced by placing at his disposal a vast pool of information that should result in fewer crimes and a higher clearance rate. Information

and intelligence can be disseminated to foot patrolmen on a periodic basis so that they may take preventive action or follow-up possible leads when alerted to new crimes or possible violations. . . . The inevitable result of a computerized mass of police information will be a synthesis of data that will both facilitate and make more meaningful the job of the foot patrolman. The possibility of increasing efficiency by the application of computers and electronic systems to police operations and tactics is most promising. (p. A-13)

Interestingly, although the department had created a centralized crime analysis unit (known as the Crime Analysis Section) years earlier, it was not until 1978 that the department developed a coordinated, precinct-level system of analysis. During the early 1970s, some precincts were performing their own analysis, but many were not. Those precincts that did perform an adequate degree of analysis did so on an as-needed basis and rarely, if ever, shared their information. Perhaps more importantly, their analysis was performed manually (O'Connell, 2001a).

In 1977, the department developed the 26/30 Automated Crime Analysis Experiment that tested the feasibility of automating precinct crime analysis. The project was successful, insofar as it: (1) demonstrated the feasibility of an automated basic crime analysis system (by developing a working prototype); (2) demonstrated that precinct personnel could be trained to use such a system effectively; (3) identified a small number of computer techniques that were "extremely valuable for manipulating crime data"; (4) recorded the most common types of errors made in entering and analyzing data; and (5) indicated that a database manager (software system) would be the most effective way of providing similar capabilities through the department-wide (FATN) computer system. Perhaps its most significant contribution was in providing the first steps toward the development of procedures for evaluating deployment (O'Connell, 2001a).

By 1978, the department had implemented a formalized precinct-level crime analysis program for the entire city. That is not to say that precincts had failed to perform any analysis prior to that time. On the contrary, robbery was always identified as a key indicator for overall crime rates. Commands were therefore required to maintain up-to-date records regarding this one offense (O'Connell, 2001a). Unfortunately, during that time the amount of analysis that was actually performed in the precincts often depended on the orientation and personal preferences of the commanding officers (O'Connell, 2001a, p. 98).

Prior to 1978, the centralized crime analysis section only obtained information from the field that was necessary for reporting purposes and for a nominal amount of analysis. Precinct and borough commanders often possessed a great deal of information that was simply not forwarded to headquarters, primarily because no mechanism existed for such an information transfer.

The procedures established for precinct-level crime analysis attempted to standardize the type of analysis that was performed in the field by establishing minimal baseline bookkeeping procedures to be performed by each precinct. In order for crime analysis efforts to succeed, the department recognized that it must be viewed as a system.

> Data is collected and collated. It is then analyzed in terms of accessing operationally useful information, and deployment and tactical decisions are then made and evaluated in terms of their relative effectiveness. In short, crime analysis represents a rational system of data analysis for enhancing and validating decision making relative to crime reduction efforts. (NYPD, 1980, p. ii)

The new procedures noted that the crime analysis function

> is a cyclical process (self-improving). As the analyst gains experience and familiarity with the data and system (including feedback), problem recognition and monitoring capabilities are increased. This in turn increases the quality of the data, resulting in an increase in the effectiveness and efficiency of the operational use of the information. (p. 3)

Noting that the "UF-60 sheet" (a summary listing of all complaints recorded during a tour) was insufficient as a primary source for crime analysis, the new procedures called for the creation and use of ongoing chronological lists of certain crimes (burglary, robbery, and "purse snatch"). They also required the preparation of spot maps and cross-tabulations (i.e., tables) for those crimes—and encouraged the same preparation for other crimes on an as-needed basis. "Through the examination (analysis) of comparative statistics relating current to prior crime complaint incidence, a supervisor, with the assistance of crime analysis personnel, should be able to identify the precinct's current crime situation (problems)" (NYPD, 1980, p. 1).

Unfortunately, while the department's enhanced crime analysis capabilities did provide a great deal of useful information, it is unclear whether that information was actually used effectively. An overriding limitation was the hierarchical bureaucratic structure that continued to exist. All significant management decisions were still being made at the headquarters level. In sum, this was perhaps the department's most significant restriction, a reactive orientation towards policing that was based on the fundamental notion of looking to headquarters for direction prior to taking any decisive action. Elizabeth Reuss-Ianni (1983), who performed an extremely thorough case study analysis of the department during this period, provides insightful observation.

> Planning is at the heart of the management function and is essential to the efficient and effective operation of police work. There is virtually no planning at the precinct level where the planning officer is primarily a conduit for statistical information requested by higher administrative levels. As a result, precincts appear to be reactive to whatever

situation develops within their boundaries. In actuality, precinct terri-toriality provides both the precinct and the department with an excel-lent opportunity for organizational intelligence based on the intimate knowledge which the street cop has of his territory. Conversely, much of the policy and decision making at higher levels of administration are perceived by precinct level personnel as arbitrary and unrelated to local needs and conditions. Further, to the extent that precinct level personnel were not part of the planning and feel no stake in the suc-cess of the plan, they will not exert much effort toward the realization of those goals or objectives. (p. 125)

By the 1980s, the NYPD suffered from several deep-seated structural and operational limitations that restricted the ability of field commanders to anticipate and to react quickly to crime and criminogenic conditions. These limitations stemmed from flaws in its organizational orientation (see Silverman, 1999). Change would have to take place if the department wished to significantly impact crime rates.

A Turning Point in Crime Analysis Capabilities

Despite advances in crime analysis and information management tech-nologies, U.S. law enforcement agencies suffered from one critical flaw. Almost without exception, system design and development occurred "in an ad hoc and incompatible manner" (Tyworth & Sawyer, 2006, p. 2). This piecemeal approach to system design led to stovepipe systems that created information silos. In other words, agencies adopted a variety of new infor-mation systems over the years. Unfortunately, older systems were retained as new systems were brought on-line, primarily due to financial concerns. This resulted in an array of functioning but incompatible information sys-tems, none of which was considered the primary system. This caused information to be buried in discrete areas throughout the organization, often within outdated systems that made retrieval quite difficult. This situ-ation was further complicated by another reality in human organizations: as knowledge is associated with power, people are often quite hesitant to divest themselves of control over data and subject themselves to retraining and a variety of new demands. Law enforcement agencies were therefore "burdened with inflexible-but-entrenched [information technology] sys-tems that [were] generally incompatible with other law enforcement sys-tems outside of the organizational boundaries, and occasionally even incompatible with other systems within the organization itself" (p. 2).

Another significant problem developed. In the absence of a proactive and logical development plan, many newly implemented information sys-tems were not properly used. All too frequently, new data systems were sim-ply used for the storage and retrieval of data. Rarely, if ever, were they used for the purpose of informing *future* business decisions. This is somewhat understandable in light of the fact that the hardware used in such systems was large and typically not located at the field level. It was only with the advent of the personal computer that field commanders regularly accessed accumulated data and began to use it as a basis for ongoing management decisions. This simple fact represents a significant paradigm shift and led to the development of such concepts as "problem-oriented" policing.

Indeed, the significance of the advent of the personal computer cannot be overstated. Without PCs, virtually all proactive field decisions would either be impossible, or unsupported by data. In the mid-1980s, few managers in professional baseball utilized computer-generated data to support their on-field decisions. By the mid-1990s, this was common practice. The same transformation occurred in the business world as well as in public service. Technologically and operationally, these organizations were completely transformed. Personal computers did not just enhance data management capabilities—they changed the fundamental manner in which these organizations operated.

Bolman and Deal (2003) explain how smaller and more powerful computers were an ideal supplement for police field operations.

> Before the proliferation of personal computers, information technology (IT) was centralized and controlled by specialists. Mainframes could do things previously impossible. But coordinating user needs with IT offerings was often very frustrating and time consuming for both sides. The spread of personal computers created a slack resource (more computing power than users needed), often reducing the need to coordinate vertically. (p. 64)

PC technology developed at a time when U.S. police organizations had embraced the concept of community policing and when decentralized decision making was quickly becoming the norm. During the 1990s, in particular, technological advances occurred rapidly in terms of "the speed and memory of computers" and the capacity of user friendly operating systems such as Windows (Boba, 2005, p. 24; see also Nunn, 2001). No longer would field commanders be required to rely on their agency's IT section as the sole source of decision-making support. Personal computers allowed field commanders to capture, analyze, and use information at the field level. Commanders could now use data to identify patterns and problems. Most importantly, they could now work to create their own unique solutions (see generally Weisburd, Mastrofski, McNally, Greenspan, & Willis, 2003).

By the early 1990s, numerous advances in computer software, hardware, and networking capabilities made crime mapping and analysis more generally available to U.S. police departments and encouraged a more open flow of information. Elizabeth Groff and Nancy LaVigne (2001) discussed the tremendous growth that occurred by the mid-1990s. By 1995, "115 agencies including 69 police departments were using STAC in the U.S." (Craglia et al., 2000, p. 712). By 1997, NIJ had provided $15 million for the establishment of the Crime Mapping Research Center to "coordinate research, disseminate information on mapping, and [to] provide training to spur development of new spatial analysis methods and software" (Rich, 1995, p. 3). A survey conducted in 1999 found that an estimated 36% of U.S. law enforcement agencies with more than one hundred sworn officers were using computer-mapping programs.

The rapid development in crime-mapping technology coincided with several significant movements in U.S. policing: (1) problem-oriented policing (see Goldstein, 1999); (2) hot-spot policing (deploying resources to areas with a disproportionate level of reported crime); and (3) community policing (a nationwide effort to create a partnership between the police and the community). Each movement had certain technological prerequisites. It is not surprising that the synergy created by these movements resulted in the development of more ambitious forms of analysis and deployment strategies. When the Community Oriented Policing Services (COPS) Office of the U.S. Department of Justice was created in 1994, its mission was to provide grants and to support police departments and sheriffs' offices in their efforts to hire officers and engage in community policing as well as to fund technology improvements. According to Melissa Reuland (1995),

> PERF [the Police Executive Research Forum] and the COPS Office have long realized that in order for community policing to be effective, citizens' and police personnel's access to information is essential. . . . These efforts have included the creation of a crime analysis software package. (p. v)

By the mid-1990s, sophisticated crime-mapping systems were becoming well integrated into overall police operations. Field commands produced and accessed a wealth of information that could support virtually all phases of police operations (e.g., patrol, narcotics enforcement, internal affairs, etc.). Sherman (1998) suggests the emergence of a new paradigm for law enforcement during this period. He supported the intelligent use of "the best available research on the outcomes of police work to implement guidelines and evaluate agencies, units, and officers" (p. 2). He called on modern police agencies to use research "to guide practice and evaluate practitioners" (p. 8). He believed that this new approach could be institutionalized and would have the potential to entirely transform the modern police organization.

Recent Developments in Crime Analysis

Police departments have clearly demonstrated that they can effectively manage crime and disorder in their communities by basing their operations on the analysis of empirically collected data. Since the terrorist attacks of September 11, 2001, the use of real-time data analysis has taken on new urgency. Local, state, tribal and federal law enforcement agencies are endeavoring to identify new platforms on which to build more sophisticated analysis and information sharing capabilities. Although significant progress has been made since the 9/11 terrorist attacks, lingering distrust between federal intelligence gatherers and local police departments, legal and security clearance issues, and incompatable technology systems have slowed the exchange of intelligence data. However, the urgency attached to improving data analysis and information sharing has significantly advanced the ability of police agencies to address crime locally as well as across multiple jurisdictions. Among other things, local departments are now assembling databases, sharing information, and establishing regional intelligence or "fusion" centers.

There are many examples of sophisticated data analysis, crime mapping, and information sharing initiatives at the local, state, and federal levels. In 2005, the NYPD launched the Real Time Crime Center (RTCC). Using sophisticated technology, detectives in the field are connected to analysts in the Center who search multiple police department, criminal justice, and other databases to identify subjects, associates, vehicles and similar crime patterns. Pictures, building profiles, and other information can be sent electronically to the field, saving critical investigative time. In 2006, the Joint Regional Intelligence Center was established in Los Angeles to support counterterrorism and criminal intelligence gathering and analysis through a collaborative effort that includes more than 200 local, state, and federal law enforcement agencies.

Intelligence centers continue to provide opportunities for small and medium size police departments to leverage resources and work collaboratively to address crime issues. For example, the Rockland County (NY) Intelligence Center (RCIC) was established in 1995 to coordinate and disseminate intelligence information. Representatives from ten police agencies including the district attorney's office, the sheriff's department, and county corrections staff the RCIC. The RCIC's operations are governed, and its priorities set annually, by an oversight committee composed of the county's police chiefs and three municipal and two county representatives. Personnel are assigned to "desks" responsible for gathering, analyzing, and disseminating intelligence related to burglaries/robberies, organized crime, gangs, identity crimes, corrections, and terrorism. The RCIC disseminates intelligence bulletins regarding emerging crime trends and high-priority issues. It also provides monthly burglary/robbery analysis reports, gang awareness bulletins, telephone toll analysis, and crime maps for police agencies in the county. Since 9/11, the RCIC monitors counterterrorism intelligence and works closely with state and federal law enforcement agencies to investigate threats and to disseminate critical information.

In Westchester County (NY) the district attorney (DA) coordinates a multi-level strategy to reduce violent and other crimes. The DA chairs monthly CountyStat meetings attended by the police commissioners/chiefs from the five largest cities, the county police commissioner, and representatives from corrections, probation, parole, the New York State Division of

Criminal Justice Services, the United States Attorney's Office, the Federal Bureau of Investigation, and the Bureau of Alcohol, Tobacco and Firearms. The CountyStat team reviews crime patterns and trends identified by police field intelligence officers during prisoner debriefings and investigations. Armed with the data, the executives develop and implement coordinated prevention and enforcement strategies. For example, the group is working with David Kennedy, Director of John Jay College's Center for Crime Prevention and Control and former director of the Boston Gun Project, to implement coordinated gang call-ins in three of the participating cities. In addition, a countywide intelligence center is being developed to facilitate real-time data analysis, crime mapping, and information sharing. In the future, the Westchester intelligence center will be linked to the New York State Division of Criminal Justice, the NYPD's RTCC, and other intelligence centers. It is likely that developments of this type will continue as both the availability of and demand for such data continues to grow.

Ideally, high-performing law enforcement agencies will be able to link their PBM systems to one another, so as to develop large cooperative networks with enhanced resources, capabilities, and a unified mission. If carefully created, perhaps the whole can become greater than the sum of the parts.

THE "LEARNING ORGANIZATION"

AN EXPECTATION OF RESPONSIVENESS

This chapter will discuss knowledge management and organizational learning. It will describe how an understanding of these concepts is essential for any administrator or student of police management who wishes to understand the theory and potential of PBM systems.

Modern police managers should be thoroughly familiar with the intricacies of internal and external organizational communication. Police organizations must actively manage information and ensure that channels of communication remain open, so that the organization can detect subtle changes in the internal and external work environments. Police managers must continually ask themselves: "What is it that we *do know*? and what do we still *need to know*?" In the past, information was all too frequently released only on a "need-to-know" basis. This was particularly true with regard to the traditional relationships between patrol officers and their colleagues assigned to more specialized duties, such as detective or undercover units. Some individuals actually prided themselves on their ability to hoard information, thus creating the impression that they were indispensable to their agency's crime-fighting efforts (endorsing the *knowledge is power* axiom in the extreme). This dynamic is not restricted to police organizations; it applies to federal law enforcement and intelligence agencies as well (Neidorf, 2002).

> The culture of agencies feeling they own the information they gathered at taxpayer expense must be replaced by a culture in which the

agencies instead feel they have a duty to the information—to repay the taxpayers' investment by making that information available. (National Commission on Terrorist Attacks Upon the United States, p. 417)

Police administrators, like all public and private sector managers, should understand the concept of knowledge management (KM). KM is generally defined as "the development of tools, processes, systems, structures and cultures explicitly to improve the creation, sharing, and use of knowledge critical for decision making" (Luthans, 2005, p. 43). It has been described as a common-sense methodology for organizing the internal information of an organization, "much of which is experiential and integrated into the more formal information flows in ways that help [it] stay competitive" (Kamarck, 2005, p. 9). It is a popular movement within the public and private sectors that recognizes the importance of proper management and use of *tangible knowledge assets* (records, files, reports, and other data) as well as *intangible knowledge assets* (the experience, skills, and ideas of employees and other stakeholders) that can inform and support management decisions (Cook & Brown, 1999; Duffy, 2001; Stromquist & Samoff, 2000). In other words, "knowledge" is an asset, a commodity and a resource. The term should include, "*any* information that can further an organization's goals" (Loshin, 2001, p. 56; emphasis added).

> Though some people use information and knowledge interchangeably, its important to realize they aren't the same. Information basically refers to any content that can be communicated. . . . Knowledge refers to content communicated in a context. In other words, knowledge includes information, as well as the context that makes the information useful and meaningful. Think about the people we call knowledgeable. A knowledgeable person not only carries a lot of information in his or her head, but is also capable of identifying and communicating the information that's most relevant for a given situation. (Oakes & Rengarajan, 2002, p. 75)

Within police organizations, knowledge is acquired and maintained through several distinct methods that include: "(1) formal training and on the job experience; (2) knowledge sharing through briefing and debriefing; and (3) knowledge structures including paper-based manuals and computer data-bases" (Collier, Edwards & Shaw, 2004, p. 459). Organizations vary on these three important aspects of managing knowledge.

The fact that knowledge is not always effectively transferred within police organizations is disturbing, but not surprising. Most organizations struggle with this task. As James Lee (2000) notes, "knowledge by its nature is highly personal and extremely difficult to transfer with [the same nuances understood by . . .] the original holder of the knowledge" (p. 35).

By viewing knowledge as an asset, it stresses the importance of developing an effective means of recording, storing, accessing, and using organizational knowledge. It stresses the importance of recognizing and understanding the importance of patterns and relationships, and assessing the true importance of given pieces of information (Dineley, 2001; Loshin, 2001).

KM is not simply a branch of an organization's information technology (IT) function. It is a technique that needs to be mastered in order for the organization to understand the entire landscape of organizational challenges and opportunities. In today's environment, the most successful police organizations will be those that create and use a system whereby upper-level management knows and uses the information that is possessed by field personnel. All police organizations should designate a chief information officer (CIO), who is generally charged with managing and operationalizing hard data stored in the organization's IT system. This individual should, however, be granted the authority and support to perform a wider role. The CIO should be available to work with upper level management to integrate the most up-to-date information into the development of organizational goals and strategies. The CIO should be charged with providing a means of sharing and leveraging human/intellectual capital for the purpose of informing virtually all business decisions. Specifically, this person's goal should be to make organizational knowledge more locatable (i.e., categorized) and accessible (searchable). All organizations must have the ability to assess "the difference between the amount of information required to perform the task[s] and the amount of information already possessed by the organization" (Galbraith, 1973, p. 5). However, simply possessing this information is not sufficient. The organization must also have the ability to actually *use* this information—to process it quickly and to act on it.

All too frequently, police agencies fail to understand the importance of knowledge management and allow their internal information systems to develop spontaneously, without any overriding plan or logic. Years of developing and deploying individual information systems without a view toward an enterprise-wide architecture often leads to a system filled with distinct "information silos" or multiple stovepiped applications. If this occurs, "any individual in any stakeholder group could have information and insight directly relevant to another individual's need. But the structure as a whole does not provide a way for those knowledge resources to be shared" (Neidorf, 2002, p. 61).

Similarly, police organizations often fail to capture or properly transfer tacit knowledge. This is not unusual, as most organizations (both within the private and public sectors) often have only ad hoc systems or methods to address this. This is, nevertheless, still quite troubling.

> In most organizations, the majority of knowledge is tacit—meaning it resides only in the heads of the employees. [Perhaps] as much as eighty percent of the knowledge in any company is tacit. Unfortunately, for most of those companies, when an employee walks out of the door, a significant amount of knowledge goes with him or her. (Oakes & Rengarajan, 2002, p. 76).

Intangible knowledge assets must be recorded, so that they can later be searched and located in the right context for further use. Perhaps the first step is for police administrators to review the posted job descriptions of their personnel. For example, the positions of police officer or detective are generally described in terms of specific duties and responsibilities associated with the ranks, but are rarely described in terms of what *knowledge* is required for each job. It is difficult to transfer knowledge assets that are not formally recognized by the organization.

Organizations must be cognizant of, and actually utilize, the various ways in which learning takes place.

> Employees may come and go, and leadership may change. But an organization's memories preserve behaviors, norms, values, and "mental maps" over time. As an organization addresses and solves problems of survival, it builds a culture that becomes the repository for lessons learned. . . . As members of the organization leave and new ones join and are socialized, knowledge and competence are transferred. (Gephart & Marsick, 1996, p. 38)

As John Thomas, Wendy Kellogg, and Thomas Erickson (2001) note: "Knowledge is inextricably bound up with human cognition, and the management of knowledge occurs within an intricately structured social context" (p. 863). This is an inherently social process. Management must take both human and social factors into account and design an efficient system to "enhance knowledge sharing, collaboration, and expedite decision-making" (Charles, 2002, p. 24; see also Baltazar, 2001). This, however, often "represents a cultural transition for which most organizations are not fully ready" (Neidorf, 2002, p. 60).

Federal law enforcement agencies (such as the Central Intelligence Agency and the Federal Bureau of Investigation) are currently quite concerned with mastering the skills of KM, particularly in light of the perceived intelligence lapses leading up to the September 11 attacks on the United States (see, e.g., Goodridge, 2001; Verton, 2003). State and local police agencies are doing the same (Kelling & Bratton, 2006). Many federal, state, and local agencies and departments are now expending a great deal of energy and resources to develop effective means of managing their organizational knowledge. There is a tendency, however, to simply "throw money" at the problem by retaining an outside consultant or attempting to purchase a "turnkey" IT system. This approach is foolhardy and expensive. A more intelligent option is to develop a socially informed KM system gradually by instilling an appreciation, on the behalf of all members of the organization, for the importance of tangible and intangible knowledge assets that can inform management decisions.

Police organizations must be designed and understood as "open systems." That is, police managers must recognize the inevitability of change and view the external environment as a source of significant input. Indeed, all public managers must "continuously respond to external and internal organizational phenomena with varying rhythms and timing" (Kiel & Seldon, 1998, p. 247). Such systems involve input, transformation, and output (Luthans, 2005). Thomas Chapel (2004) provides the following definitions:

Inputs are the resources on which the organization depends for effective performance of its activities.

Activities are the actual works performed by the program and its staff.

Outputs are the direct products of a program's activities, often tangible services or products that can be counted.

Effects, often called outcomes or impacts, are the hoped-for changes that may result from program activities and outputs (ranging from short term to long term).

In the field of policing, the inputs are varied and continuous; there are, for example, variable levels of support and resources. It is up to the agency to react to and transform these inputs through various processes and subsystems into outputs, such as safer neighborhoods, declining crime rates, etc. *All* members of the organization, from patrol and support staff to the highest levels of management, must understand the goals and processes of the organization, as well as their respective roles, responsibilities, and duties relating to them. Senge (1994) refers to this as "systems thinking."

> What is changing today is the scope of systems thinking. As power and authority are distributed more widely, it becomes increasingly important that people throughout the organization be able to understand how their actions influence others. To do so, local actors need better information systems so they can be aware of system-wide conditions. (p. 12)

In a provocative article, William Geller (1997) addressed the general air of skepticism at that time about such transformations. He detailed a variety of steps that could be taken to help "learning disabled" departments *learn how to learn.*

The concept of the *learning organization* was originally developed during the 1970's by Chris Argyris (Argyris & Schon, 1974) and further refined by Senge during the 1990s. The term generally refers to "an organization that is continually expanding its capacity to create its future" (Geller, 1997, p. 3).

> All organizations learn, but not always for the better. A learning organization is an organization that has an enhanced capacity to learn, adapt, and change. It's an organization in which learning processes are analyzed, monitored, developed, managed, and aligned with improvement and innovation goals. Its vision, strategy, leaders, values, structures, systems, processes, and practices all work to foster people's learning and development and to accelerate systems-level learning. . . . In any organization, learning occurs at multiple levels:

individual, group, and organizational. Although individuals and teams or groups are the agents through which organizational learning occurs, learning organizations focus primarily on systems-level organizational learning. (Gephart & Marsick, 1996, pp. 36–37)

In other words, learning organizations develop a culture of learning. They continually monitor and assess their ability to learn how to learn.

In the field of policing, this mind-set is often the exception rather than the rule; most bureaucratic organizations favor the familiar and the status quo. Individuals working within these bureaucracies "have a limited capacity to accept change because it disorients them" (Boyne, Gould-Williams, Law & Walker, 2004, p. 464). Bureaucracies are generally not known for embracing the concepts of inquiry and experimentation, which serve as the foundation of the learning organization.

> Most organizations exhibit a deterioration in vital signs that is inconsistent with—in fact, often destructive to—their ambitions and purposes. . . . As organizations grow older and larger. . . people often develop a sense of resignation in response to seemingly insurmountable obstacles or to lack of support from their superiors in the daily hassle of getting things done. As organizations become more complicated and demanding, people strive to carve out private patches of turf where they can exercise responsibility, protect themselves, and keep the world at bay. When it comes to their identity, therefore, employees lose their sense of teamwork and alignment with the entire enterprise and begin to seek the safety of their particular profession, union, function, team, or location. People in mature organizations tend to avoid conflict for fear of blame or of having someone take their disagreement personally. Alternatively, they may take part in a succession of routine collisions that lead to stalemate rather than resolution. As for learning, larger and older organizations tend to be less receptive to new ideas than their younger counterparts. In place of inquiry and experimentation, ideas get studied to death in hopes of ferreting out every possible weakness before making a commitment. The precondition for action is certain knowledge. (Pascale, Millemann, & Gioja, 1997, p. 130)

Argyris and his colleagues identified two distinct types of organizational learning, "single-loop" and "double-loop" learning, which they distinguish as follows.

> Single-loop learning involves improving the organization's capacity to achieve known objectives. It is associated with routine and behavioral learning. Under single-loop, the organization is *learning without significant change in its basic assumptions.* Double-loop learning *reevaluates the nature of the organization's objectives and values and beliefs surrounding them.* This type of learning involves changing the organization's culture. Importantly, double-loop consists of the organization's learning how to learn. (as cited in Luthans, 2005, p. 112)

The key is to move toward a system of double-loop learning. Single-loop learning simply "produces behavioral changes that are adaptive in a particular instance, but do not produce significant value changes" (Van Wart, 1998, p. 577). On the other hand, double-loop learning "produces a values change from which behavioral changes flow" (p. 577). Here, "decisions are based on rethinking of existing competencies/methods, which have proved inadequate . . . existing knowledge is challenged and this type of learning is closely related to continuous improvements in TQM [total quality management] and business excellence" (Eskildsen, Dahl-gaard, & Norgaard, 1999, p. 524).

Argyris (1993) argued that single-loop learning is associated with sophisticated defensive routines that produce "skilled incompetence." That is, it develops "the behavior patterns that overprotect us from threat or embarrassment as well as significant learning" (cited in Van Wart, 1998, p. 578). He argued that double-loop learning is more difficult, but it can be taught to individuals and to groups, and "can replace more limited and more defensive single-loop learning in entire organizations" (p. 577).

Senge further developed these concepts by distinguishing between adaptive and generative learning (Luthans, 2005, p. 112). Adaptive learning consists of merely adapting to environmental changes. Generative learning involves "creativity and innovation, going beyond just adapting to change to being ahead of and anticipating change" (p. 112). It is associated with a spirit of continual feedback, experimentation, and reassessment of core beliefs and assumptions. Under this view, failure is viewed as an opportunity for feedback, and not merely as a setback. Organizations that are adept at this skill continuously learn from their experiences and widely disseminate this learning. In other words, it becomes part of the organization's normal functioning (MacDonald, 1995; Snyder & Cummings, 1998).

Strategic management is built on the concept of learning. However, in many respects, the learning organization is an ideal. It implies a system whereby employees are provided with all necessary information, without even asking (Lee, 2000). It suggests an organizational culture that:

- supports and rewards learning and innovation
- promotes inquiry, dialogue, risk-taking, and experimentation
- allows mistakes to be shared and viewed as opportunities for learning, and
- values the well-being of all employees (Gephart & Marsick, 1996, p. 39; see also Luthans, 2005).

Martha Gephart and Victoria Marsick (1996) find learning organizations are "people-centered," providing "a caring community that nurtures, values, and supports the well-being, development, and learning of every individual" (p. 38). Police administrators might struggle with this concept, particularly since paramilitary organizations are not run as democracies and are not designed primarily for valuing the well-being of all employees. They have "ranks, levels of command and uniforms" and are designed primarily for the rapid execution of orders from above (Bennett & Hess, 2001, p. 3). Rarely, if ever, will police supervisors solicit attitudes or opinions from their subordinates regarding their professional development or the overall quality of their work life. Charles McClintock (2004) suggests that the goal of becoming a learning organization is a difficult one to achieve: "The notion of the continuously changing and learning organization is often a fiction that is not feasible, given the limits of human dynamics, resources, or political constraints" (p. 598).

Nevertheless, becoming a "learning organization" is not an either/or proposition. Organizations can take a variety of affirmative steps to help move *in the direction* of becoming one (Senge, 1996). In this sense, we are dealing with a continuum; all organizations can measure their relative ability to perform generative learning. Gephart and Marsick (1996) describe five distinct phases that organizations pass through on their way to becoming a learning organization.

1. the *Forming* Organization

2. the *Developing* Organization

3. the *Maturing* Organization

4. the *Adapting* Organization, and

5. the *Learning* Organization (p. 44).

It is likely that most U.S. police agencies are currently either *maturing* or *adapting* organizations. Police organizations can make substantial progress and achieve success by increasing the overall amount of individual, team, and strategic learning that takes place within the organization. The key is to create an atmosphere where the more adaptive and flexible *double-loop* learning can take place. As Richard Pascale and Jerry Sternin (2005) state, the goal is to "make it safe to learn" (p. 74).

Whether management recognizes it or not, learning *is* continually taking place within their organizations. The problem occurs when management is not cognizant of this process, when learning is haphazard, and when lessons are not used as the basis for intelligent management decisions. Police managers must be tuned into knowledge gaps (essentially being aware of what they are unaware of) and must utilize their internal systems of communication and training to help foster an atmosphere where true organizational learning can occur.

Open Communication

In the past, police administrators often naively assumed that they could control the flow of communication within their organizations.

Unfortunately, communication is a dynamic social process that is often quite complex. In reality, formal lines of communication carry only a portion of the information that is actually exchanged within an organization. Managers use downward communication to send orders and directives, to state goals, objectives, policies, and practices. However, they frequently fail to account for the various informal lines of communication that exist and often carry additional or contrary messages. Managers need to recognize that existing horizontal lines of communication are necessary "if the subsystems within a police organization are to function in an effective and coordinated manner" (Swanson, Territo, & Taylor, 2005, p. 317). These communication channels and networks supplement formal channels and help establish social bonds and facilitate teamwork; they are essential to the effective operation of the organization. Unfortunately, they can also rapidly transmit false or harmful information that can frustrate otherwise well-designed organizational plans or initiatives. Police managers must recognize and formalize horizontal lines of communication and ensure that information is openly and accurately transmitted whenever possible. They must understand that the strength of the ties between units and subunits will govern how effectively information will be transferred among them (Hansen, 1999).

Modern police managers must also recognize and understand the variety of factors that can inhibit communication and knowledge sharing within organizations. These factors often exist, despite the fact that the organization employs highly skilled or professional personnel. Argyris developed the term "skilled incompetence" to describe his discovery that, "the more intelligent and highly trained a professional—for example, a Harvard MBA or a professional management consultant—the greater his skill at defensive routines that prevent open dialogue" (cited in Fulmer, Gibbs, & Keys, 1998, p. 9). Many other inhibitors develop simply as a result of organizational structure, such as problems that result from "the lack of direct relationships and extensive communication between people from different subunits" (Hansen, 1999, p. 82). Managers must confront and remove these impediments so that strong vertical and horizontal lines of communication can be established and used effectively.

Because of their bureaucratic nature, however, police agencies are designed to focus on downward communication. Unfortunately, if most information flows downhill, upward communication is often impeded or completely blocked. As Donald Kettl (2005) notes, this inevitably leads to operational dysfunction.

> Hierarchical organizations give power according to position. Those who hold the information [needed for effective operations] might well not be those who have authority in the hierarchy. So there is great potential for internal organizational conflict if information-based power wins out—or ineffective response if position-based power triumphs. (p. 20)

Upward communication in police organizations can frequently be frustrated by: (1) the difficulty of overcoming the *rank structure* (e.g., a patrol officer would be hesitant to approach a commanding officer with a question or comment; additional ranks can often represent additional impediments); (2) *organizational culture* (that might discourage entirely open exchanges with superiors); and/or (3) the barrier of *physical distance* (since the parties frequently would not associate or share the same physical space during the work day) (Swanson et al., 2005).

Most police practitioners are quite familiar with the phenomenon that exists whereby lower-ranking officers prefer merely to tell their supervisors "what it is they want to hear," rather than providing an accurate assessment of true opinion. Unfortunately, as Reuss-Ianni (1983) notes, "If headquarters continues to solicit data from people who are unwilling to surrender it due to their understanding of the personal implications for the bearer of bad tidings, the data supplied will be of questionable value at best" (p. 125). She further explains that this frequently results in a situation where "those who have the necessary information do not have the power to decide and those who have the power to decide cannot get the necessary information" (p. 125).

Effective managers now recognize that information is the key to effective policing. The days of the careerist commanders who worked tirelessly to maintain the status quo (and believed that "no news was good news"), are gone. Today's police managers realize that virtually everything is in flux; change is inevitable and should be welcomed. Skilled managers recognize that accurate and timely information drive all management decisions, that things change, and that there is always news that must be interpreted and acted upon. Managers can no longer be inaccessible. They cannot merely assume that they know what their subordinates are thinking; they need to ask them directly.

> Some executives feel that they are too involved in daily problems and responsibilities to provide adequate time for listening fully to their subordinates' ideas, reports, and criticism. Nevertheless, many time-consuming problems could be minimized or eliminated if superiors would take the time to listen to their employees, for in listening they can discover solutions to present problems or anticipate causes for future ones. (Swanson et al., 2005, p. 316)

In sum, police managers must work to create and maintain an organizational climate that values accurate information and open channels of communication. All members of the service must understand the critical link between accurate and timely information and well-considered and effective management decisions.

Effective Training

If an organization is to achieve success, it must "create a change-oriented environment where the creativity of the employees is nurtured, developed and sustained *through education and training*" (Eskildsen et al., 1999, p. 531; emphasis added). Training plays a vital role in transforming organizations by creating a learning environment (Peak, 1997).

Police training, however, is quite distinct from training that normally takes place within private sector organizations. As paramilitary organizations, police agencies have traditionally approached training in a militaristic fashion. That is, they designed a system to transform large numbers of civilians into a group of highly skilled and competent professionals. For example, few would disagree with the contention that police firearms training programs accomplish their training goals remarkably well. Within a relatively short period of time, most departments can transform citizens unfamiliar with weaponry into competent marksmen. This process is extremely efficient for transmitting specialized skills, but many would argue that the flow of information is entirely unidirectional, that it utilizes relatively simple pedagogical tools, and that it provides absolutely no opportunity for experimentation or innovation on the part of trainers or participants. Nowhere is the training versus education contrast more stark.

This is, however, not necessarily a bad thing. Due to the inherent nature of firearms training, there is an understandable demand for uniformity, regimentation, and excellence. The problem develops when police organizations apply this methodology and mind-set to their general approach to training. Some training topics however, such as the proper means and methods of community policing, require some open discussion and interaction between trainer and student. Ideally, this would include inviting select members of the community (clerics, council members, educators, etc.) to make presentations to members of the service and attempt to engage them in a dialogue. Unfortunately, the spontaneity and unpredictability of such interactions typically strikes fear in the hearts of police administrators. Nevertheless, there is no logical reason for precluding civilian involvement in police training, provided it is well prepared, approved in advance and well-delivered. Unfortunately, the traditional paramilitary conception of police training involves either: (1) a "jack of all trades" uniformed trainer who has personal expertise in each and every training topic (very big shoes to fill!); or (2) someone skilled in the efficient delivery of any and all prepackaged training modules. Both understandings of police training are flawed in that they are based on a belief in the fungibility of both trainers and their material and the notion that the individuals receiving the training should have neither the desire nor the ability to comment on their own training. For the sake of uniformity, police organizations have traditionally limited themselves (either intentionally or unintentionally) to a training process that restricts upward communication and resembles indoctrination and mass consumption more than education.

Real training must include a vital feedback process that can ultimately inform and influence the organization's operations and strategic decisions.

> Today, training is seen as an opportunity for bringing about necessary change within [a] department and as a means for rapidly replacing or modifying outdated or ineffective practices. Rather than being a static process of mass production (i.e., routinized classroom instruction for large numbers of employees), training is now seen as a dynamic and interactive process whereby both the student and the organization can learn.
>
> In-service training is a particularly effective tool for identifying, defining and sharing "best practices." A particularly useful tool or practice could virtually move throughout the entire department in a matter of weeks. . . . This ensures that the organization reacts quickly and effectively to changing conditions. . . . By viewing training in this new light, the department can break down institutional barriers to learning and create a supportive climate for knowledge transfer. (O'Rourke & O'Connell, p. 26)

Police administrators who are dissatisfied with the quality of internal training should, therefore, consider the relative effectiveness of their training personnel and curricula in terms of affording a two-way exchange of relevant information. Luthans (2005) suggests that "the people closest to the problem usually have the best ideas regarding how to solve it" and that "learning flows up and down, so managers as well as employees can benefit from it" (p. 113). All too frequently, however, there is no dialogue; training occurs simply for the purpose of "getting on the sheet" and making a record that all personnel have received it. In such instances, true understanding is often lacking and performance at the street level ultimately suffers.

Another important issue is the fact that a great deal (perhaps the vast majority) of police training occurs informally. Despite the growing scope of mandated recruit school and in-service training curricula, much training occurs outside of the control and auspices of police administrators. This is especially true where police tactics are concerned. Newly assigned officers are often quick to adopt many of the habits and techniques of their more senior and more well-established colleagues. For example, a young officer might learn from a senior colleague to respond to a call of "shots fired" in a high-rise building by taking an elevator to the floor *above* the incident. (This would provide the officer with somewhat of a tactical edge as a violent suspect would not ordinarily expect the police to respond by walking *down* the stairs to the scene.) Such a technique might be employed by many officers within an agency, yet might never have been recognized, discussed, and/or evaluated as a formalized procedure.

Police officers learn a great deal from their colleagues, particularly during the early part of their careers. Police administrators must recognize this and work to eliminate any negative, counterproductive, and/or dangerous techniques or habits. They should also attempt to utilize this informal mode of communication to implement necessary procedures and to reinforce organizational goals. The role of field training officer (FTO) is of critical importance in this process. All too frequently, police organizations fail to understand the impact that FTOs have on the professional development of newly assigned officers (Anderson, 2004). FTOs must be properly selected, trained, supervised, and supported. Ideally, FTOs are professionals who demonstrate a level of professionalism and commitment that distinguish them from their peers. Although FTOs need not have advanced degrees of formal education (such as a master's degree), additional education can be helpful. Most importantly, the ideal FTO should demonstrate a heightened degree of personal integrity and practical reasoning and decision-making skills. FTOs must lead by example but should also be able to communicate clearly, so that trainees can benefit as much as possible from their expertise.

Finally, police administrators must understand that even the most effective technologies become virtually useless without well-trained personnel. For instance, any advanced technology, such as a computer-aided dispatch (CAD) system, may actually complicate a task or jeopardize safety if it is not operated properly. Katie Hafner (2004) notes

> any new technology, whether it is a microwave oven or the controls of a Boeing 777, has a learning curve. And often the user interface, the all-important gateway between person and machine, is a dizzying array of buttons or keys that have to be used in combinations. It can take weeks, sometimes months, of training and adapting for people to become comfortable with a new system. (p. G1)

Most police agencies actually do recognize this. Typically, departments ensure (by contract) that the vendor of the new technology provides useful and effective training to immediate users. In large departments, however, this means that many end users will not actually receive training by the vendor. The department must ensure that training is incorporated into the department's ongoing in-service training program, so that new employees will learn as effectively as those in the initial training program. The ultimate success of incorporating this new technology will depend on the quality, scope, and effectiveness of the department's internal training mechanisms. It will also depend on the system's ability to identify field problems quickly and accurately, so that they can be corrected before they develop into large-scale threats to organizational effectiveness.

Police training is therefore intimately linked with technological advancement and the overall management of the organization. It is not a stand-alone function that serves only to develop skills and provide information. It is a dynamic and interactive exchange that must be incorporated into the organization's day-to-day management and planning activities.

Developing a Learning Culture

It is widely accepted that the unique mission and paramilitary nature of police organizations has lead to the development of a distinct, complex, and particularly strong organizational culture (see Crank, 1997; Niederhoffer and Blumberg, 1976; Paoline, 2001; Wincelowicz, 2004). The values and practices associated with this culture affect employee behavior and performance and can either foster or inhibit organizational change efforts.

The term "organizational culture" is generally defined as

> a pattern of basic assumptions—invented, discovered, or developed by a given group as it learns to cope with its problems of external adaptation and internal integration—that has worked well enough to be considered valuable and, therefore, to be taught to new members as the correct way to perceive, think, and feel in relation to those problems. (Luthans, 2005, p. 122)

Organizational cultures are generally characterized by: (1) observed behavioral regularities; (2) norms (i.e., standards of behavior); (3) dominant values; (4) philosophy; (5) rules; and (6) organizational climate (Luthans, 2005). They tend to be stable and resistant to change. Culture is learned both formally and informally, through a complex system of human interaction, whereby meaning is derived from shared understandings (Langan-Fox & Tan, 1997). As Reuss-Ianni (1983) notes, often

> it does not happen in the police academy and . . . one cannot learn it from books or criminal justice courses. A cop learns it from his [or her] own street experience, as an apprentice to officers already on the job and from contact with a peer structure of working cops in a precinct. The lessons are constantly reinforced by the "war stories" and experiences of other officers and through the traditions of police practice which developed in these networks. As the officer is socialized into the precinct social structure and into one of its subunits, the job comes to be governed by a series of conventions or mutual understandings among the officers. (p. 67)

However, as Luthans (2005) notes, "A common misconception is that an organization has a uniform culture. . . . There can be a dominant culture as well as subcultures throughout a typical organization" (p. 124). Often, multiple cultures can develop and vie for dominance at any particular point in time. Their existence and impact can positively or negatively affect organizational performance (Strati, 1998).

Harry Levinson (1994) provides a list of psychological "truths" about organizations that are quite helpful in understanding how and why cultures develop and persist over time. He notes that:

1. All organizations recapitulate the family structure and the behavioral practices of the culture in which they are embedded.

2. All animals and human beings differentiate themselves into in-groups and out-groups and develop what might be called an in-group narcissism, the "we-they" phenomenon.

3. All organizations, by definition, being made up of people, are living organisms. They have developmental histories and evolve adaptive patterns that deal with different levels of complexity.

4. All living organisms experience continuous change, both within themselves and in their environments. . . .

5. All groups follow a leader. Different groups at different times in their life experience require different styles of leadership, but the founding leader's policies, practices, and organizational structure frequently endure (p. 429).

Reuss-Ianni (1983) identified a dichotomy of culture that was specific to police organizations in her work, *Two Cultures of Policing: Street Cops and Management Cops*. As the title suggests, she believed in the emergence and functioning of two competing, and sometimes conflicting, cultures within police departments. She contended that the competition (and sometimes open antagonism) between "street cops" and their "bosses" was at the heart of the organizational dilemma of modern urban policing. This dichotomy is certainly not limited to police organizations. Many other public service organizations experience this general split between practitioners and supervisors. Indeed, even in the private sector, one can normally identify distinct subcultures based on one's overall level of motivation to conform to established rules and to achieve organizational (as opposed to personal) goals (see, e.g., Lipman-Blumen & Leavitt, 1999). Her findings were consistent with the work of Edgar Schein (1997), who identified disabling learning dysfunctions that often exist in organizations due to the existence of multiple subcultures (such as the *operator culture* and the *executive culture*).

Nevertheless, the U.S. police culture has been altered on several occasions. For example, many large-scale programs are currently underway throughout the country to foster integrity and to sensitize personnel to the cultural diversity that exists throughout our nation's communities. Another excellent example of a planned and well-executed cultural shift is the one that occurred during the early 1990s within the NYPD during the tenure of William Bratton. Bratton determined that the existing management culture was restraining organizational performance and that it needed to be changed (O'Connell, 2001a). He set out a series of well-designed reengineering efforts that ultimately altered the rigid hierarchical structure of the department, providing greater flexibility in terms of decision-making and experimentation (see Silverman, 1999; Silverman & O'Connell, 1999). Bratton succeeded in bringing about a cultural shift, particularly with regard to the worldview of managers within the organization.

If an organization attempts to move toward the goal of becoming a learning organization, top-level management must recognize the significance of organizational culture. They must understand their organization's dominant culture, as well as any other significant subcultures that could challenge progress. Any efforts, no matter how well-planned or well-exe-cuted, can and will be frustrated by a culture that does not truly value learning and the power of knowledge. The only way to ensure that this appreciation develops and takes hold within the organization is through continual reinforcement. This would include: (1) reiteration and rein-forcement of mission and organizational goals via memoranda and various regular communications from top-level management; (2) incorporating "learning skills" and ability to manage and use information as formal crite-ria in regular performance reviews of mid- and upper-level managers; and (3) including learning techniques and the importance of organizational learning as topics in the organization's executive development and in-ser-vice training programs.

The bureaucratic model can be modified to produce a more intelli-gent, cooperative, and proactive form of police organization. The key is to ensure that this shift is permanent, and not merely transitory. To do this, one must take into account the personal element, the human factors at play. In order to ensure long-term success, we must first obtain then main-tain buy-in from all stakeholders, particularly the men and women who will actually be performing the work. Progressive change efforts frequently fail, since "the whole burden of change typically rests on so few people. In other words, the number of people *at every level* who make committed, imaginative contributions to organizational success is simply too small" (Pascale et al., 1997, p. 127). Lasting change will only come about with the active participation of all levels of the organizational chart.

At the end of the day, police organizations will continue to be bureau-cracies, albeit modified ones. No organizational change effort can over-come the civil service or rank system that exists in U.S. police agencies; the chain of command will remain intact. Nevertheless, development of a pos-itive and strong organizational culture that is geared toward continual performance improvement can lead to "desirable organizational outcomes such as increased member identification, commitment, cooperation and greater consistency in decision making and performance" (Langan-Fox & Tan, 1997, p. 275). Police organizations must overcome the tendency to "overlook distant times, distant places, and failures" (Levinthal & March, 1993, p. 95). Police organizations are perpetually under construction (O'Hara, 2005). Modified and proactively oriented bureaucracies can be, and often are, quite effective in accomplishing organizational goals (Rainey & Steinbauer, 1999) The key is to recognize, understand, and align organizational culture and any attendant subcultures with the over-all mission and goals of the organization.

PROACTIVE POLICE MANAGEMENT AND THE DEVELOPMENT OF EVIDENCE-BASED POLICING

Police organizations, like all other organizations, need to engage in a proactive form of strategic management that entails, "assessing strengths and weaknesses, identifying opportunities and threats, determining where the organization should be going, and then establishing goals, strategies, and tactics for getting there" (Kissler, Fore, Jacobson, Kittredge, & Stewart, 1998, p. 353). They must be able to anticipate where their resources will be needed (i.e., hot-spot policing techniques) or, at the very least, react immediately with an effective intervention or response.

Unfortunately, as Edward Maguire (2004) notes, police agencies

> like many other public agencies are often unable to state with any degree of precision how their performance has changed over time or how it compares with that of their peer agencies, particularly those situated in similar community contexts. (p. 1)

The public now demands accountability from the police. This entails providing credible explanations in response to continuous inquiries such as what was done? was it effective? and how much did it cost? Police officials no longer have the luxury of merely shrugging their shoulders as crime rates and costs continue to rise. They are now rightly expected to justify their efforts and expenditures.

Police forces are increasingly accountable to government at various levels and to the community at large for various aspects of their performance and are expected to communicate with government and the public about what they are doing. (Collier et al., 2004, p. 458)

They need to demonstrate that they have a plan; that the plan is being followed; and whether or not their efforts are having any measurable effect.

Crisis Situations

In the aftermath of the September 11th terrorist attacks and the devastation wrought by hurricane Katrina, police leaders have now recognized that they must have the ability to react, adapt, change, and cope with myriad problems that are clearly "nonroutine." In these situations, police administrators are afforded little time to react and face the likelihood of failure and its attendant costs. The Los Angeles Police Department's *Plan of Action, Book 1* notes that one of the primary needs of the department is to establish an efficient internal system

whereby incident-related information is received, analyzed, investigated and disseminated accurately and as rapidly as possible. The successful management of past disasters has shown that timely and accurate intelligence in the hands of experienced planning and operations personnel creates a synergy enabling effective critical incident detection, prevention and response. (Hahn, Cunningham & Bratton, 2004, p. 63)

Unfortunately, few police organizations are adept at basing the majority of their routine or crisis decisions on hard data. In traditional, hierarchical police organizations, the chief and his executive staff are the "repositories" of information and the sole decision makers. The rest of the organization is charged with execution.

Problem Identification

Goldstein (1990) advocated a radical overhaul of the policing mindset. He suggested that merely responding to repeated calls for service did little to impact crime and to improve the lives of citizens. His view coincided with the results of the Kansas City Preventative Patrol Experiment (Kelling, 1974), which suggested that routine patrol practices (i.e., random patrol and response to calls for service) were far too reactive and largely ineffective. He suggested that the police seek proactive, effective solutions to underlying and persistent problems. Unfortunately, not every solution (or problem, for that matter) is obvious. Problem identification requires timely and accurate information, as well as a trained eye. The form of "problem-oriented policing" promoted by Goldstein required not only a new mind-set but also a new methodology for obtaining and processing information.

Lawrence Sherman and Dennis Rogan (1995) similarly suggested a more informed and more effective method of policing. By identifying and deploying personnel into areas with clusters of reported crime (hot spots), they suggest that the police can have a greater impact on crime reduction. This approach was almost immediately recognized as a more intelligent form of policing, and departments across the country quickly sought the most effective means of identifying and patrolling their respective hot spots. Like problem-oriented policing, the hot-spot method had one critical requirement—timely and accurate information. Modern police agencies began to place a premium on usable data and quickly (almost imperceptibly) grew accustomed to basing many of their most critical tactical and strategic decisions on data. Data-driven decision making became the norm and developed as an effective means of ensuring that police decisions were logical and supported by something more than anecdotal information or instinct (Brown & Brudney, 2003).

Evidence-Based Practice

The concept of evidence-based practice was originally developed in the field of medicine (see Roberts & Yeager, 2004). Doctors use "treatments for which there is *sufficiently persuasive evidence* to support their effectiveness in attaining the desired outcomes" (Proctor & Rosen, 2004, p. 193; emphasis added). Medical practice suggests that practitioners in other fields should be in a position to provide a persuasive rationale for their practice/business decisions. Decisions should be "based, to the fullest extent possible, on the best available and most appropriate research evidence" (p. 194; see also Davenport, 2006).

Evidence-based practice has two distinct components: (1) using the best available evidence to select the most appropriate and best-fitting intervention to use; and (2) deciding whether the intervention implemented is having its predicted results—meaning, has it reached its desired outcome or should it be abandoned (Proctor & Rosen, 2004). Continually monitoring and evaluating performance measures (discussed later in this chapter) provide the inputs to determine intervention effectiveness, success, and/or failure (Pfeffer & Sutton, 2006).

To be effective, evidence-based practice must be collaborative; people at all levels of an organization should be involved in assembling, sorting, and presenting a variety of data. As previously mentioned, the collective approach differs greatly from the traditional method of police decision making, whereby the chief or top administrator issued directives from "on high" with little consultation or input from individuals outside the "inner circle" of the highest level of command. The knowledge-creating model sees the organization as continuously engaged in knowledge conversion. Under the knowledge-creating model, "the personal knowledge of each member is leveraged so the whole organization can use it to develop new products and services" (Choo, 1998, p. 14).

Participative management has been quite successful in the corporate realm but, unfortunately, "power-sharing arrangements seem to have found little acceptance in law enforcement circles" (Wuestewald & Steinheider, 2006, p. 48). An interesting paradox exists, however, whereby "discretionary authority tends to be greatest at the bottom of the police organization where patrol officers apply laws, policy and regulations to situations that do not fit neatly into the rulebook" (p. 48). In other words, patrol officers tend to be more autonomous and creative in their work than what is typically acknowledged. Officers assigned to street patrol possess a wide array of knowledge and opinions that can certainly inform many important management decisions. Patrol officers are similarly the first members of the organization to detect whether or not a particular tactic or initiative is having its desired effect. They therefore possess a great deal of useful knowledge—evidence—that should not go untapped, particularly when the organization is attempting to employ problem-solving or community-based methods to reduce crime.

By "closing the gap between research and practice," evidence-based practice is designed to review measurable outcomes and identify best practices as well as the most efficient and effective interventions and action strategies available (Camasso, 2004, p. 243). It means that "practitioners use theories and interventions based on the empirical evidence of their effectiveness, apply approaches appropriate to the client[s] and setting, and evaluate their own practice effectiveness" (Knox, 2004, p. 324).

Police agencies have enjoyed much success in the application of statistical and other crime data to inform crime control and prevention strategies. As mentioned in chapter 2, August Vollmer in 1909 became the first police chief to use crime records for short- and long-term planning (Spelman, 1998). Since Vollmer, an array of evidence-driven strategies have been developed and implemented to control crime. The systematic analysis of reported crime data serves a number of purposes: to identify potential suspects in specific crimes; to spot geographic and temporal crime trends; and generally to account for police response to it. For example, situational crime prevention, a theory developed by Ronald Clarke and Marcus Felson (1993), identifies specific forms of crime and the environmental context in which they occurred. Policing strategies are developed based on this analysis and implemented to increase the risk associated with committing the crimes and to reduce rewards perceived by the offender. Hot-spot policing and crime mapping focus police resources on the places where, and during the times when, there are significantly high occurrences of crime; these methods depend on in-depth analysis and the plotting of crime data.

In the mid-1980s, the Newport News (Virginia) Police Department, under the leadership of Chief Daryl Stephens, developed a technique known as SARA to insure the effective use of data to address police issues. This four-step methodology entails: (1) *scanning* the work landscape for potential problems and threats; (2) *analysis* of these problems, similar problems, potential problems, prior organizational responses, and identification of available options; (3) *response,* which includes implementing comprehensive and effective solutions, with the assistance of outside agencies when necessary; and (4) *assessment,* the evaluation of the impact and effectiveness of actions taken (Swanson et al., 2005). The SARA technique has been adopted by many police agencies because it encourages managers to become more reflective and forces them to base their operational and strategic decisions on objective, verifiable evidence.

Sherman (1998) was one of the first researchers to suggest that police agencies should adopt evidence-based practice as a means for "continuously improving [their management practices] with ongoing feedback" (p.2) Sherman contended that research could be used to guide police practice, evaluate practitioners, and enhance operations. According to Sherman, the evaluation of ongoing operations is the "crucial missing link in many recent attempts to improve policing" (p. 1). It can also help police agencies become more reflexive or "smart" institutions. Sherman argues that "police practices should be based on scientific evidence about what works best" (p. 2). Unfortunately, in many police departments, existing "knowledge resources" are not organized in ways that support strategic decision making or are limited to specialized research and evaluation units. These units, while valuable, may not draw sufficiently on resources throughout an organization and sometimes stifle knowledge exchange because of misguided perceptions of protecting their specialized knowledge. Robert Hayward (2004) notes that, "The most difficult task in information management is to present data, information, and knowledge in ways that facilitate the accrual of wisdom about how to make the entire system perform better" (p. 45).

Cultural Transformation

If evidence-based practice is to become a defining feature of modern policing, it needs to be part of a wider cultural transformation that goes beyond crime control and/or prevention. In many ways, this cultural transformation began in 1993, as a result of the Clinton administration's interest in developing and deploying effective performance measurement systems throughout federal agencies. The Government Performance and Results Act (GPRA) mandated that all federal agencies provide concrete evidence of organizational goal achievement. It also directed that future funding would be tied to each agency's ability to provide evidence of their effectiveness. GPRA was "an effort to legislate conformity with the principles of performance-based management" (Simeone et al., 2005, p. 191). Similar efforts were underway in the private sector at the time, where new technologies and management approaches were being explored to develop effective organizational performance measurement systems (see, e.g., Jensen & Sage, 2000; Schaffer & Thomson, 1992). The GPRA was designed to improve the overall quality of public services being delivered by requiring all federal agencies to: (1) develop strategic plans, with clear and obtainable goals and objectives; (2) define how they intended to achieve those goals; and (3) demonstrate how they would actually measure agency and program performance in achieving those goals (Artley, Ellison, & Kennedy, 2001). In essence, it required all federal agencies (including law enforcement agencies such as the FBI and DEA) to create a management system that could be used to demonstrate organizational effectiveness. Another primary goal was to "strengthen accountability for program results" (Hatry, Morley, Rossman, & Wholey, 2003, p. 5).

Will Artley and his colleagues (2001) define a performance-based management system as "a formalized framework within an organization for the implementation, conduct, and maintenance of a performance-based management approach to business operations" (p. 1). They explain how such a system focuses on results, not just activities, and is an absolute necessity in light of the new business realities created by the GPRA. They also provide a helpful framework for public service agencies wishing to develop such a system. They assert that the essential steps in developing a performance-based system are:

1. Define organizational mission and strategic performance objectives

2. Establish an integrated performance measurement system

3. Establish accountability for performance

4. Establish a process/system for collecting performance data

5. Establish a process/system for analyzing, reviewing, and reporting performance data, and

6. Establish a process/system for using performance information to drive improvement

There is a subtle but very important distinction between the terms "performance-based management system" and "performance-based *management*." The latter term describes a discrete set of business skills needed for *using* the data generated from a system. In other words, a system of performance-based management is used not only for data gathering and report writing but also to "steer the ship."

> Performance-based management is a systematic approach to performance improvement through an on-going process of establishing strategic performance objectives; measuring performance; collecting, analyzing, reviewing, and reporting performance data; and *using that*

data to drive performance improvement. (Artley et al., 2001, p. 3; emphasis added)

The GPRA's legislative mandate forced federal agencies to begin developing such management systems. Many other public organizations (state and local) also looked to establish their own systems and by the late 1990s, many state and local legislatures began to develop legislation similar to the GPRA. What started out as a federal legislative initiative quickly spread as a national reform movement. Performance-based management resonated with politicians and their constituents who sought cost-effectiveness and efficiency, but it also appealed to administrators who were searching for better data that would support more effective decision making and ultimately improve organizational performance.

There are six primary benefits associated with performance-based management (Artley et al., 2001).

1. Providing a structured approach to focus on strategic performance objectives;
2. Providing a mechanism for accurately reporting performance to upper management and stakeholders;
3. Bringing all interested parties into the planning and evaluation of performance;
4. Providing a mechanism for linking performance and budget expenditures;
5. Providing a framework for accountability; and
6. Sharing responsibility for performance improvement.

Performance-based management presumes that the organization is able to avail itself of "accurate, timely, and complete information" (p. 9; see also Maple & Mitchell, 1999). This information is obtained through a process known as environmental scanning, whereby data concerning the internal and external work environments are gathered from a variety of sources and carefully analyzed (Kanji, 2002). This information is then used to inform strategic planning and day-to-day operational decision making.

Although the GPRA held much promise in terms of enhancing overall efficiency and effectiveness, many federal agencies initially struggled to establish acceptable management systems. Congress was generally dissatisfied with the quality of the early reports submitted by federal agencies and concluded that "most agencies lack the reliable data sources and systems needed to develop, validate, and verify performance information" (Pane, 2004, p. 612).

Despite the fact that federal agencies submitted performance management plans for many years, critics continued to note that genuine outcome information was lacking. For example, a report from the General Accounting Office in August 2000 noted that most federal agencies had not yet established plans that linked all of their performance measures to strategic goals (Saldarini, 2000). This may be due, in part, to the fact that identification and measurement of outcomes for public programs is often an extremely difficult task (see Wulczyn, Kogan, & Dilts, 2001) because outcomes "commonly cut across organizational lines" (Kowalewski, 1996, p. 2). As a result, many agencies simply "retreated to simple output or workload measures" (Bernstein, 1999, p. 86).

As previously discussed, over the past decade the requirements imposed by GPRA have gradually made their way to the state and local levels (Melkers & Willoughby, 2004). Top-level police administrators understand a simple reality—federal, state, and county funding sources increasingly require proof that service interventions have been effective. Police managers, like their colleagues in the health and education fields, are now often required not only to account for the resources they use but also to "document and measure quality of service, program, and client *outcomes*" (Dziegielewski & Roberts, 2004, p. 200; emphasis added). As a result, police administrators find themselves actively seeking methods to measure organizational *outcomes*, such as a safer city or a reduction in the public's fear of crime, rather than mere organizational *outputs*, such as the number of arrests made or responses to calls for service.

Performance Measures and Outcomes

GPRA and similar initiatives emphasize performance and accountability, using empirical methods for evaluative inquiry. State and local police agencies, like their colleagues in federal law enforcement, must now "report not only how much they spend, but how much work they do, how well they do it, how efficiently, and, ideally, what their actions achieve" (Ammons, 1995, p. 37). In other words, they must demonstrate the consequences of their actions and activities. Ideally, outcomes should be directly linked to organizational goals, which are logically and clearly linked to the overall mission of the organization.

Unfortunately, while the mandate to directly link program activities to outcomes is clear and unambiguous, "there is often disagreement about what outcomes to measure or how to operationally define them" (McClintock, 2004, p. 603). Since virtually all program activities should be clearly linked to *outcomes*, it is imperative that senior management: (1) identify desired outcomes; (2) clarify priorities; and (3) establish and ensure accountability for the attainment of desired outcomes.

In the field of policing and law enforcement, this is often easier said than done. Identifying and "distinguishing outputs from effects or outcomes is often problematic" (Chapel, 2004, p. 638). Robert Behn (2004) notes that

> unfortunately, government agencies (like all organizations) do not
> produce outcomes. Organizations produce outputs. The outcomes are
> what happens outside the organization. Automobile manufacturers do

not produce transportation: they produce cars. . . . Citizens might like to believe that government produces societal outcomes (so that they need not worry about their own contribution), but public agencies can produce only outputs. (p. 11)

Organizations such as the Federal Drug Enforcement Administration have become adept at identifying and recording organizational outputs, such as the number of drug seizures made, amounts of drugs seized, number of arrests, number of warrants executed, number of successful prosecutions, etc. They experience more difficulty in assessing outcomes. They can say what the organization did, but they have greater difficulty determining if their efforts are having the desired impact. For example, information about the amount of illegal narcotics seized is useful and may reflect enforcement successes, but it does not indicate the quantity or quality of narcotics still available in the community. Additional measures, such as the number of drug overdose admissions to area emergency rooms or the relative purity of seized illegal narcotics, might be more accurate indicators of availability (i.e., supply). Extrapolating from the available data provides additional information on whether enforcement efforts are having an impact.

A variety of performance *measures* can and should be used to provide an accurate picture of how well organizational *outcomes* are being achieved. For example, if a desired outcome is stated as "enhancing the safety and security of local residents," an agency should collect data concerning: (1) the number of crime prevention/security surveys performed; (2) the number of criminal convictions obtained; (3) the number of weapons seized; (4) the results of citizen satisfaction surveys, etc., whereby the rate of reported crime can be examined relative to population density (Tran, Gardon, & Polidori, 2004).

The process of selecting outcome measures is difficult, though, particularly for police organizations. As Burt Perrin (2006) explains, it entails an entirely new way of thinking.

Implementing an outcome focus represents a fundamental shift in the nature of thinking, acting and managing within the public sector, away from a focus on *process* and on what one needs to do, to a focus on *benefits*. (p. 7)

Mission statements and stated goals must be reexamined and, if necessary, rewritten to be consistent with performance measure efforts. Often, broadly stated goals (such as the maintenance of a "safe community") cannot be measured by one or even several measures. Rather, a variety of indicators must be developed and used to gain an accurate performance assessment. For example, in the field of policing, we should regularly examine the number and type of: (1) calls for service, (2) average response time, (3) arrests, (4) warrants executed, (5) summonses issued, (6) civilian complaints, (7) line-of-duty injuries, etc.

The selection of useful performance measures is obviously of the utmost importance. They should be tangible, clear, and specific. Genie Stowers (2004) suggests the following criteria for selecting outcome indicators:

- **Relevance to the mission/objectives** of the program.

- **Importance to the outcome** it is intended to help measure. (Does the indicator measure an important aspect of the outcome?)

- **User comprehension** of what is measured and reported.

- **Program influence or control over the outcome.** (If the program is expected to have some tangible, measurable effect on a specific outcome, an indicator of that outcome should be a candidate for inclusion—whether the effects are direct or indirect.)

- **Feasibility** of collecting reasonably valid data on the indicator.

- **Cost** of collecting the indicator data. (Sometimes, however, the most costly indicators are the most valuable.)

- **Uniqueness.** (To the extent that an indicator overlaps with other indicators, it becomes less important.)

- **Manipulability.** (Do not select indicators that program personnel can easily manipulate to their advantage.)

- **Comprehensiveness.** (Indicators should include outcomes that identify possible negative effects. Does the list of indicators cover all the characteristics of concern to customers? Does the list of indicators include relevant feedback from customers relating to the outcomes? Performance measures should extend beyond mere *reporting*. (Teague, Trabin, & Ray, 2004).

Since police performance is multidimensional, a great deal of thought must go into the selection of indicators. They must be identified through a process of trial and error. When engaging in this process, it is best to err on the side of "overinclusiveness." That is, it is better to select more indicators. As it becomes apparent over time that some are unwieldy or not cost effective, those can be discarded. Measures need not be flawless. At the very least, however, they must be accurate and valid. It goes without saying that the overall quality of a performance-based system is only as good as the measures that support it.

Behn (2004) suggests that organizations analyze a large number and wide variety of quantitative and qualitative indicators. For example, a police agency should use an array of indicators to measure police service delivery, including the number of criminal complaints received or the number of summonses issued (quantitative) as well as the narrative results of a citizens' satisfaction or citizen contact survey (qualitative).

Ideally, performance measurement is tied into an organization's strategic planning process as a way of measuring the implementation of goals and objectives derived from an organization's mission and strategic value statements and SWOT (strength, weaknesses, opportunities, and threats) analysis. Stowers (2004) suggests that the "results and the measures themselves should be available and visible, not just the purview of those in management or in the budgeting area" (p. 9). The relative weight of importance that is given to each measure depends on a host of factors, all of which relate to what the organization believes is most critical at the time.

It should be noted that performance-based management can also have a "downside." In England, for example, where a great deal of emphasis has been placed on organizational efficiency within the public sector, critics have pointed to the damaging effect of an overemphasis on benchmarking and goal attainment. Some suggest that target/goal attainment has become such a priority for administrators and such an administrative burden that quality of service has almost become a secondary concern. Moore (2003) echoes these sentiments in the United States and suggests that the demand for accountability entails more than meeting preestablished performance targets. Thomas Ward (2000, 2005) expressed similar concern about the overemphasis that has been placed on the "beating the numbers approach." An agency's obsession with reducing crime statistics may be demoralizing, discourage middle managers from ascending to more senior positions, breed organizational dissonance, and alienate the community because of the use of overly aggressive police tactics to drive down crime.

Knowing Organizations

Information, regardless of whether it is used to inform crime strategies and/or management practices, must be treated as intellectual capital that can be acquired, channeled, and warehoused to continuously improve the efficiency and effectiveness of the organization's process (Hayward, 2004). If it is managed appropriately, this "evidence" can be readily accessed and will contribute to the generation of organizational knowledge and wisdom as well as the "continuous process of reformulating and refining theory" (Chaiklin, 2004, p. 96). What is absolutely necessary is a system designed to maintain strategic focus, ensure data quality, provide continual monitoring, and the dissemination of necessary information.

Police agencies must become "knowing organizations."

> A knowing organization is well prepared to sustain its growth and development in a dynamic environment. By sensing and understanding its environment, the knowing organization is able to prepare for adaptation early. By marshalling the skills and expertise of its members, the knowing organization is able to engage in continuous learning and innovation. By applying learned decision rules and routines, the knowing organization is primed to take timely, purposive action. At the heart of the knowing organization is its management of the information processes that underpin sense making, knowledge building, and decision making. (Choo, 1998, p. xi)

The Compstat system provides an effective model for police and other criminal justice agencies to build knowing organizations, formalize evidence-based practices, monitor performance, and support continuous learning and innovation. Chapter 5 reviews the development and implementation of that system in the New York City Police Department under then Commissioner William Bratton.

"COMPSTAT"
ITS PHILOSOPHY, PRACTICE, AND PROMISE

This chapter will examine Compstat, arguably the first truly effective PBM system to be established in a U.S. police department. It will also consider how PBM techniques can alter and improve the overall quality of organizational communication and decision making.

Beginning in 1994, the NYPD began a carefully planned redesign of its entire organizational structure. Under the leadership of newly appointed Commissioner William Bratton, the department employed a variety of management strategies designed to reengineer its business processes and to create a flatter organizational structure based on geographic decentralization, teamwork, information sharing, and managerial accountability (Silverman & O'Connell, 1999). This rapid redesign of the department's organizational architecture was based on the concept of continuous improvement of performance (benchmarking and the sharing of "best practices") and the ability to utilize timely and accurate information to manage and control change. Stated in other terms, the department attempted to correct its "knowledge-inhibiting activities" (Snyder & Cummings, 1998) and to institutionalize the organizational learning process described by Argyris (see chapter 3).

The overall rate of reported violent crime in New York City declined dramatically and far outpaced reported crime drops across the nation (Horowitz, 1995). From 1993–1998, New York experienced a 53% drop in the burglary rate, a 54% drop in reported robberies, and an incredible 67% drop in the murder rate (Silverman, 1999). Philip McGuire (1999) contends that, "No other major American city recorded as significant or sustained a reduction in crime during so short a period, or any comparable period, in the modern crime-reporting era" (p. 134). These extraordinary achievements were attributed in large part to the department's unique and innovative model of police management (Kelling & Sousa, 2001).

Eli Silverman (1999) explains that prior to 1994, the NYPD, like most police organizations, was addicted to formal rules and procedures and subject to an occupational culture that had proven itself to be particularly resistant to change. It was characterized by strict hierarchical structures, organizational rigidity, and a culture that was generally unreceptive to change. Such organizational constraints are common within police organizations. Virtually all police organizations prefer regulatory supervision and have a general aversion to change.

In accordance with classic bureaucratic structure, the overall orientation of managers within the department was downward, rather than outward (towards the external environment) or upward. Precinct commanders "did not see crime reduction as their foremost responsibility" and were "essentially on their own in combating crime" (Silverman, 1999, p. 98). Commissioner Bratton quickly altered this mind-set by making a variety of high-level personnel changes and by redefining the department's overall purpose and mission. (Bratton, 1996b)

An emphasis was placed on the realignment of organizational resources. An ambitious reengineering effort shifted the department from being a centralized, functional organization to a decentralized, geographic organization (Silverman & O'Connell, 1999). A number of centralized, functional units were broken up, and their functions (and personnel) were redistributed to new geographically decentralized units (precincts). An entire level of the department's organizational chart was removed (divisions were dismantled during this time period) in the belief that decisions should be made at the lowest operational level. Precinct commanders were given unprecedented authority and responsibility. An effort was made to identify high-performing commanders who were willing to assume greater responsibility (see generally Huselid, Beatty, & Becker, 2005). Nevertheless, top-level administrators still retained control. Despite the operational latitude granted to precinct commanders, authority was still exercised at the top, but within a better informed context based on results (Silverman, 1999).

Functional specialists were placed under the command of newly defined geographic managers, moving decision making down the organizational hierarchy (Silverman & O'Connell, 1999). This resulted in greater empowerment, more participation in decision making, and less hierarchical communications within the organization. The "information silos" previously used by managers to hoard information (resulting in suboptimized organizational performance) were dismantled.

Bratton clearly described the direction in which he intended to move the organization and highlighted with specificity the strategically important managerial work to be achieved. To accomplish these goals, a variety of intelligent crime-reduction strategies were developed and implemented. The instrument used to implement and monitor these strategies was Compstat.

Immediately after taking office, Bratton shocked his subordinates by establishing new, exacting standards of operational performance. He and his top aides recognized that data needed to be gathered and analyzed in a timely manner if effective crime-reduction strategies were to be implemented (Bratton & Knobler, 1998). Periodic meetings were scheduled at headquarters whereby precinct commanders were required to report and react to crime data generated from their commands. Over time, these data-based informal discussions between department executives and field commanders developed into formal biweekly strategy meetings (known as Compstat meetings) whereby all levels of the department participated to identify precinct and citywide crime trends, to deploy resources, and to assess crime control strategies.

Utilizing real-time crime data and sophisticated computer mapping technology as basic crime-fighting tools, Compstat enables senior level administrators to engage in face-to-face discussion of issues and proactive practices that draw on the collective expertise of the entire organization. It has developed as an interactive management device that enables the organization to view, discuss, and understand varying needs for police services and cross-unit performance comparisons. Compstat is used to teach, supervise, and evaluate personnel, all in one central forum. According to the former mayor of New York, Rudolph Giuliani, Compstat has "transformed the N.Y.P.D. from an organization that reacted to crime to a police department that actively works to deter offenses" (Giuliani, 1997).

Bratton credited Compstat with moving the department "from a micro-managed organization with very little strategic direction to a decentralized management style with strong strategic guidance at the top" (Bratton, 1995, p.2). By utilizing a system of internal benchmarking and the open transfer of best practices, Compstat moved the department in the direction of the learning organization described by Argyris—one that is able to analyze, reflect, learn, and change based on experience (Argyris, 1999; O'Dell & Grayson, 1998).

Today, Compstat has become synonymous with a more intelligent and proactive style of police management. It is founded on four core principles: (1) accurate and timely intelligence; (2) effective tactics; (3) rapid deployment of personnel and resources; and (4) relentless follow-up and assessment (NYPD, 1996b). Visitors from around the world have traveled to New York to participate in Compstat conferences or to sit in on the department's Compstat meetings (Dodenhoff, 1996). Many police agencies have successfully implemented this style of management, and it has been successfully adopted in a variety of other public service agencies. Some examples include the New York City Department of Correction's version known as TEAMS; New York City's Traffic Stat; and Jobstat (Marzulli, 1998; Straub & O'Connell, 1999). Public managers and academics alike have recognized Compstat's utility as a public management device. In 1996, Compstat was awarded the prestigious Innovations in American Government Award from the Ford Foundation and the John F. Kennedy School of Government at Harvard University.

Compstat was designed not only to solve problems but also to identify their causes. It is a system that continuously performs needs assessments—a "formal process that identifies needs as gaps in results between what is and what should be" (Leigh, 2004, p. 622).

What Is Compstat?

Compstat was originally intended as a mechanism for the production of real-time crime data that could be discussed and used by top-ranking officials as they formulated strategic and operational plans for their department. Senior administrators were summoned to police headquarters to respond to targeted questions about crime reports and related conditions within their specific areas of responsibility. Prior to the advent of the Compstat system, real-time data were not routinely being assembled, distributed, and used in this manner within the organization (see O'Connell, 2001a).

During the first few months of 1994, there was a certain degree of experimentation with regard to the format of the meetings as well as with the physical layout and setting. As the number of participants grew, the meetings moved to a larger venue (Gorta, 1998; Maple & Mitchell, 1999). Representatives from other agencies participated, including "district attorneys from each of the five boroughs, the New York State Department of Parole, the City Probation Department, . . . the City Corrections Department . . . consumer affairs, social services, and environmental protection" (McGuire, 1999, p. 137). Their participation was critical, particularly if "the problems or strategies to be discussed require[d] inter-agency coordination and cooperation" (p. 14) The seating arrangement during these meetings "shifted from rows to a horseshoe shape to encourage more interaction" (Silverman, 1999, p. 102).

As additional personnel participated, oral presentations of field commanders became much more thorough. Similarly, the briefing books that contained the crime data that were to be discussed became more comprehensive.

> The Compstat staff began supplementing its oral briefings to [senior administrators] with increasingly refined briefing books. These books summarize each precinct's unresolved investigations and patterns of criminal activity, particularly homicides, shootings, rapes, and robberies. . . . (Silverman, 1999, p. 114)

> Briefing books were at first prepared only for the chief of department, deputy commissioner for crime control strategies, and police commissioner. Although bureau chiefs attended meetings and occasionally participated, their involvement was originally less central to the ques-

tioning process. Eventually, these chiefs (chief of detectives, organized crime control, transit, and housing, plus the first deputy commissioner) became more involved and were also provided with briefing books. (Silverman, 1999, p. 117)

The questioning of precinct commanders also became more intense as the system developed. They were now required to possess an in-depth knowledge and understanding of a wide array of crime-related topics, as well as "qualitative information about precinct and community conditions and their relationship to effective crime fighting" (Silverman, 1999, p. 106). More importantly, they were being held responsible for crime reductions. As Commissioner Bratton noted, "having given the precinct commanders increased power, I had to make sure they were handling it properly through accountability and relentless assessment" (Bratton & Knobler, 1998, p. 231). Many commanders were unprepared for this new level of responsibility. During this time, there was a particularly high level of turnover at the precinct commander level.

McGuire (1999) reported that a precinct commander's success depended in large part on his/her ability to understand the demands of the new administration.

> A commander's success at the meeting requires a detailed and careful study of precinct conditions, an understanding of the success or failure of recent tactics, and the ability to use this insight to respond to questions and present appropriate plans for the next period. (p. 138)

In order to ensure accountability and to foster a sense of ownership, precinct commander profile sheets were developed.

> As time went by, we incorporated color photographs of the commander and his or her executive officer on the profile sheets. When it was their turn to report, each precinct's leaders came loaded with information, statistics, and ideas, ready to fire. We called that being "in the barrel." (Bratton& Knobler, 1998, p. 233)

Initially, there was no formal process for recording or assessing the operational plans and performance of commands. The assessment of how well the NYPD was complying with Compstat decisions depended on the memories of Deputy Commissioner Jack Maple and Chief of Patrol Louis Anemone (Silverman, 1999). By the spring of 1996, detailed minutes were compiled, which served as an institutional record. Pre- and post-Compstat meetings developed over time and evolved "from informal, oral interviews to more systematic, in-depth briefings" (p. 114). The format of the meetings changed to accommodate the type of questions necessary to the information needed.

> The Compstat meeting timetable scheduled precincts by patrol borough, with the expectation that eight to twelve precincts would be represented at every meeting. It quickly became apparent, however, that

only three to five precinct commanders could be adequately questioned at a typical Compstat session. Briefings became more selective
and concentrated as precinct presentations were streamlined, crime
data mushroomed, and Compstat staff became more familiar with precinct problems. (p. 114)

By the summer of 1995, the department abandoned the established schedule for Compstat meetings and gave precincts and boroughs only a few
days prior notice if they were to appear at a meeting. Silverman contends
that this was done due to a concern that "some precincts were slacking off
because of the predictable Compstat schedule" (p. 118).

In May 1997 and 1998, the NYPD sponsored three-day Compstat conferences, each time attracting over 400 attendees, including representatives from more than seventy-five police departments in the United States
and other countries. Silverman (1999) suggests that Compstat also contributed to Giuliani's successful 1997 reelection campaign, which featured
television adds saluting New York City's crime drop. The Compstat system
continues to be employed within the NYPD and it has been replicated with
success in a variety of police and nonpolice settings (O'Connell, 2001b).

Moore (2003) has characterized Compstat as "a combined technical
and managerial system that embeds the technical system for the collection
and distribution of performance information in a broader managerial system designed to focus the organization as a whole" (p. 470). It is designed
specifically to create "internal accountability and organizational learning"
(p. 473).

When implemented and used, Compstat can be an "integrated, holistic
system of gauging . . . business process performance on a regular basis"
(Kueng, 2000, p. 67). David Weisburd, Stephen Mastrofski, Ann Marie
McNally, Rosann Greenspan, and James Willis (2003) refer to Compstat as
a system for strategic problem solving based on management techniques
of data analysis and use customized into a single program for police organizations. They identify six management principles as the core of Compstat's design.

1. Clarify the agency's mission by focusing on its basic values and
   embodying them in tangible objectives.

2. Give priority to operational objectives over administrative ones.

3. Simplify managerial accountability for achieving those objectives.

4. Become more adept at scanning the organization's environment to
   identify problems early and to develop strategies to respond (data-
   driven).

5. Increase organizational flexibility to implement the most promising
   strategies.

6. Learn about what works and what does not by following through
   with empirical assessment of what happened (p. 423).

It is important to emphasize again that Compstat is a management model that includes many interdependent components: data gathering, analysis, and *use* via interactive staff meetings. Organizational policies, management structures, practices, and the technologies that support them are all deeply dependent on one another.

Technology is only one element in the Compstat package (Illich, 1973; Kling & Dutton, 1982). New and emerging approaches to studying the success of information systems sometimes use the term *ensemble technology* to describe the context of use and the influence of organizations on technology as well as the influence of technology on organizations (Orlikowski & Iacono, 2001). Committing additional resources such as training, skilled staff and support services plus the development of organizational arrangements, policies, and incentives to enable the effective management and use of new technologies can create a "web of computing" (Kling & Scacchi, 1982). Seeing Compstat as a black box solution functioning independent of the environment in which it is embedded, rather than as a "web of computing" or an ensemble technology, is a shortcut to failure.

The interaction that typically takes place during Compstat meetings is quite far removed from a "typical staff meeting." Once again, the entire organizational chart is present and all units/divisions are expected to participate actively. This level of participation is perhaps the most distinguishing characteristic of the Compstat process.

Lance deHaven-Smith and Kenneth Jenne (2006) refer to this process as "management by inquiry." They describe a process whereby an organization conducts "regularly scheduled, highly formalized meetings between top executives, middle management, and line personnel to discuss the performance and operation of individual units" (p. 66). They conclude that such structured discourse, which examines reasoning, attitudes, and motives, is actually quite effective and unique.

> Although discursive processes are often employed by upper management when formulating agency objectives and strategies, they are generally considered to be incapable, by themselves, of directing administrative behavior down through the ranks. . . . If structured discourse is used at all for administrative personnel beneath the upper echelons, it is typically a pseudo-democratic effort to foster buy-in and defuse employee dissatisfaction, not a genuine dialogue across administrative levels to set and adjust the course of administrative action. (p. 66)

They contend that this unique form of discourse is used by Compstat (and similar systems, such as the Powertrac program used by the Broward County, Florida Sheriff's Office) to adjust both activities of units and administrative procedures of units to improve performance, increase efficiency, and respond to evolving conditions or changing priorities. They suggest that this process is successful, since it is "based on the belief that motives and actions are shaped primarily by interpersonal communications and agreements" (deHaven-Smith & Jenne, 2006, p. 68). In essence, it helps to create an accountability system by recognizing the "tendency for people to feel bound by their promises, to give reasons for their beliefs and actions, and to accede to the better arguments and more justifiable claims of others" (p. 69). In this way, all participants help to brainstorm, plan, explain, and evaluate current initiatives and proposed courses of action.

Management by inquiry is only effective, however, when it is based on authentic and honest dialogue. Unfortunately, Compstat-like performance measurement systems can devolve into a forum for negative reinforcement, whereby field commanders can be subjected to embarrassing or harassing questioning (see O'Connell, 2001a).

> Top managers need to be wary, however, of using inquirement processes to lay traps for subordinates. When performance data or other information causes top managers to suspect administrative problems in one of their subordinate units, they need to avoid prejudgments and remain detached. Otherwise, their questioning of unit administrators and their analyses of data on unit performance will be designed not to reach consensus on conditions and tactics, but to entrap or embarrass. To the extent that administrative discourse is seen as a game of "gotcha," it will reinforce rather than expose and dissolve defensive thinking, and the communicative weakness of performance management will be amplified rather than corrected. Hence, it is essential that inquirement processes be carefully structured to facilitate discursive problem solving, discourage heavy-handed questioning, and respect the dignity of all participants. (deHaven-Smith & Jenne, 2006, p. 74)

Compstat's Impact on the NYPD

While Compstat had a profound positive impact on many of the NYPD's most basic operations, it is important to note that many of these benefits were (at least initially) unintended and unexpected. For example, Bratton notes, "It started as the simple monitoring of a briefing. It became an extravaganza. We had started panning for gold and had struck the mother lode" (Bratton & Knobler, 1998, p. 233).

The NYPD's successful development and use of Compstat resulted in tangible changes in three distinct areas: (1) the flow of information within the department; (2) the department's decision-making processes; and (3) the department's organizational culture.

Communication and Information Management

Prior to the advent of Compstat, information did not flow freely throughout the NYPD (Silverman, 1999). A great deal of information was maintained by the department's many specialized units, and was only released on a need-to-know basis. Information that did flow to headquarters from the field commands typically did so in a formalized and deliberate manner. Lateral communications (i.e., those between the commands) were informal and generally limited (Maple & Mitchell, 1999). Information flowed primarily through official channels, and field commands (both the precincts and boroughs) were not communicating freely and candidly with headquarters (Silverman, 1999).

Commissioner Lee Brown, who preceded Bratton, had introduced an ambitious community policing reform program. He lamented the fact that in a large department "many units do not have the opportunity to interact with other units on a regular basis" (Silverman, 1999, p. 109).

Bratton set out to change that. He believed that the department would only succeed in coordinating its many crime-fighting efforts if it could open the channels of communication. Both he and Jack Maple believed in the concept of transparency, where all units operate from the same general information base and understand the operations and goals of one another. An official department publication (NYPD, 1996b) made the following claim: "The barriers that long separated the Department's Patrol Services Bureau, Detective Bureau and Organized Crime Control Bureau have been broken down, and a new spirit of cooperation is resulting in the rapid deployment of appropriate resources" (p. 2). In many respects, that statement appears to be true. The way in which it was accomplished was to change people's attitudes towards information. Bratton and the department's upper echelon wanted to show clearly that no one unit or administrator had a proprietary interest in information. The hoarding of information was no longer tolerated.

Information and ideas were openly shared during Compstat meetings. The system utilized both textual and graphical news to present large amounts of data from various sources. It also included a drill-down function, whereby managers could obtain additional levels of detail. Issues that had previously taken weeks to resolve were quickly addressed since most (if not all) necessary parties were assembled in the same room. In a major departure from previous practice, "all NYPD informational arrows [were] in one quiver, targeting crime conditions for all key decision makers at their crime-fighting meetings" (Silverman, 1999, p. 109). Interaction and information sharing now integrated into the system.

> Until this time, a precinct commander would never in his or her career expect to talk consistently and directly to the chief of department, the first deputy, or the police commissioner, but there we were, sitting at the command table. (Bratton & Knobler, 1998, p. 233)

This communication led to better coordination. In essence, it enabled the organization to distribute sheet music to its members so that everyone would know what everyone else was playing. Or to change metaphors, Compstat was "the informational cement of reform, the central mechanism that provide[d] communication links to traditionally isolated specialized units" (Silverman, 1999, p. 186).

Jack Maple and Chris Mitchell (1999) described Compstat as a "mechanism for sharing good ideas throughout a department and for keeping good ideas from ever being forgotten" (p. 187). Phyllis McDonald (2002) suggests that Compstat achieved its goal of an open exchange of information by increasing the vertical flow of information and opening new channels for lateral communication.

> Compstat demands that communication occur throughout the police hierarchy, up and down. . . . Executive officers who do not communicate with or involve supervisors and officers will be unable to respond effectively to issues raised at Compstat meetings. Compstat demands that communication occur across districts or precincts and units within the agency. (p. 18)

It is interesting to note that the ten copies of the original February 1994 Compstat book were designated for internal use only and specifically stated they were not to be released to the public or other agencies. "Three years later, more than 200 Compstat books were issued weekly to all NYPD units, representatives of the city's district attorneys, probation departments, courts, the State Division of Parole, federal agencies, and numerous outsiders" (Silverman, 1999, p. 123).

The Bratton administration made other changes as part of its overall reengineering process to open the internal flow of information. These included the creation of new administrative positions, such as Domestic Violence Prevention Officer, and the transfer of some units and positions for the purpose of coordination of information. However, many changes are attributable solely to Compstat, such as the recurrent theme of follow-up and reinforcement of successful tactics, and the dissemination of best practices (Maple & Mitchell, 1999).

Compstat opened existing lines of communication within the organization but, perhaps more importantly, also created new ones. The Chief of Patrol (situated at the top of the organizational chart) could now frequently engage in lively and in-depth conversations with precinct anti-crime sergeants or detective squad commanders (individuals who rarely had direct access to upper-level managers at headquarters). Operational questions and concerns that typically required a flurry of memos from the field to headquarters and back again could now be addressed immediately via candid discussions between all levels of the organizational chart.

Compstat resulted in *more* communication taking place within the organization. While the NYPD formerly had many official reporting requirements and mandated notifications, these communications were the equivalent of a series of one-way streets running parallel to one another. Thanks to the Compstat meetings, these communication channels were converted to two-way streets—broad two-way highways with several lanes of traffic running in many different directions at the same time. The meetings themselves, as well as the preparation that was required beforehand, helped to remove blockages and correct what was in many ways a faulty intraorganizational communication system (see generally Pandey & Garnett, 2006).

Compstat ensures that information is no longer just meticulously compiled; it is *used*. It is openly shared for the express purpose of collaboration and the development of effective new strategies. By analyzing the relative performance of each operational unit, upper-level managers can now determine, relatively promptly and accurately, whether or not a planned course of action is succeeding. It informs their efforts with regard to strategic planning and problem solving and provides them with a direct and effective means of setting and communicating organizational goals, then monitoring and evaluating performance vis-à-vis those objectives.

There is ample evidence to suggest that Compstat is far more than an efficient performance monitoring system. It is a knowledge management device that enables the agency's chief decision makers to tap into and use the intellectual capital of the entire organization. This includes not only what is expressly known by the organization and its key administrators (explicit knowledge), but also what is known and understood intuitively or instinctually by the individuals who actually perform the work (Cook & Brown, 1999). Compstat is a useful mechanism for the identification and harnessing of individual competencies, successful practices, skills, and routines. It is a particularly effective form of internal benchmarking that enables senior management to identify top performers, to analyze and pinpoint any significant distinctions that contribute to superior performance, and to communicate and/or adapt them to the entire organization.

Compstat also facilitates the transfer of knowledge among subunits (by the sharing of best practices) and corrects factors and/or structures that inhibit the transfer of knowledge. Compstat has drawn together otherwise disconnected groups and facilitates both the vertical and horizontal transfer of knowledge. It also confronts the powerful forces "that oppose productive dialogue and discussion" within the organization (Senge, 1994, p. 237). Compstat encourages teamwork and collaborative responses to problems and challenges.

The Compstat process enables administrators to take a holistic view of the entire organization. It views the organization as an open system and discourages linear thinking. Rather than merely reacting to what is perceived as simplistic cause-and-effect chains, Compstat encourages administrators to search continually for the interrelationships of events and processes that hinder or facilitate peak performance. Senge refers to this as "systems thinking" (as cited in Silverman, 1996, p. 11). Rather than basing one's managerial decisions on a series of random snapshots or glimpses of the performance of isolated parts, this management approach enables decision makers to keep "the big picture" in focus at all times.

Most organizations are unaware of the specific ways in which their strategic vision is limited. A variety of factors can prevent managers from "seeing, seeking, using, or sharing highly relevant, easily accessible, and readily perceivable information during the decision-making process" (Bazerman & Chugh, 2006, p. 90). Compstat can be readily used to combat this phenomenon known as *bounded awareness*, in which managers fail to see or seek out relevant and necessary information.

Compstat also manages tension, strain, stress, and conflict within the organization. All organizations experience tension caused by the discrepancy between current reality and the desired state (see generally Fritz, 1996). Compstat enables the department to *redirect* the tension toward desired goals. It entails a continuous process of analysis→action→reevaluation→adjustment that keeps the department continually moving forward. By proceeding in this manner, the department learns, reacts, and gets smarter each time around.

Analyzing these findings in light of the "competing values framework/approach" developed by Robert Quinn and John Rohrbaugh (1981), it is clear that the NYPD formerly operated in a hierarchical style. Prior to the development of Compstat, it operated as a monopoly and rarely saw the need for immediate action. Hierarchical organizations value predictability and security.

Compstat prompted the department to adopt a new style of information management known as the *rational style*. This style also operates in an environment of relatively high market certainty; the overall mission of police departments will always be monopolistic. However, the new style includes immediate action (Quinn & Rohrbaugh, 1981; 1983) as a hallmark, constantly analyzing patterns and selecting the best available strategy. The competing values approach can also be used to document how the NYPD moved from an overall internal organizational focus to an external one (Van Wart, 1998).

Decision Making

As mentioned above, prior to the development and implementation of Compstat, the NYPD was a highly structured and hierarchical bureaucracy. Traditionally, "precinct commanders were hampered by central management from headquarters. They were not given broad authority to formulate and implement crime fighting plans in their own precincts, appropriate to precinct conditions" (NYPD, 1996a, p. 9). Bratton had found the department to be "a centralized bureaucracy" that was overspecialized and not capable of responding to the many different needs of New York city's residents. (Bratton & Knobler, 1998, p. 199).

A document distributed at the 1998 Compstat conference describes how this "overspecialization" occurred.

> With the rise of the so-called "professional model," police agencies created a host of specialized units to deal with specific (and often temporary) problems, while executives attempted to retain tight control over the direction and scope of officers' activities. This attempt at special-

ization of police functions was predicated upon prevailing management theories which emphasized rigid organizational and supervisory structures as the key to efficiency—theories that worked quite well on assembly lines and other highly routinized private organizations, but less effectively in large public service organizations charged with a broad mandate to achieve a wide range of social objectives. Like barnacles on the hull of a ship, these overlapping and often-duplicative specialized units accreted upon the organizational structure and slowed its progress. (NYPD, 1998, p. 3; see also Silverman & O'Connell, 1999)

Bratton (1996b) altered this situation by giving more authority to precinct commanders who, in his view, were in the best position to effect local strategies that would yield dramatic crime reductions.

I decentralized. I gave away many of my powers not—as my predecessors wanted—to the cop on the beat, but rather to the precinct commander. I did not want to give more power to the cop on the beat. They were, on average, only 22 years of age. Most of them never held a job before becoming New York City police officers, and had only high school or GED qualification. These kids, after six months of training, were not prepared to solve the problems of New York City. . . . My form of community policing, therefore, versus former Police Commissioners Lee Brown's and Ray Kelly's, put less emphasis on the cop on the beat and much more emphasis on the precinct commanders. (p. 12)

Bratton's views regarding the most effective means of implementing the community-policing philosophy are echoed in official department documents.

In New York City and elsewhere, agencies [began] empowering patrol officers, in accord with the ideology that every officer should in essence be the chief of his or her beat, responsible for coordinating or directly providing virtually all police services within that sphere of responsibility. In many respects this overreaching effort to force the implementation of community policing was flawed, since it naively assumed that every young police officer on patrol possessed the requisite knowledge, experience and wisdom to judiciously utilize the considerable discretion and authority they were given. Moreover, it effectively cast supervisors and superior officers in a supporting role and diminished their authority to manage, direct and control the beat officer's activities.

The New York City Police Department has departed from the traditional wisdom of police management and has modified conventional community policing ideology by recognizing that in order for the agency to be effective in reducing crime and in responding to the needs of communities, many operational decisions must be made by commanders at the precinct level. Precinct commanders are in a far better position than Headquarters executives to appreciate and meet the particular needs of their communities and to direct the efforts of the 200 to 400 officers they manage. They are also in a better position than beat officers to understand and harmonize the agency's policies with the social dynamics operating within their geographic areas. To operationalize this, the NYPD's policies were revised to empower precinct commanders and to significantly expand their authority, responsibility and discretion, as well as the degree of control they exercise over personnel and other resources. The corollary of that expanded authority, responsibility and discretion is increased accountability. (NYPD, 1998, p. 4)

The role of the precinct commander was redefined during the Bratton administration.

- Precinct commanders were given more freedom to manage their own commands.
- Precinct commanders were told that they would be responsible for reducing crime in their commands.
- The NYPD refocused its strategy of community policing, giving the main responsibility for problem solving and for getting concrete results to precinct commanders.
- Compstat meetings were held in which precinct commanders discussed crime conditions in their precincts and, more importantly, what they planned to do to address them. These meetings shortened the chain of command between the supervisor in the street and the executive staff, allowing high-level managers to get timely information directly from their subordinates in the field.
- Specific, department-wide strategies were developed to address particular crimes and conditions, all of which stressed urgency. The department would no longer simply wait for crime to happen; it would become proactive and search for solutions (NYPD, 1996b, p. 9).

These changes all contributed to a significant alteration to the department's overall decision-making processes. By

treating the precinct commander as the focus of attention, and treating the commander's problems as the ones that the organization as a whole is supposed to try to solve, an important change is created in the status and working relationships in a police department. (Moore, 2003, p. 475)

Compstat was central to this change. The NYPD

made enormous strides in feeding information to appropriate decision-making levels. Traditionally, NYPD headquarters was perceived as the nerve center of the department's decision-making apparatus. Changes in operational police tactics were conceived, formulated, and issued from headquarters, primarily on a city-wide basis, and often with very little input from field commands. The post-1993 restructuring and crime-control strategies provided field commanders with far more leverage over their own troops. . . . The post-1993 NYPD leadership also realized that uniform, city-wide crime-fighting decisions were not as effective as individualized strategies designed for particular communities. . . . By increasing the authority and responsibility of precinct commanders, the NYPD freed them from having to forward information along the chain of command simply to receive high-level confirmation or reassurance. (Silverman, 1999, p. 182)

McGuire (1999) explains how Compstat enabled and encouraged top administrators to become intimately familiar with specific conditions and crime-fighting strategies, an unprecedented situation.

> The discussions [during Compstat meetings] frequently involve details of specific crime patterns and ongoing investigations that previously would not have been brought to the attention of top management. The result is a familiarity and knowledge of week-to-week operational results at the executive level that helps flatten the organizational pyramid—an accomplishment that many thought impossible before Compstat. (p. 136)

Bratton and his senior staff were extremely active. Indeed, Bratton (1996b) viewed himself as a corporate CEO, who constantly examined his organization's bottom line. He used Compstat as his primary monitoring mechanism.

> We began to run the NYPD as a private profit-oriented business. What was the profit I wanted? Crime reduction. I wanted to beat my competitors—the criminals—who were out there working seven days a week, 24 hours a day. I wanted to serve my customers, the public, better: and the profit I wanted to deliver to them was reduced crime. All of my franchises—my 76 precincts—were measured, not on how many calls they responded to, but on how much crime was reduced. (p. 13)

Giuliani (1997) provides a similar understanding of how Compstat's process of continual monitoring helped the department operate as a private institution.

> The analogy which I often use is that of a major banking institution which each day at the close of business contacts its branches to assess the transactions of the day so that it can develop strategies to enhance its measure of success, namely, profits. For years, the NYPD's measure of its performance was based on arrest statistics—an indicator that while important is not a measure of its success. After all, the primary mission of a police force is to prevent and deter crime, a mission which is measured by crime statistics, not arrests, since arrests represent a police response to crimes that have already occurred. Through the use of Compstat, the NYPD captures, retrieves and analyzes crime statistics on a daily basis, and, like a bank, is able to quantify its successes and develop strategies or deploy resources to build upon that progress. (p. 3)

Compstat helped to institutionalize this new management philosophy. By 1996, the department recognized that a dramatic change had taken place.

> The gathering of field intelligence, the adapting of tactics to changing field conditions, and the close review of field results is now a continual, daily process rather than an annual or biennial event. The NYPD can make fundamental changes in its tactical approach in a few weeks rather than a few years. (NYPD, 1996b, p. 2)

Compstat was intended to provide guidance and support to field commanders without engaging in micromanagement. "Although overall strategy guidance flows *down* to the precincts, many of the tactics that are accomplishing the strategies flow *up* from precinct commanders, squad commanders, and rank-and-file police officers and detectives" (NYPD, 1996b, p. 2).

> Ultimately, Compstat's significance lies in its impact beyond the confines of its data and its war room—crime strategy meetings. This innovation process radiates throughout the NYPD as the energizer of strikingly creative decision making at headquarters and in the field. (Silverman, 1999, p. 124)

To understand Compstat's influence on the department's decision-making capabilities, one must realize that it was designed to have impact far beyond the formal crime meetings.

> There are four levels of Compstat. We created a system in which the police commissioner, with his executive core, first empowers and then interrogates the precinct commander, forcing him or her to come up with a plan to attack crime. But it should not stop there. At the next level down, it should be the precinct commander, taking the same role as the commissioner, empowering and interrogating the platoon commander. Then, at the third level, the platoon commander should be asking his sergeants, "What are we doing to deploy on this tour to address these conditions?" And finally you have the sergeant at roll call . . . all the way down until everyone in the entire organization is empowered and motivated, active and assessed and successful. It works in all organizations. (Bratton & Knobler, 1998, p. 239)

Compstat forced the organization to engage in a productive form of self-reflection that enabled it to discern environmental changes and to react accordingly. It provided the ability to "modify behavior and strategies in accordance with changing conditions" (Yohe, 1997, p. 15). The competing values framework would characterize the foregoing findings as moving from process—an overall concern for means, to outcomes—ends that meet the organization's goals (Van Wart, 1998).

Organizational Culture

Aggressive crime fighting seemingly was not the primary focus of NYPD precinct commanders prior to 1994. Some commanders contended that an aggressive stance toward crime would actually impair a precinct commander's career. As one senior field commander noted: "We were there to keep the lid on and not to be an embarrassment. The main thing was don't make waves, something might go wrong. You were put through the wringer if you really did your job" (Silverman, 1999, p. 87).

A department publication issued in 1996 provides similar evidence that there was no clear directive to field commanders that their primary focus was to fight crime.

> Like many large bureaucracies, the NYPD had been organized around avoiding risk and failure. For years, precinct commanders had been constrained on every side by regulations and procedures. Many police operations, such as prostitution sweeps and executing search warrants, could only be conducted by centralized units, reflecting an abiding distrust of precinct personnel and resources. Yet, despite all the micro-management, the Department was providing very little in the way of genuine strategic direction. It was clear what precinct commanders and personnel weren't allowed to do, but much less clear what they *ought* to be doing to combat crime, disorder, and fear. (NYPD, 1996a, p. 1)

Prior to 1994, there was a general impression that the surest way to succeed as a precinct commander was to maintain the status quo. McDonald (2002) attributes this sentiment somewhat to the conclusion of the 1973 Kansas City Preventive Patrol Experiment that random patrol did not deter crime. McDonald believes that this view was overblown and dominated police thinking for two to three decades. Bratton (1996b) concurs.

> Somehow, in the 1960s and in the increasingly permissive society of the 1970s, we began to excuse police from having any responsibility for the prevention of crime. We began to espouse that there were so many causes of crime that were beyond the control of police: How could we hold the police accountable for preventing crime when so many of the things that we believed caused crime were beyond their control? . . . By the 1980s, American police by and large were excused from controlling behavior in our streets or changing behavior that was aberrant, to the extent that they were also excused from doing anything about the prevention of crime. (p. 3-4)

The bureaucratic structure of the department also influenced the development of a unique occupational culture. The department's

> hierarchical accountability structures generated many administrative rules, bureaucratic regulations, operational protocols and excessive paperwork. Important as these formal accountability structures seemed to the fulfillment of management's concerns, the police officers who actually delivered services to the public saw little value or purpose to them, often deriding the structures as unnecessary and burdensome. This dynamic—born of two distinct and incompatible spheres of interest and activity—contributed to the emergence of two occupational cultures within the agency: street cops and management cops. As a result, the Department lacked a central focus and unanimity of purpose since both

groups had different agendas and approached crime problems from different perspectives. (NYPD, 1998, p. 3; see also Reuss-Ianni, 1983)

Bratton's initial selection of top personnel was critical to the establishment of a new mind-set. Several experienced commanders were selected by Bratton *because* of their aggressive attitudes and fundamental belief that crime could be dramatically reduced. As experienced crime fighters, these men were able to identify bona fide efforts to reduce crime and to challenge insufficient procedures.

> Sometimes the grilling got tough. . . . You didn't want to lie at Compstat—you'd get caught and get hung out to dry. The people who did best had given thought to solving their precinct's problems; the people who did worst tried to fudge them. "The two biggest lies in law enforcement," says Maple, "are 'We worked very closely together on this investigation,' which means they don't work at all together, and 'We're doing this as we speak,' which means, 'We haven't done it yet.' They're holding actions." (Bratton & Knobler, 1998, p. 235)

Bratton believed that Compstat had a positive effect on morale.

> Over time, commanders brought in beat cops from their precincts who had done an exceptional job. . . . They described the circumstances and heard the whole room burst into applause. You can imagine the effect on a young cop and his or her career to stand there and be applauded by everyone in the department from his commanding officer up to and including the police commissioner. Compstat became a rallying point to encourage and reward people for good work. (Bratton & Knobler, p. 237)

Bratton believed that the earlier reform efforts of his predecessors had been stymied because they had "left the old guard at the top in place" (p. 205). He made personnel changes whenever they were deemed necessary. Compstat was used to facilitate the selection process.

The Compstat mechanism was critical to this overall change in the organizational culture. It served as a constant reminder that a "business as usual attitude" would not be tolerated.

> The central strategic direction of the Department became far stronger and the lines of accountability far clearer. Avoiding failure [was] no longer a formula for success. Instead, the positive efforts of commanders and cops at reducing crime, disorder, and fear [were] being recognized and encouraged. (NYPD, 1996a, p. 1)

Several prior reform efforts had failed, primarily because of a lack of "buy-in." Due to its persistent nature and its reinforcing (almost self-perpetuating) message, Compstat helped achieve the necessary buy-in for Bratton's reforms (Silverman, 1999).

Compstat forced managers to develop cross-functional skills and an aggressive mind-set that no doubt altered the culture of the entire organization. "Compstat transformed the NYPD from an organization that reacted to crime to a police department that actively works to deter offenses" (Giuliani, 1997, p. 2). Howard Safir (Bratton's successor) referred to Compstat as, "a shot of adrenaline to the heart of the NYPD" that remolded the department (Silverman, 1999, p. 124).

As a management philosophy, Compstat reinforces the need for continuous performance improvement and a general dissatisfaction with the status quo. Compstat is founded on the belief that "things can always be done better." It empowered field managers and encouraged them to sense and to create opportunities. This sense of entrepreneurialism is quite distinguishable from the philosophies of traditional hierarchies (and of the NYPD in particular), which are often characterized by "timidity and caution on the part of subordinates who fear criticism from superiors and thus fear to pass unpleasant information up the line" (Perrow, 1972, p. 39).

Compstat released the creativity in NYPD managers by promoting innovation and experimentation. By pushing decisions down the organizational chart and distributing power more widely, it encouraged fresh thinking and expanded possibilities. Thinking "outside the box" quickly became the norm. In essence, each field command began to formulate and assess new methods and approaches to routine tasks, as well as unexpected challenges.

Although the overall direction of the organization was still monitored and controlled by senior administrators and policy makers at headquarters, Compstat enabled most decisions to be made in the field. Field units began to perform functions that would ordinarily be reserved for a "research and development" section or a "skunkworks" unit. Commanders were encouraged and empowered to try new things and to take necessary steps to address the needs and challenges of their particular commands.

> We encouraged creative thinking and backed our people up when they practiced new techniques. We freed them from old restraints, gave them responsibility, held them accountable, and were very pleased with the results. We were often amazed. Commanders came up with solutions and innovations that none of us on the command staff had thought of. It was great to watch their minds at work. (Bratton & Knobler, 1998, p. 237)

The innovation, creativity, and experimentation that resulted yielded significant results in the form of rapidly dropping crime rates and enhanced organizational performance.

Compstat enabled the NYPD to welcome and to manage change rather than to fear it. It institutionalized a general dissatisfaction with the status quo and resulted in an organizational philosophy based on the continuous search for better practices. "What Compstat really stands for is a zero tolerance approach to shrugged shoulders, shoddy workmanship and shirked responsibility" (Gorta, 1998, p. 41).

As Tom Junod (2000) notes, Compstat helped change the way the department thought.

> What has generally escaped notice . . . was the simple and fundamental and revolutionary change Bratton inspired in the way the NYPD thought. What has generally gone unrecorded is the day Bratton held his first retreat for his executive officers, and John Timoney [the NYPD's Chief of Department] stood before them, before the entire command structure of the NYPD, before all the chiefs and captains, before all his peers, before everyone he knew, before all those freaking cops, and said that they were wrong, and had been wrong all along, the last twenty-five years, for they had built an entire organization on the probability of failure when they ought to have built one on the possibility of success. They were out reacting when they should have been anticipating; they were out containing crime when they should have been attacking it; they were out cleaning up dead bodies when they should have been out saving lives. (p. 154)

Compstat moved the department from a hierarchical culture characterized by security, stability, order, and routine toward an adaptive culture characterized by creativity, risk, and flexibility. Such a shift is understandable under the circumstances. As Montgomery Van Wart (1998) indicates, "hierarchical cultures flourish when the environment produces recognizable cues of higher certainty and the time-line for action is long-term" (p. 94). The Bratton administration deemphasized tradition and the status quo, and emphasized instead the values of innovation and change, conveying a very clear message to members of the entire organization that the internal and external work environments had changed radically.

The historical record is clear that Compstat represents the department's first attempt at creating a comprehensive information management system to coordinate *all* of its crime-fighting efforts. It amounted to a new operating model whereby performance data for the entire organization could be examined via an information "dashboard" (see Edwards & Thomas, 2005).

The distinguishing feature of Compstat is not the technology behind it but the philosophy and process that support it. The technology was not new; what was new was *how they used it*. "Elements of strategic problem solving had begun to be implemented more widely across American police agencies before the emergence of Compstat" (Weisburd et al., 2003, p. 421). This is true both in terms of available technology and the use of various problem-solving techniques. What is distinctive, however, about the NYPD experience is the fact that these techniques were being employed comprehensively. For the first time in the department's history, *all levels of the organizational chart* gathered in one central forum for the sole purpose of discussing crime. This had never before occurred within the NYPD or, for that matter, in any other major U.S. police department. Bratton and his colleagues succeeded in reorienting the department back to its original (core) mission—crime fighting (Maple & Mitchell, 1999; Bratton & Knobler, 1998). This mission resonated with the rank and file, altered the character of the organization, and spurred an unprecedented level of productivity. This shift did not eliminate the police bureaucracy, but it helped to modify it dramatically and to make it far more efficient.

The philosophy of strategic deployment of resources and continuous improvement and accountability clearly predates the implementation of Compstat, which was fueled by the department's overall reengineering process. In order for this philosophy to take root and permeate the entire organization, however, some new mechanism or process was needed. Compstat served that purpose. In light of the department's ambitious plans to reengineer itself, some monitoring mechanism was needed. It would have been naïve to assume that the department could radically overhaul its most fundamental practices and processes without creating an effective monitoring device.

The Viability of the Compstat Model

Moore (1995) provides a diagnostic framework with which to gauge the relative effectiveness of public sector action and management practices. The *strategic triangle* focuses managerial attention on three key questions: (1) is the action publicly valuable; (2) is it politically and legally supported; and (3) is it administratively and operationally feasible? Compstat has proven to be an extremely valuable and effective mechanism for police management; it is both feasible and readily replicated (see generally O'Connell, 2001b). It has survived the administrations of a new mayor and subsequent police commissioners, evidence of its political support.

Robert Fritz (1996) notes that "all organizations have success—but not all success succeeds in the end" (p. xiii). He contends that "the only way that organizations can really change is not by a change in behavior or process systems, but by a change in structure" (p. 133). He adds that, if change has been imposed on existing inadequate organizational structures, the organization is likely to experience a period of oscillation, a distinct period of reversal where "success is neutralized" (p. 7). This has not been the case with Compstat. The historical record indicates that Compstat significantly altered the department's organizational structure; it also suggests that Compstat is both viable and sustainable.

Compstat marks not only a unique period in the history of the NYPD but also in the history of police management generally. It stands as one of the most significant innovations in the field over the past several decades. Its full impact and influence have yet to be seen. Compstat developed out of a broader technological, social, and intellectual context. As GIS, knowledge management, and decision support technologies advance, the entire field of U.S. policing will continue to advance (albeit perhaps slowly) towards the Compstat paradigm, perhaps fueled by a process known as "mimetic isomorphism" (see Galaskiewicz & Wasserman, 1989). The day is now gone when a simple recapitulation of arrests and index crime reports will suffice. Police managers must have an array of performance indicators to accurately assess the current organizational landscape. These data must be used not simply for the purpose of generating reports; they should be used as a data dashboard to proactively "steer the ship."

Whether the term Compstat will survive is irrelevant; indeed, the term is inherently limiting. Technology will continue to develop, and police managers will continue to require an effective PBM system to monitor data. Police agencies are now considering the use of a variety of emerging technologies, such as placing advanced audio and video systems at high crime locations to detect gunshots. Will we use acoustic triangulation only for precise calculation of where a particular crime was committed, or will we create a real-time detection system to apprehend those with illegal firearms and thereby protect citizens? It is easy to see a future where such advanced systems will be more generally employed and their data monitored by the police for the express purpose of solving crimes as, or immediately after, they occur. The monitoring systems (a sophisticated array of cameras, microphones, and sensors) employed in London's Underground is perhaps the best example currently in use.

Any study that attempts to establish whether Compstat "works" must first clearly establish what exactly it is that Compstat is intended to accomplish. If we believe that the ultimate measure of success is dropping crime rates, then we expose ourselves to several quantitative challenges. Several researchers have concluded that Compstat should only be viewed as having had moderate success, due to the fact that some of the agencies under study failed to achieve the expected reduction in reported crimes rates. Still others point out that agencies that have not employed Compstat-like systems reaped equal or greater levels of crime reduction without availing themselves of this new innovation. They would like us to conclude that Compstat cannot fairly be considered the "cause" of crime reductions in any agency.

Compstat developed in a milieu that included the developing concepts of "hot-spot policing," "problem-oriented policing," and "evidence-based policing." While these differ in some ways from one another, they all involve the notion of "smarter" policing. A study in 2001 that examined the development and implementation of Compstat within the NYPD concluded that it (1) opened existing lines of internal communication; (2) created new channels of vertical and horizontal communication; (3) shifted ongoing operational decisions to the field level; and (4) significantly altered the organizational culture of that agency (O'Connell, 2001a). The study concluded that the NYPD benefited in measurable ways from each of these changes. This is one of many critical measures that could be used when asking whether Compstat works.

It would be premature to discount Compstat based on an analysis of crime statistics alone. Ideally, evaluative studies should be supplemented by a longitudinal analysis of the changes to the organization's communication and decision-making structures, as well as an ethnographic study of the evolution of its organizational culture. While certainly ambitious, this is the most comprehensive and accurate means of assessing the true impact of Compstat.

Implementation of some elements of a Compstat-like information system does not mean that Compstat has been adopted. Some suggest that Compstat meetings are merely "glorified staff meetings." Real Compstat meetings involve the representation and active participation of the *entire organizational chart*. They also necessarily involve accountability and relentless follow-up. Absent this, the meeting will remain a staff meeting. Similarly, if the Compstat philosophy is not adopted and internalized (that is, the belief that the police can make a difference and that performance can always been improved), then the experiment will fail. Unless the philosophy is understood and willingly adopted, the exercise becomes mere mimicry. Compstat requires a critical mass of people committed to change.

The potential for success is directly related to the agency's desire for real change. Compstat is most likely to succeed if it is incorporated into a wider reengineering or organizational change program, as it was in the NYPD and in White Plains. Compstat appears to be most successful in settings where administrators are dissatisfied with the status quo and experience some sense of immediacy.

James Swiss (2005) notes that results-based management systems often do not produce the expected positive effects in government agencies because of the lack of an incentive system. The civil-service system has certainly caused the demise of numerous police change initiatives in the past. Collective bargaining ensures that the rank and file have a place at the table to discuss the creation and implementation of such performance-based management systems. Fear is often a strong motivation, but it cannot be the primary one. For this reason, there is a need for a continuing dialogue regarding the creation of both intrinsic and monetary incentives to instill a sense of personal accountability if any Compstat-like system is to endure.

The Limitations of the Compstat Management Model

Compstat has now been closely studied in a variety of settings and contexts (see, e.g., O'Connell, 2001b; Weisburd et al., 2003; Willis, Mastrofski & Weisburd, 2003). While its many successes have been widely publicized, researchers have noted several limitations.

James Willis, Stephen Mastrofski, David Weisburd, and Rosann Greenspan (2003) provide perhaps the most complete examination of the proliferation of the Compstat model and have identified numerous problems that are associated with its implementation in one particular agency, the Lowell, Massachusetts Police Department. The researchers suggest that Compstat has yielded several specific benefits to the agency but that, in many respects, the "potential is unfulfilled" (p. v). They specifically note the following deficiencies:

1. lack of training in data analysis
2. reluctance among managers to share resources
3. the absence of systematic follow-up
4. a variety of technical information technology (IT) problems
5. the exclusion of rank-and-file officers from most meetings
6. a general attitude of indifference toward the program among some members of the agency.

Their research suggests that several problems are inherent to the philosophy and design of Compstat and that some problems might be particularly acute in smaller departments and agencies (10–30 people). For example, while some degree of "brow beating" might be inevitable, it should not become a defining feature of this management model. Compstat is best defined by its emphasis on collaboration. Rather than pointing fingers, participants use their collective abilities to identify problems and to develop effective responses. While accountability is a key feature of the model, it does not supersede the collaborative aspect of the process.

Compstat will certainly fail if it is imposed on an agency and its managers. If each individual field commander is left adrift to arrive at his/her own solutions and explanations, Compstat becomes an adversarial process whereby the primary goal is to outshine one's competition. This concept is anathema to the most fundamental notion of policing in the United States. Field commanders must be free to speak openly, to think creatively, and to seek the insights and expertise of their peers. This must be communicated at the outset to everyone in the organization and endorsed by all participants. Without united cooperation efforts, Compstat will not be an effective crime-fighting strategy and could, in fact, cause untold harm in terms of morale and overall organizational effectiveness.

Compstat must not be viewed as a panacea for police inefficiency and ineffectiveness. It is not a quick fix for an otherwise poorly run organization. If the organization does not understand and/or accept the philosophy and practice of Compstat, the entire process can devolve into a charade. It must be supported by individuals who sincerely want to identify operational deficiencies and to correct them.

There is another inherent limitation associated with implementing Compstat in a small police department. It entails the art of effectively balancing accessibility with confidentiality. All organizations that currently utilize Compstat with success recognize that some information, particularly information concerning ongoing internal or external investigations, is simply not appropriate for general consumption and will be limited to a "need-to-know basis."

For example, a small agency might justifiably be hesitant to discuss information concerning the execution of an upcoming search warrant, since information tends to travel quickly in small departments and small towns. Similarly, an internal investigation regarding an allegation against an officer of serious malfeasance of duty will generally only be disseminated to those individuals participating in the investigation. Large police departments typically have little trouble guarding this information, as such agencies generally have their own internal affairs units (that many times conduct separate Internal Affairs Compstat Meetings). Smaller agencies, however, will have much more difficulty in protecting this information, particularly if all such investigations are performed by the chief. Small agencies must be cognizant of these issues and take steps to ensure that the Compstat concept of a free flow of information throughout the entire organization can be limited under very specific circumstances.

One hallmark of PBM systems is the generation of data from which managers can discern patterns and identify problems that require immediate attention. This issue of pattern recognition is quite similar to prediction. If a persistent problem is identified, the next logical step is to act in some way to discontinue the problem or condition. Police managers, for example, must predict which problems will persist absent police intervention, then intervene as necessary.

In the corporate world, this form of prediction is quite common. Corporations base pricing, earnings estimates, market-share calculations, and a host of other performance measures on predictive modeling. That is, rather than merely describing in numbers what is currently occurring, they use more advanced statistics such as multiple regression to predict what is likely to occur. This enables the organization to deploy resources with maximum effect. This method, generally referred to as analytics, allows the organization to "use sophisticated experiments to measure the overall impact . . . of intervention strategies and then apply the results to continuously improve subsequent analyses" (Davenport, 2006, p. 101).

It is unlikely that there will ever come a time when the majority of police management decisions will be made by using these techniques. The unpredictable nature of day-to-day police operations dictates that discretion and spontaneous decision making will always be a necessary part of effective policing. Nevertheless, when police administrators decide where to deploy personnel or consider whether or not to discontinue an ongoing enforcement or investigative initiative, they would benefit from some form of predictive modeling. Analytics of some type could also be used to analyze the cost-effectiveness of certain long-term strategic decisions (in terms of overtime incurred, or reduced crime rates).

Numbers do not speak for themselves; but they certainly do speak. They speak a language that needs to be interpreted by skilled police professionals as they observe correlations and interactions among the data. These relationships will have meaning to experienced police managers as they bring their skills and expertise to bear when noting both expected and unexpected findings. The key is to provide meaning to the numbers. Unexpected findings are fine; unexplained findings require more thought and the asking of additional questions. Police managers will note the dynamic nature of the data. They will observe that, as one figure changes, others do as well. For example, as the number of directed patrol assignments within an agency increase, the amount of overtime incurred might similarly increase, while some other measure(s) (such as the total hours expended in the performance of routine patrol) might drop. It is up to the police professional to provide the "story" behind these numbers by asking such questions as "Why?" and "What if?" It is the job of the PBM system to ensure that these numbers are both timely and accurate.

As efficient as any PBM system might be, it will always need to be operated and used by practitioners who are skilled in the art of policing. As Peter Kueng (2000) notes, PBM systems "cannot tell a manager—based on the observed level of performance—what action he or she should initiate. However, a [PBM system] can direct attention to relevant facts that were, in the absence of a [PBM system], barely visible" (p. 71).

In sum, the technology is now available to provide a police organization of any size with sufficient data to support an information-based strategy that should improve the overall quality of decision making, as well as the quality and effectiveness of services provided. Vincent Hughes and Peter Love (2004) note, however, that technological advancements to date have far outpaced the development of police managers' information and communication technology skills. What is needed is an effective and intelligent management strategy and the requisite skills for understanding and using the modern technological tools that are now available.

The question about the utility of Compstat is only one example in a wider debate over whether PBM programs, with their focus on organizational outcomes and predetermined benchmarks, "really result in more effective and efficient delivery of public programs" (Perrin, 1999, p. 105; see also Jaggi, 2003). Perrin (1999) does not imply that performance measurement systems are ineffective, or uniformly detrimental. He merely suggests that a performance measurement system, in and of itself, should not be seen as a panacea for a struggling organization.

> Instead of judging programs [or organizations] by the degree to which they have met predetermined qualitative indicators or targets, why not instead hold them accountable for demonstrating that they do actively question and assess the effectiveness and impact of what they are doing? Hold programs accountable for demonstrating how they seek feedback and make use of evaluation in program improvement and in strategic planning. Hold programs accountable for demonstrating that they have in place, and make use of, appropriate monitoring systems, which may very well include performance measures. (p. 107)

Police administrators are accountable to both politicians and the public; they continually face the challenge of reducing crime. A problem develops, however, if they adopt a strategy based on overly simplistic views. Arbitrary performance targets, such as "a 10% reduction in the rate of reported violent crime," can be detrimental. Unless such goals or benchmarks are reasonably based (and actually obtainable), they may result in a misperception of poor performance or, worse still, manipulation of the data to ensure compliance. Those responding to directives must be experienced in the use of data to generate statistics on performance trends. When utilizing Compstat, for example, one must recognize and understand the phenomenon of "regression towards the mean." This, in layman's terms, is the process whereby a precipitous drop in reported crime "levels off" after a certain period of time. In other words, a 25% crime reduction during period one, followed by a 20 then 15% reduction, *does not* mean that the crime rate is rising. Politicians and senior officials often seem to be blind to this fact and other complexities of statistically based performance measurements. If authentic discussions about crime are to take place, data analysis and potential problems with it must be thoroughly understood. Any given performance target simply cannot be beaten consistently. As David Bernstein (1999) notes, "the challenge for evaluators is to convince stakeholders that performance measurement is limited in its ability to explain apparent results" (p. 92). Reasonable performance targets should only be set once baseline performance levels have been examined, and those who monitor, report, and use those statistics must understand their meaning and appropriate use.

This point cannot be overemphasized. Any and all performance targets or benchmarks must be derived from within the organization with the active input of key stakeholders. If external benchmarks are imposed prior to an assessment of what constitutes normal operations for the organization, the likelihood of success will be greatly diminished. Newly developed PBM systems must run for a time before baselines are established. That is, equivalent units must be identified and data must be acquired and analyzed so that "apples-to-apples" comparisons can be made. Once seasonal or geographic variations are accounted for, there can be an understanding about average performance, and reasonable and challenging targets may be set.

Another important concept is that no single measure or indicator is dispositive of organizational performance. Unfortunately, "managers are not always well versed in causal inference and are likely to assume causality falsely from correlational data" (Perrin, 1999, p. 105). In other words, correlation does not equal causation. If data show that ice cream sales and the incidence of drownings in the United States are highly correlated (rising and falling at the same time), does that mean that ice cream consumption somehow leads to swimming deaths? Certainly not. Frequently, there is a third "lurking" variable, such as temperature, that can fully explain the situation. Unfortunately, public managers and the individuals they are accountable to are often too quick to accept easy explanations. As a group, they are generally unaware of the complexities of the interactive effects associated with many performance measures.

The Benefits of a Compstat-Like Performance Management System

PBM systems have the potential to be the solution police agencies are looking for, provided the adopters understand that it is not a prepackaged product that can merely be inserted into the organization's ongoing management processes to ensure success. PBM systems must be thoughtfully and collaboratively developed with the active input of all stakeholders (Bernstein, 1999; Theurer, 1998). Further, the adoption of a PBM system as an organizational decision-making model requires consistent and active support by managers and leadership if its true potential is ever to be realized. The system can help to answer the question of whether an organization's performance is better than yesterday's and to what degree target values have been fulfilled (Kueng, 2000). For policing, PBM systems incorporate concepts such as hot-spot and evidence-based procedures (Sherman, 1998) and are based on the fundamental belief that the police *can* make a difference in fighting crime, and that continuous improvement is possible. PBM systems perform an effective monitoring function and have great potential for agencies operating under special circumstances, such as consent decrees resulting from civil rights litigation (Walker, 2003).

PBM systems have great potential in terms of interoperability with other criminal justice data systems (such as probation and parole agencies). As technology evolves and as the need for collaborative action (as in the war on terror) increases, PBM systems could be used as a vehicle for the coordination and analysis of a wide array of data (Foldy et al., 2004; Kamarck, 2005).

PBM systems have been found to serve as a training tool, opening the lines of communication and aiding in the selection of future managers and leaders. They help communicate the general direction of the organization, foster the recognition of problems, and initiate corrective action so that problems do not escalate. Performance information can be communicated directly to work teams "to improve resource allocation and process output . . . to give early warning signals, to make a diagnosis of the weaknesses of a business process, to decide whether corrective actions are needed and to assess the impact of actions taken" (Kueng, 2000, p. 72). PBM systems have been found to help bypass lengthy preparation rituals and accomplish measurable gains quickly (Schaffer & Thomson, 1992).

The PBM process is also an excellent means of providing continuing evaluation of middle managers and identifying talented new ones. All organizations should "identify their strategically important 'A' positions—*and then*—focus on the 'A' players who should fill them" (Huselid et al., 2005 p. 112). Public service performance reviews generally suffer from a variety of shortcomings, such as the fact that they are rarely candid; occur infrequently (usually annually); tend to rate most employees the same;

and typically are not based on a truthful continuum of work quality. By contrast, an effective PBM system provides a continuous flow of evaluative information to top administrators. Similarly, meetings provide a stage on which field commanders can exhibit their skills relative to their peers and the organization's stated vision. Civil service requirements often dictate who is "selected" for these key positions/ranks. In order to ensure adequate skill sets for these middle managers, an effective program of executive development or in-service training must be created and regularly used.

Like all models and tools, PBM systems must be used properly. They should serve primarily as a means of managing organizational knowledge, not as an auditing and oversight device. There is a very real risk associated with measuring numbers for their own sake. One of the major criticisms of the GPRA is that it "invariably results in measuring what is easy to count rather than what most appropriately reflects the complexities of social programs" (Perrin, 1999, p. 103). Another is that management focus tends to turn to those things that are systematically measured—and often those things are the wrong things.

A number of studies of performance measurement in the public sector focus on the utilization of performance measurement systems to generate real change. In one study, Patria de Lancer Julnes and Marc Holzer (2001) point to Michael Patton (1978) who advocated a focus on utilization as a process, not as a singular event, and to Martha Marshall (1996) and Ara Merjanian (1996) who emphasized that developing and using performance measures often involve changes that are threatening to an organization, regardless of the potential value of the change. de Lance Julnes and Holzer conclude that utilization of performance-measurement information is a two-stage process—the first being the development of measures and the second, being the actual use of those measures. Caution is encouraged in both phases—the identification of measures must be sound, and their use must be supported if performance measurement systems are to have the expected impact.

Clearly, any PBM system is subject to abuse by otherwise well-meaning administrators or politicians. Mere mimicry of the original NYPD Compstat model will invariably result in a lack of authentic buy-in and ultimate failure unless those individuals adopting it understand that Compstat is a philosophy as well as a process. In order for Compstat or any other PBM system to flourish, it must be understood that the system must be developed from within the organization, not imposed from the outside. Any mandate given to a public organization (such as a police department or agency) to adopt the system will certainly ensure its eventual demise. An essential feature of successful PBM systems is that the list of performance indicators that will eventually be monitored is developed with the active input and participation of field personnel (those actually doing the work). While the basic features of PBM systems are surprisingly fungible, the system's design must be tailored to the particular challenges and capacities of the organization (see, e.g., Kowalewski, 1996).

Index crimes and overtime rates can and should be easily monitored, but the PBM model has far greater potential. Since performance is multidimensional, particularly regarding the field of policing, an array of measures must be thoughtfully chosen and carefully used. By soliciting the input of police officers and individuals who actually perform the work, a more valid list of indicators will be obtained. This will also increase the level of buy-in from the field and optimize the system's chances for success.

A police organization that attempts to replicate a PBM system like Compstat quickly (perhaps by means of readily available federal funding) will invariably find that implementing a PBM system is a challenge. In order to succeed, the newly created PBM system must become part of the organizational architecture and "as much a part of the organization's culture as are styles of dress and unquestioned forms of conduct" (Eggers & Brown, 2000, p. 181). The organization must first undergo a reexamination of its mission and core business goals and objectives (both stated and unstated), before any PBM system can be successfully used (see generally O'Connell, 2001a). In order for a reform such as PBM to succeed, it must alter both the culture of the organization and the day-to-day behavior of its people.

Agencies should also not expect to realize a financial savings as a result of the implementation of a PBM system. Reasonable start-up costs, such as equipment expenditures and training, should be anticipated. Operational efficiencies may be realized after the system is online and functioning properly.

The PBM model has tremendous potential for improving the overall quality of police services being delivered in this country. It has the potential to provide an organization with a new perspective, a new operational strategy, and a new long-term outlook. It can also be used to develop an effective business plan "that could be used to guide priorities and drive decisions at every level of the organization" (Kowalewski, 1996, p. 3). Organizations, however, must be willing to truly "transform" themselves. The necessity of an enterprise-wide transformation should alert organizations considering the adoption of a PBM system to maintain a sense of cautious optimism and realistic goals. In a sense, they must keep their eye on the prize, while taking deliberate, well-informed steps toward a new PBM focus.

In most instances, the organizational architecture must be adjusted (sometimes radically) to accommodate and realize the maximum benefit from the PBM system (see generally Brickley, Smith, & Zimmerman, 1997; Ottaway & Burns, 1997). If necessary adjustments are not made, and if the PBM model is forcefully inserted or imposed on an unwelcoming organization, conflict will undoubtedly occur.

PBM systems are not simply an add-on to existing systems. In order for them to be effective, they must become the primary management system for the organization. All too frequently, PBM systems are simply added via stovepipe development practices and fail to yield expected benefits. Ideally, the PBM system should be used to develop an information dashboard that can inform and coordinate all strategic and operational decisions.

Fritz (1996) suggests that organizations sometimes move forward in a vigorous and determined way toward some stated organizational goal or target, only to oscillate, move away from, and ultimately abandon that goal. This phenomenon, which he refers to as "structural conflict," occurs in U.S. police organizations and has stymied myriad change initiatives over the years. (For an interesting historical account of a failed "management-by-objectives" initiative in a large police department, see Reuss-Ianni, 1983.)

> When organizations initiate change, other forces are often simultaneously working to maintain the existing situation, causing the organization to oscillate back to the status quo. In this situation, several deep structural elements are in conflict with each other. These elements include the cognitive focus, organizational structure, and actions of the various participants. A resolving structure, on the other hand, is designed to lead to the accomplishment of the desired results. (Coe, 1997, p. 168)

The Compstat model has certainly not been immune to criticism. Since its very inception, critics have identified the very real potential for abuse in terms of the "grilling" of field commanders, which necessarily takes place at times (see generally Bratton & Knobler, 1998). Many suggest that unfair or harsh questioning during meetings can have an immediate (and dramatic) adverse effect on the morale of other commanders as well as the rank and file. Some suggest that the entire issue of "accountability" is inherently unfair, in that field commanders are being called to task for the criminal actions of others (O'Connell, 2001a).

This point requires further discussion. The originators of Compstat never intended to hold commanders accountable for the criminal activity of others. Rather, they wanted to design a management system that would hold field commanders accountable for using *best efforts* to detect and apprehend criminals; it was hoped those best efforts would lead to a reduction in the overall rate of crime within the community. At the core of Compstat's philosophy was a fundamental belief that the police can actually make a difference in terms of crime reduction. Some level of crime will always exist in our society. It is the job of the police to use their collective best efforts to reduce that overall rate as much as possible. Compstat is a mechanism specifically designed to track and evaluate those efforts.

Perhaps the most detailed criticisms of Compstat are those contained in a research report conducted by James Willis, Stephen Mastrofski, and David Weisburd (2003) entitled *Compstat in Practice: An In-Depth Analysis of Three Cities*. The authors argue that U.S. police departments cannot always provide a fertile ground for Compstat's demanding agenda (p. v). They cite a variety of factors that might restrict a department's ability to successfully adopt Compstat: "scarcity of resources and political pressures may limit departments' freedom to allocate resources to specific crime problems" and managers might "lack the training to take full advantage of Compstat data when they are making decisions" (p. v). While these factors are no doubt relevant and can certainly hinder implementation they are, to a certain extent, extraneous issues. Both training and funding can always be supplemented. These issues, however, do not speak to the inherent utility of the model. The true question is whether Compstat's success can be effectively reproduced in other agencies and, if so, how best to implement the program in order to ensure success.

It is entirely possible that Compstat and other PBM models can, and should, only be implemented as part of an overall change management program, as it was in New York. Simply inserting a Compstat-like PBM mechanism in a dysfunctional police organization will not yield any tangible benefit. Indeed, that is not why it was originally designed. It developed as part of a wider reengineering program in which the NYPD reassessed and redesigned many of its most fundamental practices and policies. It is this fertile field of change that provides the best opportunity for a program like Compstat to take root and flourish. The adoption of Compstat or any other form of PBM system will not guarantee any concurrent change in organizational behavior. Harold Sirkin, Perry Keenan, and Alan Jackson (2005) identify four factors that have been found to determine the outcome of any transformation initiative: (1) the duration of time until the change program is completed; (2) the project team's performance integrity; (3) the commitment to change that top management and employees display; and (4) the effort over and above the usual work that the change initiative demands of employees (p. 111; see also Kotter, 2007).

Perhaps those documented instances where Compstat has yielded disappointing results are more attributable to other deep-seated organizational dysfunctions (such as a lack of training or strategic planning) or simply are due to the fact that the organization was not properly oriented toward or prepared for a program of change. In several instances, middle managers used their fledgling Compstat system in a

> pattern of organizational response to crime spikes in hot spots that was analogous to the Whack-a-Mole game found at fairs and carnivals [where] a premium is placed on responding quickly, rather than monitoring problem holes continuously to try to discern patterns. (Willis, Mastrofski, & Weisburd, 2003, p. 75)

Compstat is not designed as a tool to enhance efficiency at responding to reported crimes. On the contrary, it is designed to provide knowledgeable managers with a means to discern patterns and (proactively) predict where their efforts will have the most impact. Just as a hammer is most useful in the hands of a skilled carpenter, Compstat is best used by people who are already quite knowledgeable and skilled in the philosophy and practices of problem-oriented policing and the art of "managing for results" (see generally Goldstein, 1990).

Since its inception, Compstat seems to have flourished in agencies where middle managers possess these skills. All organizations that consider adopting Compstat must understand that the field commander serves a key role. In many respects, they are linchpins in the entire process and often have a direct strategic impact. Great care must be used in selecting and/or training them.

The following section describes the "best practices" of any Compstat-like PBM system—one that utilizes interactive meetings as an essential component. It contains various recommendations for obtaining the maximum benefit from this particular form of PBM system.

Regarding Implementation

- In order for any PBM system to function properly, top-level management must express and reaffirm its dissatisfaction with the status quo. PBM is based on ongoing organizational learning and continuous improvement; it adheres to the idea of "better" rather than "best practices."

- To achieve success, traditional bureaucratic management models should be replaced with a more intelligent and experimental form of problem-solving policing. The Compstat philosophy is based on a presumption that field commanders are best suited to make field decisions. Field commanders must receive adequate resources, personnel, decision-making freedom, and support from the uppermost levels of the organization. In return, upper management can expect a higher degree of personal accountability from commanders. While some aspect of reported crime rates is clearly beyond the field commanders' control, what is under their control is the commitment to use best efforts to reduce crime. Some percentage of violent crime is unavoidable and unpreventable, due to the fact that it is spontaneous (such as a stabbing in a night club); however, diligent and effective policing techniques can reduce the likelihood of tragic occurrences (such as aggressive enforcement of alcohol beverage control laws, local noise ordinances, etc.).

- PBM systems should monitor more than the organization's relative success at achieving short-range goals (i.e., a "snapshot" or "dip-stick" measure of current performance). They should be used to *set* and to *monitor* short-, medium-, and long-range goals.

- PBM systems help the organization "identify emerging conditions, problems, needs and issues [and to] view them as change opportunities" (Downes, 1998, p. 657).

- To ensure success, there must be a modern organizational and information technology (IT) infrastructure in place. GIS capabilities might not be necessary if analysis is not going to be based on geographic comparisons (modern spreadsheet capabilities might be sufficient to produce descriptive statistics, graphs, etc.).

- There must be an auditing and inspections unit to ensure the timeliness and accuracy of the data used. Sometimes, data are simply too old to be useful. Some data do not have "the currency program managers usually need to react" (Hatry, et al., 2003, p. 13).

- The process should always be understood as evolutionary, not stagnant; it must be modified and perfected constantly. There is always room for improvement in seeking better practices.

- The PBM system must be the prevailing management philosophy throughout the entire organizational chart. To maximize effectiveness, it must be pervasive—not limited to disciplinary or auditing functions, nor to one particular unit or section. It requires a buy-in by all members of the organization.

- Selection of performance indicators must be a collaborative and fluid process focused on what is important to the organization. Managers should consider the existence of multiple plausible measures to capture each concept (Nicholson-Crotty, Theobald, & Nicholson-Crotty, 2006).

- When selecting indicators, it is important to address core business practices. Identify the organization's most important functions and focus on those first. The list of performance indicators can always be expanded and refined at a later date. It was only after the NYC Department of Correction was able to control inmate violence (one of the first things measured by TEAMS), that they were able to address other issues (such as tracking and addressing inmate complaints and grievances, or producing inmates for court appearances in a timely fashion, etc.). Since virtually nothing could be accomplished until the organization provided a safe and secure environment for both staff and inmates, it was important to address violence (a "reactive" process) before more constructive (proactive) measures could be taken.

- The purpose and practices of a PBM system should be incorporated into the training curricula for all personnel, from the initial hiring through in-service training for all personnel.

- Whenever a PBM system is adopted, the organization must afford its managers ample opportunity to adjust to the new management system and to alter their practices accordingly. This involves training and emphasis on the transition process. Too rapid a shift in organizational philosophy and management approach could do more harm than good, particularly in a struggling organization.

- Implementation is only the "tip of the iceberg." A considerable amount of time and energy must be expended to assure that the mechanism survives. Short-term success is encouraging but not sufficient. Continual cooperative effort and commitment are mandatory ingredients for further success.

- In order to ensure the long-term viability of a PBM process, agencies must utilize a sufficient number of motivated and creative administrators who are both students of, and believers in, the process. High-level personnel changeovers can provide opportunities for creativity and innovation, as long as there is also continuity and strong leadership.

Regarding the Meetings

- If a PBM system includes interactive strategy meetings, the entire organizational chart must be represented at all meetings.
- There must be a competent and creative chief inquisitor, a top-level administrator who leads the discussions at all meetings.
- The dais must include one or more "operational" people with extensive field experience and the respect of those in the field. Young "corporate CPA types" with little or no operational background can be stonewalled or more easily misled. You must know the job in order to monitor the work properly and to move the organization forward.
- Meetings should be held at headquarters away from many of the distractions in the field. This serves a symbolic purpose and draws on additional resources (personnel, equipment) that are rarely available in the field.
- There must be an authentic and spontaneous dialogue during meetings—a lively discussion, not an inquisition. Similar to the Socratic method of inquiry used in most U.S. law schools, it involves point, counterpoint, and thoughtful responses to questions. It should not, however, resemble a deposition, where the respondent is interrogated. It is an art, a skill developed over time.
- The meetings are not disciplinary tools—there is a need always to address successes as well as failures. A negative connotation for these meetings is bad for morale and will severely limit their utility.
- All presentations should include a profile of the department/unit, as well as its highest ranking administrator. This would include date of appointment, geographic area(s) of responsibility, personnel and resources under command, a photograph, etc. This alleviates the need to have introductions, which take time and detract from the overall quality of the presentations (this would obviously not be necessary in small departments or agencies).
- Meetings must be scheduled early in the workday, preferably 7:00 or 7:30 AM, so that participants will not be distracted by other issues and matters.
- All meetings should be recorded (if not actually broadcast). It is always preferable to send presenters back with a tape or steno-

graphic record of what was said. This is necessary for follow-up purposes and for critiques of one's own performance.

- Nonpresenting units or agencies should send a representative to
  attend meetings if it is anticipated that the agenda will include
  issues pertinent to them. Ultimately, meetings should all be available
  online and interactive so that the entire organization, jurisdiction,
  or city could observe (and perhaps participate).

- Someone on the dais must be chiefly responsible for recognizing
  instances of micromanagement (detailed discussions that are not
  pertinent to the entire organization which should be discussed by
  the interested parties at a later time).

- Participants must always be on the lookout for collaboration opportunities with outside agencies.

- A business-like atmosphere should be maintained, characterized at
  all times by mutual respect. Top-level management must constantly
  be alert for personal attacks or unwarranted criticisms. One person
  at a time should have the floor.

- Meetings must be scheduled frequently, based on the needs of the
  specific organization. The process is the equivalent of the organization checking its own pulse; better health depends on proper monitoring. If departments and subunits are obtaining useful information
  and direction, they will look forward to these meetings.

- Positive comments must be communicated with the same level of
  sincerity and concern as criticisms. It is important not only to praise
  the presenter(s), but also the individuals performing the work
  within the agency as well.

- Top-level administrators should be aware not to get bogged down in
  retrospective analysis. They should look back only as far as necessary to explain what's going on now and what can be expected in
  the future. Too much attention on the past prevents progress.

- Discussions about poor performance typically lead to training opportunities, and learning takes place in both directions. Presenters
  should describe their standard operating procedures (how they do
  things). Commissioners or top administrators generally know and
  understand the ends (organizational goals) but not always the
  means (how things actually get done in the field). This process provides a perfect opportunity for bridging the knowledge gap between
  management and the rank and file.

- Preparation is the key. All data and information must be shared well
  in advance of the meetings. Comments from top administrators
  should be relayed to field units prior to the scheduled meetings. This
  does not mean everything is scripted but major issues should be

communicated so that participants can reflect on potential questions and formulate thoughtful responses.

- Field units should engage in mini-meetings to prepare for the larger, more comprehensive meetings. They should meet well in advance of the larger meeting to address anticipated areas of inquiry.

- It is very important to have a recap, "what we've learned today," at the conclusion of each meeting and to clearly articulate and record who is going to be following up with whom.

- Questioners should always be on the lookout for training opportunities (indeed, the Director of Training, or his/her representative, should be present at all meetings) in order to identify potential topics for additional in-service training. If a mistake is made by one manager, it often is likely that others will make the same mistake. Negative trends can be stopped sooner if the process includes constant monitoring for areas needing additional training.

Regarding the Flow of Information and Ideas

- Meetings are the organizational equivalent of thinking out loud: weighing options for addressing information obtained from the internal and external work environments; reflecting; brainstorming; attempting to select the most rational and effective course of action; and drawing on all organizational resources, including the practices and opinions of key personnel.

- The flow of information must be in two directions. There must be an active dialogue. All parties actively teach and learn.

- This process relies primarily on information that is compiled in the ordinary course of business, but it also draws on tacit knowledge in the organization—information that is possessed in the field and is more associated with personal skills (Cook & Brown, 1999).

- Interactive discussions "generate new knowledge and new ways of knowing" (Cook & Brown, 1999, p. 381).

- Presenters should be dissuaded from responding with statements such as, "we're working on that," or "we'll take that under advisement." Such platitudes stifle the dialogue and are nonproductive. Officials should keep the momentum moving in a positive direction: "Please get back to us with an action plan that outlines the steps you will be taking to correct this situation." Follow-up questions are important to encourage more dialogue.

- Top-level administrators should use questions like:
  —*How* did this happen?
  —*Why* did this happen? (What is causing it?)
  —*When* did this happen and how long had it been like that?
  —*What* can we do to change (or sustain) it?

- An effort should be made to develop the public speaking and critical thinking skills of individuals who will be expected to present at meetings. This can be done by creating an executive development program or by engaging outside consultants to develop necessary skills for managers and administrators. The NYPD introduced a Compstat College, where newly promoted managers are introduced to the process through practice meetings; the NYC Department of Corrections calls its program the "Leadership Institute."

- In addition to executive development courses, a system of personal (one-on-one) mentoring could be valuable. Newly promoted managers can and should learn from the experiences of more senior personnel.

- The PBM process is a philosophy as well as a mechanism. It is a new way of thinking. Agency goals and methods must be internalized by managers; they must believe in the utility of the PBM system and should begin to incorporate it into their day-to-day decisions and actions.

Regarding the Collection, Analysis, and Dissemination of Data

- The key issue is the timeliness and accuracy of the data (i.e., how quickly does the information come to the research unit from the field?). If the accuracy is questionable or if the information is stale, it gives presenters wiggle room to explain away poor performance (e.g., "Those numbers are not up-to-date, we're actually doing much better than that today!" or "We've already corrected that condition.")

- In order to be truly meaningful, *all data* must be reviewed by senior management (both positive and negative performance information). They should not view performance indicators in a vacuum. They must at all times have a "global" perspective in order to truly understand the overall health and performance of the entire organization.

- Managers should be vigilant to avoid pitfalls associated with the "paradox of data overload" (Kamarck, 2005, p. 9). In many instances, so much information is made available that it makes analysis and effective use virtually impossible.

- Managers who are being reviewed should be geographically accountable. That is, they should have a proprietary interest, or a specific responsibility for the work being performed in a particular area or by a particular group of people. They need to have a "stake" in the work being performed if they are to be held "accountable."

- Accountability only goes so far. There will always be instances where a crime wave occurs spontaneously despite the best efforts of the police or where a school district's test scores drop precipitously from the rapid influx of immigrants. Events are explainable and understandable if we see them in context and use the information provided to us by statistics. Statisticians refer to these situations as *outliers*. There will always be "unusual" situations that fall on the extreme ends of the bell curve. The key is to understand the uniqueness of these situations and to learn from them. We need to create and use institutional memory.

• It is important to identify equivalent units (e.g., case loads, libraries, precincts, etc.) in order to have effective comparisons, so that comparisons are "apples to apples."

• All performance measures must be meaningful and must address the core mission and basic goals of the organization.

• Performance measures must be relevant—they must be meaningful and of real use to the organization. Managers must resist the tendency to measure the measurable—"focusing on what's easily measured leads to 'looking good without being good'" (Senge, 1994, p. 304).

• Performance indicators must continually be reviewed/revised. It is imperative that the entire organization understand the *meaning* of each of the indicators and that they use a common definition. There must be a common understanding. Perhaps the number of recorded public "complaints" are, on further reflection, actually requests for information.

• Numbers do not have a meaning unto themselves, they must be interpreted. Police managers must familiarize themselves with the concept of bounded rationality (Jones, 2003), whereby decision makers tend not to fully explore all possible options and explanations.

• Managers must recognize that they will never have *all* of the information regarding any upcoming decision. The key question to ask is whether you have all the information you need.

• Police managers should also be aware of the phenomenon known as the confirmation bias. This occurs "when people observe more, give extra emphasis to, or intentionally look for evidence that would validate their existing beliefs and expectations and are likely to excuse or completely ignore evidence that could reject their beliefs" (Byrd, 2006, p. 511).

• When measuring an agency's efficiency, a key question is, "efficient for whom?" Administrators must at all times have an understanding of the needs of their end users and stakeholders (i.e., the public). An efficiently performing public service organization can nonetheless be "inefficient" if it fails to meet the goals and expectations of the public.

• Positive trends or increases in productivity must be sustained and thoroughly examined. Focus must be placed on sustaining positive trends, not just identifying and eliminating negative ones.

- Top-level managers or individuals on their staff must have a working knowledge of statistics. They should know how to use and interpret comparative statistics; they should also understand the phenomenon of regression toward the mean (see p. 107). "Bottoming out" is a natural phenomenon.

- A fundamental knowledge of statistics includes familiarity with the terms *correlation* and *causation* and the distinction between the two.

- Managers should be aware that "even when a program is doing what it should, there may be a long time lag between program activities and observable impacts" (Gilmour, 2006, p. 28).

- Management must understand that statistics can always be interpreted in a number of ways; however, they must always be *intelligently* interpreted. This applies to all types of performance measurement systems, not just police management systems. For example, if sanitation trucks are completing their routes more quickly, one would assume that to be a good thing. But perhaps not. Maybe they are coming in too soon by not making all of their pickups. Sometimes quality is far better than quantity; it depends what you're measuring. Managers need to look at the big picture rather than a single performance category. They need to use the entire constellation of performance measures for the entire agency. That's where the true story is. Police managers can, for example, compare the relative performance of officers assigned to patrol, investigative units, community affairs, etc.

- Managers must always be aware of similarities and distinctions between units. Returning to the waste disposal analogy, perhaps one garbage route in a downtown area is inherently more difficult and slower than many others (just like sectors or commands in different neighborhoods differ from one another). Managers obviously need to know their agency, the nature of the work, and their people. Once appropriate baselines are established (means, medians, and modes) for each unit, they will have a proper frame of reference. Then they will be in a position to judge overall performance of different units.

- Managers need to establish "reasonable" (obtainable and sustainable) baselines for each unit and supervisor. Geography remains the same, it is therefore taken into account in the establishment of baselines. It is unreasonable to assume that baselines will be identical for all units, although one could expect them to be substantially similar if their overall mission and operations are similar.

- The increases or reductions indicated in performance measures should never be viewed as absolutes but rather as a basis for intelligent inquiry and discussion. Without meaningful dialogue (among decision makers and rank and file) top-level managers run the risk of relying *exclusively* on data reflected in performance indicators and might only obtain a partial view of organizational performance (Buckmaster, 2000).

- Data must be delved into and truly analyzed. There should be a constant search for statistically significant variations and possible correlations.

- It appears that there is a generic "fiscal response" used by presenters to deflect criticism: "I'm aware of that [condition or deficiency] but I don't have the resources available to address that, I have more important issues to address." Such a response could stifle further discussion. In effect, it insulates the party from further criticism and justifies deficiencies in performance. Budgetary constraints should be no surprise to either party. If a particular corrective measure cannot be undertaken for fiscal reasons, it should be discussed in detail, either during the meeting or at a later time with interested parties in attendance.

- Every effort should be made to ensure that a form of tunnel vision does not develop, whereby managers become overly "stat conscious" and work exclusively on crimes and matters included as performance indicators. "Constantly holding district commanders accountable for the same crimes at Compstat [meetings] may lead to potentially useful crime-related information being overlooked" (Willis, Mastrofski, Weisburd, & Greenspan, 2003, p. 34).

- Other agencies, such as probation departments and offices of the district attorney, should participate in the process. For a variety of reasons, other agencies might not be able to send a representative to participate in the meetings. If this is the case, the police agency should ensure that relevant information is forwarded to the necessary parties, either through one-on-one meetings or via an ongoing transfer of analyzed data.

- Some recapitulation of periodic meetings should be made available to the public, preferably via a department Web site.

- Although meetings should not generally be open to the public (due to the sensitive nature of many of the data and discussions concerning criminal activity and ongoing police investigations), select members of the community should periodically be invited to attend and participate. Their observation of the proceedings will strengthen police-community relations (akin to the benefits of a citizens' police academy) and their insights could be used to provide the police with community members' perspectives and insights. The importance of public involvement cannot be overstated. As Mark Moore and Anthony Braga (2004) suggest, the important question that lies at the core of developing any adequate measure of police performance is for citizens and their elected representatives to decide what it is that they as a political community value in the activities and operations of a public police department (p. 4; see also Collier, 2001).

- A PBM system will ultimately fail, unless it is utilized for true organizational brainstorming. The system must be used to identify organizational strengths, weaknesses, opportunities, and threats (both internal and external to the organization). It should be used not only to identify and close performance gaps but also to ensure that they stay closed.

- Performance indicators must have the ability to detail the measurable evidence necessary to demonstrate that an intervention has achieved desired results. For that reason, each and every performance indicator should be tied, logically and expressly, to the stated strategic goals of the department. These, in turn, should be directly linked to the overriding organizational mission (as expressed in the agency's mission statement); there should be no guesswork involved. All employees should understand the importance of these indicators and why they need to be tracked continually.

- Practitioners must understand that progress might be made in a certain performance category despite the fact that the PBM system does not yet detect any significant improvement. This occurs due to the phenomenon known as nonlinearity.

  There is probably a dynamic of change that we all misunderstand. We must recognize that all of us have a predisposition to linear thinking (A leads to B, B leads to C, etc.) when in fact an awful lot of change comes from situations where things get worse before they get better. It's similar to the case of non-linear thermodynamics, where we talk about the system having to become more and more in disequilibrium, or disharmony, in order to move to a new state of order. (cited in Fulmer & Keys, 1998, p. 37)

- Brainstorming and innovative problem-solving techniques should be employed by all participants. Managers should be free to "think outside the box" and suggest innovative solutions to pressing problems. The key is to engage these individuals. Pascale and Sternin (2005) stress the need for identifying "positive deviants." That is, individuals who are "on the periphery of their organizations . . . who are far removed from the orthodoxies of mainstream change endeavors. These innovators' uncommon practices and behaviors enable them to find better solutions to problems than others in their [organizations]" (p. 72). Police managers can become hesitant to concern themselves with issues that arise outside of their geographic area of responsibility (Willis, Mastrofski, & Weisburd, 2003). They might also refrain from rendering opinions for fear of casting their colleagues in a bad light, particularly during meetings. These problems can and will undoubtedly occur unless the tone is set from above. The PBM model will only succeed with a full and open exchange of information. This involves not only timely and accurate crime data but also the collective wisdom of all participants. While it is no doubt difficult to establish this type of atmosphere, it can be accomplished if the top levels of management encourage it. Each department or agency head must continually reinforce the need for open channels of communication. Opinions should be solicited and freely offered. As problems occur, the overriding question should be, "Why is this happening?" The manager with geographic responsibility for that area will obviously be in an ideal position to understand the who, what, when, and where of the incident, but not necessarily the *why*.

In many instances, scores, if not hundreds, of years of policing experience is assembled in one room. It would be foolhardy to neglect to tap into this knowledge base. Some problems will continue to exist, but many can be solved by using the collective wisdom of all participants. When any proposed course of action is suggested, an essential feature should be the cost-benefit analysis. As a manager proposes a certain tactic or response, others should be encouraged to voice their opinions regarding possible ramifications and to identify all relevant pros and cons. For example, a tactic proposed by a field commander might prompt a response from a legal, budgetary, or union perspective.

- During meetings, some individual or unit needs to be charged with identifying and discussing the relative costs and benefits of all proposed action plans, versus ignoring those particular needs and tasks. In a financial sense, this function is generally referred to as "cost-consequences analysis" and seeks to determine "prospective return on investment estimates for potential solutions" (Leigh, 2004, p. 625). Discussions that are entirely theoretical or utopian in nature will only generate unfeasible or impractical solutions that will serve no real purpose for the organization. Someone should always be asking the following questions: *"Can we do it? Is it practical? How much will it cost?"* and *"How will it affect our other plans and operations?"* An often more important and provocative question is, *"How much will it cost us to ignore it?"*

- The Crime Analysis Unit (or some equivalent) should regularly interact with field managers and should be fully integrated into the agency's ongoing management operations. Unfortunately, this is often not the case (see Willis, Mastrofski, Weisburd, & Greenspan, 2003). What is desired is a state of synchrony, where managers from all units work as a team (Kamarck, 2005).

- Whenever the PBM system is used to spearhead or direct any specific initiative, operation, or program, there should be consensus among all stakeholders concerning the following:
  —The activities that constitute the program
  —The intended effects of the program
  —The order in which effects are expected to occur
  —The activities that are expected to produce the effects
  —The effects that will be used to determine the success of the program (Chapel, 2004, p. 642).

THE PROLIFERATION OF COMPSTAT-LIKE PBM SYSTEMS

PBM systems have slowly, but steadily, spread through American policing. This chapter will describe how the Compstat model has moved beyond policing and has been successfully adapted in other public sector venues. The chapter will also explore the role of auditing and inspection processes in performance-based management systems.

Shortly after its successful implementation by the NYPD, the Compstat model was adopted by the New York City Department of Correction (DOC). The Correction's model, known as TEAMS ("Total Efficiency Accountability Management System"), was initially employed to address inmate violence that was driven by unfettered gang activity. In 1993, the department recorded more than 1,100 violent incidents in its jails. July and August 1994, represented one of the worst periods of violence with 176 slashings and stabbings on Rikers Island, an average of nearly three a day (Straub & O'Connell, 1999). Inmate violence exacerbated problems caused by budget cuts that had reduced the number of correction officers from 10,700 in 1992 to 9,800 in 1994. Manpower shortages and high sick leave (officers averaged 21 days a year) spun overtime costs out of control—$2.2 million a week during the first three months of 1994 alone. According to one warden, the disorder at Rikers Island and throughout the city's jails was "a system of organized chaos" (Straub & O'Connell, 1999, p. 30).

The state of the correction system stood in stark contrast to Mayor Rudolph Giuliani's efforts to reduce New York City's crime rate and restore its quality of life. Mayor Giuliani's mandate to then Commissioner Michael Jacobson and his deputy Bernard Kerik was clear—reduce violence and restore order in the jail system. TEAMS became the foundation upon which a multi-pronged strategy was built, monitored and expanded. Under Commissioner Kerik inmate violence was reduced by 90% in four years. Overtime costs were cut in half, and sick leave reduced 25% by 1999 (p. 32).

The Department of Correction was charged with more than incarcerating individuals, it was also responsible for providing for all of their physical needs. Specifically, they were responsible for housing inmates, feeding them, providing medical and mental health treatment, administering substance abuse programs, transporting and producing inmates for court appearances, etc. The list of performance indicators monitored by the TEAMS system grew to exceed those used by Compstat and totaled approximately 600 indicators (O'Connell, 2001b).

Like Compstat, TEAMS was credited with substantially improving: overall organizational performance; the quantity and quality of training; and the flow of communication within the agency (O'Connell, 2001b). Perhaps more significantly, it also substantially altered the department's organizational culture by creating a managerial philosophy based on agency-wide accountability and the belief that performance could be continually improved. TEAMS is also important because it advanced the Compstat paradigm beyond crime control and violence reduction by monitoring and improving multiple aspects of DOC's operations and signaling its application to broad-based organizational improvement.

Building on the successes achieved using a performance-based management system in the NYPD and Department of Correction, Mayor Giuliani launched the Citywide Accountability Program (CAP) in January 2001. Under CapStat, thirty-eight agencies were directed to create and implement their own Compstat-like program. According to Giuliani, "we set four parameters that the commissioners had to submit to me:

- Data had to be collected regularly and reliably—preferably on a daily basis, but at least once a week—at a set time.

- Twenty to forty performance indicators that got at the core mission of the agency had to be established.

- A regular meeting must be convened—with a minimum frequency of once a week—including a floor plan that demonstrated exactly which agency leaders were required to be present at each meeting.

- Ten or more representative performance indicators that the agency wanted on its page of the city's Web site must be submitted (Giuliani, 2002, pp. 88–89).

By the time Mayor Giuliani left office, twenty city agencies had built Compstat-like processes, including ParkStat (Department of Parks and Recreation), HealthStat (Department of Health), and TrafficStat (Department of Traffic) (O'Connell, 2001b).

Under Mayor Giuliani, the City's social service programs underwent significant management changes beginning with the dismantling of the

massive Human Resources Administration (HRA). The HRA was established during the Lindsay administration to provide services to the City's
poor. By 1994, the HRA was an agency with a $7.2 billion budget and its
mission included administering, directly or through contracts, the food
stamp offices, day care centers, employment services for public assistance
recipients, shelters for victims of domestic violence, protective services for
adults, protective and preventive services for children, foster care programs, home care for disabled and elderly persons, social services for people with AIDS and HIV-related illnesses, child support enforcement
services, and food distribution programs (Smith & Grinker, 2005, p.16).
Under Giuliani's reorganization, homeless services were addressed under a
new agency, the Department of Homeless Services (DHS), and child welfare under the Administration for Children's Services (ACS).

In 1998, HRA implemented *JobStat* to gather and monitor performance data relative to job placements and retention rates and *VendorStat*
to monitor contracted and nonprofit service providers. In March 2006,
Mayor Michael R. Bloomberg announced the creation of *ChildStat* in the
Administration for Children's Services, following the death of 7-year old
Nixzmary Brown. According to the Mayor's press release, ChildStat will
enable ACS to use data to track and analyze its investigations, identify
high-risk cases, and assign intensive supervision to those cases.

The City of Baltimore's CitiStat program represents the most ambitious and, arguably, the most effective use of a Compstat-like PBM mechanism for monitoring a full array of public services. Regularly, the mayor,
deputy mayors, and key cabinet members meet with department heads
from the city's Bureau of Water and Wastewater, Bureau of Solid Waste,
Health Department, Bureau of General Services, Housing Authority,
Department of Transportation, Department of Recreation and Parks, in
addition to the police and fire departments to discuss performance goals
and objectives (German, 2006). The key performance outcomes measured
by the CitiStat process include, but are not limited to, agency responses to
constituent requests for city services, reducing program redundancies,
reducing employee absenteeism and overtime expenses. For example, by
monitoring trash pickups, city officials discovered that some routes took a
few hours to finish while others took so long that employees earned overtime. The routes were changed in order to redistribute pickups and to
reduce overtime costs.

Similar to the "Stat" process in New York City, Baltimore has used CitiStat to monitor specific programs and initiatives such as lead abatement,
drug treatment centers, and juvenile justice. However, CitiStat is unique
because it brings multiple agencies together in one forum to address city-
wide issues and to ensure interdepartmental coordination and cooperation. Further, the integration of department databases with the "3-1-1"
system (a centralized call center through which citizens can request information, request city services, and follow up on the progress of their

requests) enables the City to track its efficiency in responding to constituent requests.

Martin O'Malley (former mayor of Baltimore elected governor in 2007) campaigned on the success of CitiStat and has indicated his intent to bring it to Maryland state government. During 2005, Washington state governor Christine Gregoire drew heavily on this model when she created the GMAP (Government Management Accountability and Performance) program. Under this program, each of the state's 140 agencies was required by executive order to create "relevant and easy to understand measures that show whether or not programs [are] successful and to hold regular problem-solving sessions to improve performance, and report regularly to the governor" (Kamensky, 2006, p. 9).

The PBM model has proven to be particularly adaptable, provided it is thoroughly understood and carefully implemented. Its documented success outside the field of policing demonstrates not only that it is a fungible product, but also that it can be particularly effective in helping to coordinate joint initiatives and enhance inter-agency cooperation.

Auditing, Inspections, and Accountability

Aggressive businesses and industries measure performance meticulously. They carefully monitor and record the relevant dimensions of performance. They know the important facts and figures, and they act on that knowledge (Ammons, 1996). Within this context, audit and inspection teams play a critical role in performance-based management, as well as in building organizational capacity.

Unfortunately, the traditional role played by the auditor (or similar entity) in public sector agencies has been narrowly focused on examining resource expenditures and/or determining the extent to which members of an organization follow the rules. Recognizing that in a tightly controlled environment innovation is stymied, Gore (1993) condemned the auditor's "gotcha" mentality and recommended that inspectors general, specifically their audit functions, "help improve systems to prevent waste, fraud and abuse and *ensure efficient, effective service*" (p. 6; emphasis added). Further, the federal government's "reinvention" plan recommended that inspectors general (and auditors) use their role as a neutral observer to collaborate with managers to make programs work better (Gore, 1993). Since 1993, there has been a gradual, continuous shift, as government auditors and other oversight entities have increasingly defined their roles in helping public agencies serve their customers better, while securing the confidence of the public in their integrity (Osborne and Hutchinson, 2004).

Today, auditing and inspection units play a critical role in police agencies, improving management and operations, often in conjunction with a PBM mechanism, and ensuring agency-wide integrity.

Police agencies have learned, too frequently after a scandal, that information developed through audits and inspections is critical to agency integrity, operations and strategic planning (Anechiarico and Jacobs, 1996). To be effective, audit and inspection units must provide a continuous flow of information, rather than a periodic "report card." Police managers, like their counterparts in the private sector and other public agencies, can not afford to wait for the semi-annual auditors' report and hope that the news is good. Rather, real time data must be obtained and shared on a regular basis so senior managers can use it to "steer the ship."

Performance audits are one format that should be considered by police agencies endeavoring to assess the management and operations of their agencies. Performance audits are objective and systematic assessments of the performance of an organization, program, or activity in order to provide information to improve public accountability and facilitate decision making by parties with responsibility to oversee or initiate corrective action.

> Performance audits provide assurance or conclusions relating to audit objectives that provide an evaluation against objective criteria, such as specific requirements or measures, or good business practices. Performance audits provide objective analysis so that management and those charged with governance and oversight may improve program performance, operations, reduce costs, facilitate decision making by parties with responsibility to oversee or initiate corrective action, and contribute to public accountability. (Comptroller General, 2006, pp. 12-13; footnotes omitted).

Performance audits can be used to: (1) ascertain the extent to which operating units are aligned with the organization's mission and goals; (2) evaluate overall leadership skills and capabilities of managers; (3) assess the adequacy of staff training, organizational structure and community satisfaction; (4) establish benchmarks against which to measure and compare productivity and performance; (5) evaluate the extent to which technology is being used to increase productivity and improve community satisfaction; and (6) establish a reporting system that can be monitored and updated on a continuous basis by senior management (McClendon, 2001). In this regard, performance audits are consistent with PBM theory and practice and may be a valuable adjunct to the process.

Audit/inspection units are utilized in conjunction with various PBM models. For example, the TEAMS Field Unit ensures the standardization of data collection methods throughout the New York City Department of Correction. Serving as the analytical arm of the TEAMS process, the Field Unit performs research and evaluations of each of the Department's jail and service commands and provides follow-up assistance in carrying out recommendations discussed during TEAMS meetings. Similarly, in Baltimore, data is submitted to the CitiStat team which analyzes the information and prepares the presentation for CitiStat meetings. The CitiStat operations team ensures the data submitted by city agencies is accurate by conducting field inspections and examining agency files and other data sources at random.

In the Los Angeles Police Department, George Gascon, the former Assistant Chief of Operations, created CompStat Plus. According to Gascon (2005), CompStat Plus represents an enhanced application of the well-known Compstat principles of inspection and accountability as well as the use of more in-depth auditing methods, mentorship, and close collaboration to help underperforming commands. To begin, an inspection team is formed using commanding officers who are recognized experts in patrol, detectives, crime analysis, etc., well respected by their peers, and have current knowledge of the command to be inspected. The goal of the inspection team is to identify performance inhibitors in order to help the underperforming command improve its crime reduction efforts. Following an initial review of statistical data, on-site inspection and staff interviews, a road map for improving performance is developed in collaboration with the effected command. In addition, a mentoring component facilitates the interaction between the inspection team and command staff and supports the performance improvement process.

Police agencies should employ a variety of assessment methods including, but not limited to, formal periodic audits and inspections of all units and divisions; "spot" inspections and audits; qualitative evaluations, such as surveys and focus group interviews of all stakeholders (e.g., community members, patrol officers, etc.); and direct observation of programs and activities. These methods are designed to ensure accountability and data integrity. Pane (2004) described eight (8) distinct data quality standards that can prove useful:

1. **Validity:** Data adequately represents performance. Have the indicators and associated data been scrutinized to ensure they all describe the phenomena of interest?

2. **Accurate Definitions:** Definitions are correct. Have clear, written definitions of key terms (including inclusions and exclusions) been communicated to data providers?

3. **Accurate Counts:** Counts are correct. Are counts accurate; e.g., is double counting avoided?

4. **Editing:** Data are clean. Have you discussed large changes or unusual findings with the primary data providers to see if they might be due to editing errors?

5. **Calculation:** The math is right?

6. **Timeliness:** Data are recent. Do data meet decision-making needs?

7. **Reporting:** Full reporting is made. Are data quality problems at each level reported to the next level?

8. **Burden Reduction:** Data collected are used. Are all data that are collected actually used?

Police managers must assess the quality and reliability of statistical crime and other data before acting on it. Unfortunately, there are too many examples of police crime statistics being called into question. For example, questions have arisen over the underreporting of crime statistics in Baltimore (Green, 2006) and St. Louis (Kohler, 2005). The Philadelphia Police Department was accused of intentionally "downgrading" rapes and misclassifying other crimes over an extended period (Fazalollah, McCoy, and Moran, 2000). In New Orleans, five police officers were fired and a sixth demoted for improperly downgrading crime complaints. And an audit of the Atlanta Police Department's crime data discovered thousands of missing police reports and a consistent lack of data integrity. Ward (2005) questioned whether the Compstat process in the New York City Police Department had gone too far by constantly putting police commanders under pressure to beat past numbers and demonstrate further crime reductions. In most instances it seems that data manipulation occurs to keep officers out of hot water with their commanding officers, to create the false impression that crime has been reduced, or to further political and/or career aspirations. These and other scandals cast doubt on the Compstat paradigm and erode public confidence in police performance management efforts.

Auditing and inspections systems, regardless of the type or methodology employed, must have the ability to identify program deficiencies, data manipulation, and corrupt employees. In-depth discussions of internal affairs, inspectors general, external oversight commissions, etc. are available in various sources. However, one program which merits description in this text is the early intervention system or early warning system because of its emphasis on individual and organizational performance monitoring.

Early intervention systems (EIS), such as the one's currently employed in the Los Angeles Sheriff's Department, San Jose Police Department, Pittsburgh Bureau of Police and other cities throughout the country capture specific pieces of information about police officer behavior and performance to help identify problems early on. Early intervention systems are applied in a variety of ways. Some agencies use EIS to help identify officers who may be experiencing personal or professional problems that result in poor job performance. These systems generally focus on helping officers and providing intervention in a non-punitive and non-disciplinary form. Other agencies use EIS to inform performance evaluations, assignment decisions and to improve accountability. And others use EIS to identify misconduct and/or corruption (Walker, Milligan, and Berke, 2005).

The Pittsburgh Bureau of Police implemented its EIS in response to a U.S. Department of Justice consent decree (1997). The consent decree followed a series of allegations of excessive force, false arrests, improper searches and seizures, and failures to discipline and supervise officers. The decree instructed the Bureau to make comprehensive changes in oversight, training and supervision. One of the key elements required by the decree was that the Bureau develop and implement a computerized early warning system (EWS). As a result of the Bureau's reform efforts which led to wholesale changes, the decree was lifted in 2002.

Pittsburgh's Performance Assessment Review System (PARS) collects data on a wide variety of categories, such as, but not limited to: accidents, arrests, commendations, civilian complaints, civil claims, disciplinary actions, sick time, traffic stop data, use of force, and workers' compensation claims. PARS alerts the supervisory staff when an officer's conduct exceeds predetermined thresholds for any one performance category. Each month, the Bureau's command staff meets to discuss personnel management issues identified by PARS. COMPSTAR meetings, similar in form to Compstat, ensure that the data produced by PARS is acted upon. During COMPSTAR meetings, commanders discuss the performance of officers both in and out of their commands. Commanders provide details regarding special assignments, for example, vehicle and traffic enforcement, which might explain high summons issuance, and possibly complaints. COMPSTAR meetings provide a forum for open communication among command-level personnel, prevent problem officers from "falling through the cracks," strengthen accountability and facilitate the development and implementation of effective intervention strategies (Davis, Henderson and Ortiz, 2005).

The combination of PARS and COMPSTAR has proven to be an invaluable component of the Pittsburgh Police Bureau's restructuring efforts, led to the lifting of the consent decree, and continues to be an essential element of its management practices. The Pittsburgh Police Bureau case demonstrates the value of early intervention and early warning systems in enhancing accountability and integrity in police agencies.

Auditors and inspection units have become essential components of police performance management systems. Auditors can make significant contributions to an agency's mission by helping senior managers figure out what to measure, how to measure it and how to integrate findings into overall performance enhancement. A neutral, objective body is also needed to audit the data process, to keep it honest and free from political or other influence. Auditors can and should identify best practices within individual operating units and share them across the agency. A PBM system could certainly assist in this regard.

PBM Systems in the Post-9/11 Era

Perhaps the single most significant lesson learned from the September 11 attacks is the value of human intelligence and inter-agency communication and cooperation. As we have discussed, PBM systems are an effective means of closely monitoring the internal and external work environments. They enable well-trained managers to scan ongoing data systems for aberrations and anomalies that might have significance from an operational standpoint. Recently, some experts have suggested that this monitoring function can be expanded for a broader purpose. They contend that a series of inter-connected law enforcement agencies with well-established PBM systems can be used as a network of listening posts and information relay points to assist with the war on terrorism.

Kelling and Bratton (2006) suggest that the broken windows theory of policing can be adapted to counter terrorism in order to create "a hostile environment for terrorists" (p. 3). They explain that, often, terrorists commit "relatively minor precursor crimes" that can be used to fund or facilitate future attacks. For example, while a theft of police uniforms from a dry cleaner, or the theft of a fuel truck might not raise the suspicion of the jurisdiction involved, perhaps it would to others who were provided access to this information (such as the FBI or CIA). Police managers are often loathe to make mandatory notifications to other agencies, but perhaps this information could be provided to and routinely scanned by other appropriate authorities at the state and federal levels. A variety of otherwise innocuous events could be monitored, such as the sale of fertilizers (which could be used to produce powerful explosives) or the theft or forgery of important official documents, such as drivers' licenses or passports. Ideally, interconnected police agencies with functioning PBM systems could serve as a series of "listening posts" that could aid and support our nation's counterterrorist activities. Even if organizational cultural barriers compromise or prevent the proactive transmission of such data, at the very least, the technology and techniques (i.e., PBM systems) now exist for the careful monitoring of these events so that information can be immediately provided once it is requested. Agencies should move from a "need to know" to a "need to share" mind-set (Final Report of the National Commission on Terrorist Attacks Upon the United States, 2004, p. 417). PBM systems can help to bring about the type of interoperability that can enhance homeland security.

The Compstat system has recently spawned a new variation on the theme; the NYPD's Real Time Crime Center (Gaskell, 2005). While perhaps not properly classified as a PBM system, it is being used to manage data more proactively, to inform decisions, and to arrive at accurate and effective solutions. It differs from standard PBM systems in that it is not oriented toward or employed for performance measurement purposes, training, etc. Rather, its sole purpose is to access and review extremely large volumes of "real-time" data to identify individuals and to solve crimes. It is important to note, however, that the Real Time Crime Center acts as a supplement to the Compstat system, which is still being used by the NYPD with great success.

As the challenges facing the police continue to evolve, PBM systems will play an increasingly important role. Technologies continue to advance rapidly and PBM systems have now been used with great success in a variety of roles and venues. There is every indication that PBM systems will continue to be an essential feature of modern law enforcement.

How to Develop a Performance-Based Management System

The following chapter outlines both a theoretical framework and a set of practical steps for developing and instituting an effective PBM system for virtually any modern police agency.[1] The steps presented below provide the most logical and effective means of establishing a PBM system that will not only operate effectively, but endure. A preliminary word of caution is necessary, however. Police managers who wish to develop such a system must recognize that change efforts of this type are extremely complex. Unfortunately, it is not so simple as merely directing that such a system be established. It often involves contending with a host of political and cultural dynamics that can derail, or entirely frustrate, such efforts. Charles Lindblom (1997) notes that

> change is not initiated on an inert society. It is not like shaping a piece of marble into a sculpture, not like building a house on an empty lot, and certainly not like mobilizing an otherwise passive set of people into a movement. More than one sculptor is chiseling the marble. Some other builder is trying to build on the same lot or at least to alter the structure you want to create. In short, initiating change is a competitive, often hostile, activity. (p. 265)

Management must ensure that a more holistic approach is taken; one that considers and properly uses culture, politics, technology, etc. to support each and every necessary step in the process. If a new system is forcefully imposed on an unwelcoming structure, failure is inevitable. Success depends on buy-in at all levels of the organization, as well as "user involvement, strong project management and a sound structure for planning and decision making" (Harris, 2002, p. 1).

Similarly, while it is a relatively simple process to initiate an effective PBM system in any police agency, it is not a process that can be rushed. A turnkey system consisting of all of the ideal performance measures for any particular agency cannot be implemented, since such a system does not yet exist. It must be developed gradually from within. A small subset of meaningful measures must be identified, experimented with, analyzed, and revised as necessary. This process takes time and a great deal of thought and cooperation.

As described in chapter 1, the city of White Plains worked to transform its departments. As evidenced by this editorial from the local paper, the city has achieved measurable results.

> There was good news last week for all those who live, work or play in White Plains: All the building, all the new nightlife, all the new vitality have not meant a corresponding increase in serious crime. . . . Serious fell by 5.7 percent last year and by 37.1 percent over the past five years, according to new figures released by the White Plains Department of Public Safety. The numbers would be notable in and of themselves, but against expanded housing opportunities throughout the city and a boom in nightlife and street activity, they are even more impressive. . . . The number of larcenies dropped even as the city's retail sector expanded. Vehicle accidents decreased 2.4 percent, despite a 2 percent increase in traffic. [Commissioner] Straub credited the gains to the hard work of police officers and a departmental reorganization in April: "Clearly, the integration of enforcement strategies with community outreach efforts is starting to pay off." . . .
>
> Police have put additional emphasis on what matters to average people. For example, Straub said police are focusing on domestic violence cases, following them through the courts and reaching out to both victims and offenders "to make sure that service options are available." The department is involved in the "Step Up" program, a multi-agency effort to open up mentoring and job opportunities for at-risk youth. And it is committed to keeping police foot and car patrols highly visible. . . .
>
> Straub credited his predecessor, retired Commissioner John Dolce, with the police-presence initiative and applauded the efforts of Westchester District Attorney Janet DiFiore for bringing agencies together to focus on tough issues. But Straub and the White Plains police deserve their own pats on the back for their willingness to look differently at what today is clearly a different city. After the murder of a woman in a downtown White Plains parking garage in mid-2005 and a series of worrisome crimes last fall, the police did not get defensive, they got to work. They and their commissioner seem determined to face, and prevent, crime in the city—not let it define it. (Editorial, 2007, p. 6B)

The following process describes the establishment of a PBM system that is capable of measuring not only organizational success (or failure) but also of improving communication throughout the organization. The information gleaned by a PBM system is virtually useless unless it is properly analyzed and acted on. The discussion below explains how a PBM system can incorporate a rather sophisticated feedback system, whereby regularly scheduled meetings are convened for the purpose of productive interactive inquiry.

Step One: Review of Organizational Mission/Vision.

The first step in any program of planned change is to examine the organizational mission carefully. This entails the review and refinement of the existing mission or the development of an entirely new one. This involves far more than the simple review of a mission statement. It entails thoughtful and open dialogue and an authentic attempt to "figure out what your value system is. Decide what your [organization] stands for . . ." (Peters & Waterman, 1982, p. 227). Unfortunately, most organizational mission statements are vague and are merely inspirational. This is particularly true in the field of policing.

Simply stated, the mission statements of most U.S. police agencies do not guide the behavior of their personnel. A clear, direct, and understandable mission statement must be crafted so that specific organizational goals can be drawn from it and directly linked to the overriding mission. Field personnel and managers should never need to ask, "Why exactly are we doing this?" It should always be clearly understood by all. This ensures that the performance-based management system that is ultimately developed has validity and the support of all members of the organization. It also ensures that all subsequent goals and performance measures will be linked directly (and logically) to the organizational mission.

Step Two: Adjust/Realign the Existing Organizational Structure and Technology Architecture.

This often requires a considerable amount of planning. Most importantly, it requires the will and the authority to make necessary changes to the existing organizational structure. As emphasized throughout this text, Compstat and other performance-based management systems are most likely to succeed when they are implemented as part of an overall reengineering program. Those individuals wishing to adopt such a system must have a genuine desire and the ability to make necessary changes to the organization's structure, policies, and practices.

Step Three: Initial Investigation Phase.

Identify specific goals for the organization. Break them down into specific tasks and functions: what will need to be performed in order to accomplish these goals? Identify core business practices. Determine "what exactly it is that you do," and compare them to a list of needed tasks and functions.

Step Four: Develop a "Preliminary" Set of Performance Indicators for the Organization.

Select the most important or fundamental functions first, then analyze them by comparing preliminary performance indicators to the goals and overall mission of the organization. Ensure that all elements are consistent. There is one inherent problem associated with this step in the process. Police professionals are often loath to attempt to explain or quantify exactly what is meant by the term *policing*. Police administrators acknowledge that police "performance" is a term with subtle nuances. They know that there is no one definitive measure of police performance. For example, arrest activity is certainly important to a patrol officer's performance appraisal, but perhaps the better officer is the one who can resolve a situation without resorting to the sanction of arrest, or perhaps an officer is assigned to a position or detail that does not present many arrest opportunities (such as a community affairs officer).

Another way to conceptualize this step is to ask the question, "Which activities have the greatest value to the organization and its stakeholders?" Moore and Braga (2004) explain that

> the important question that lies at the core of developing any adequate measure of police performance is for citizens and their elected representatives to decide what it is that is intrinsically valuable, or what it is that we as a political community value in the activities and operations of a public police department. (p. 4)

Perhaps the best way to grasp how to properly select performance indicators is to look to a field other than policing. How would one go about listing performance measures in, for example, a library system? The obvious measure would be "number of books loaned." But isn't that like defining police performance solely by looking at arrest activity? Isn't the mission of the library system broader than that? One would need to look carefully at the mission of the library system. Most likely, its mission has been operationalized (to some extent) in terms of specific organizational goals, such as "to provide cultural activities for the community" or "to provide a safe and secure environment for patrons." From this, we can then begin to list reasonable and clear performance measures that can be tracked, such as:

1. number of public films shown
2. number of public lectures given
3. number of "special events" for children sponsored
4. number of public/civic meetings held
5. number of citizen complaints
6. results of public satisfaction surveys
7. results of employee satisfaction surveys

8. amount of funds collected as fines

9. number of articles (books, tapes, etc.) acquired

10. number of articles (books, tapes, etc.) lost/damaged/destroyed/ stolen

11. number of articles/resources donated

12. results of "outside" safety (health, fire, etc.) inspections

13. results of internal physical plant inspections (safety and cleanliness inspections of all public areas, such as parking areas and restrooms)

14. number of operational computers on-site

15. number of "user-hours" for patrons using computers

16. number of copies made at copy machines

17. number of articles placed on reserve

18. number of articles retrieved via interlibrary loan

19. head counts (i.e., number of children/senior citizens/adults observed on premises) at various times of the day

20. number of "hits" on library's online catalog system

21. results of financial audits and inspections

22. amount of employee sick leave

23. amount of employee overtime

Each library in the system can track its own performance by means of these objectives, which are accurate and verifiable measures. Baselines can be established and period-to-period comparisons can soon be made. More importantly, uniform measures allow senior administrators to assess the overall *performance of the system as a whole* and enable them to make unit-to-unit (that is, library to library) comparisons within the system, and to track performance over time.

Carolyn Heinrich (2002) describes a set of performance measures that were identified to evaluate *outcomes* of a job training program established under the federal Job Training Partnership Act (JTPA). These include:

1. participant program completion rates;

2. participant job placement rates;

3. participant wages at placement;

4. retention rates at six months after job placement;

5. wages received at six months after job placement;

6. licenses or certifications, attainment of academic degrees, and other skills-attained measures; and

7. measures of participant program costs.

As you can see, any number of useful performance indicators can be designed for these, or virtually any other, public service agency. The key is to develop them according to the mission and goals of each agency. Performance indicators should never be imposed from the outside.

Indicators for police organizations appear to be of two general types: (1) the "need to know" category, which includes rather straightforward data that speaks to the ongoing operations of the agency (such as the number of index crimes reported, the amount of overtime expended, etc.); and (2) the "like to know" type, which provide police managers with a more thorough understanding of the broader context of police operations. A good example of the latter would be an agency's interests in determining the effect that a newly opened "big box" retailer might have on a community in terms of calls for service, vehicular and pedestrian traffic flow, etc. (Parry, 2006)

Policing is actually no different from any other form of public service. Even absent a "marketplace barometer of product value," all police agencies can create "well-conceived measures of . . . services that would nevertheless offer a gauge of progress or slippage over time and . . . a gauge of performance adequacy relative to targets, standards, or comparison jurisdictions" (Ammons, 1995, p. 37). This is a creative process (and obviously goes well beyond the tracking of reported crime). The only limiting factor is the requirement that the measures must be aligned to desired organizational outcomes "to show that managers are measuring the 'right things'" (MacBride, 2006). This is only possible, however, when measures are developed both carefully and collaboratively.

Step Five: Distribute Preliminary List of Indicators to All Stakeholders.

Encourage them to reflect carefully on the suggestions for the next step.

Step Six: Solicit Feedback From all Stakeholders.

Engage in authentic dialogue.

Step Seven: Revision Phase.

Revise indicators according to the feedback received. Obtain consensus/agreement of all stakeholders, both internal and external constituent groups and clients. Create new indicators (secondary, tertiary) as necessary.

Step Eight: Data Collection and Analysis Phase.

Design a process for the collection and analysis of data. Gather data (current, as well as historical, if available) and input it in a form that will be useful for all stakeholders. Analyze the data; a simple spreadsheet analysis might be sufficient. Set baselines for current performance and begin to examine historical data for trend analysis and long-term strategic planning

Step Nine: Management Phase.

In preparation for first meeting, examine baselines and make comparisons of equivalent units. Set reasonable and obtainable goals. Identify significant distinctions in performance between units.

Step Ten: Dissemination Phase.

Disseminate results of initial analysis. Solicit individual feedback from field units (i.e., their interpretation of the data and explanations for performance).

Step Eleven: Hold Meeting.

Discuss data and trends; make inferences; and facilitate long-, medium-, and short-range strategic planning. In addition to monitoring the relative performance of individual units, the system must be used to determine the *overall effectiveness of the organization as a whole*. In other words, it should answer the question, "How are we doing?" for the entire organization. It can immediately be used to identify the organization's most consequential performance deficit and to prepare baseline measures for later comparisons.

Step Twelve: Recapitulation Phase.

Communicate the post-meeting recap (memorandum) to the entire organization, outlining future goals and strategies. Conduct post-meeting follow-up with individual units as necessary. Field units will conduct their own (internal) post-meeting assessment and prepare for next scheduled meeting. At the follow-up meeting, review list of indicators and performance baselines. Revise or include additional indicators as necessary.

Step Thirteen: Repeat Steps Six through Nine in Preparation for Next Meeting.

Obstacles to Effective Implementation

Once again, remember that any performance-based management system must be based on a sincere desire to use timely and accurate data to improve performance. Any organization that begins development and implementation but has a concern about publicizing performance data (i.e., what if the numbers are bad?) is destined to fail. Similarly stated, "Performance measurement is often implemented with a focus on assessment and reporting rather than on the use of measures to improve performance on an on-going basis" (Plant et al., 2005, p. 10). If performance data are not intended to be used, then the system devolves into an enhanced and elaborate recording system. Once again, measurement must take place for the purpose of supporting management decisions, not merely for bean counting.

Performance measurement systems frequently function "as an instrument of control, rather than as a tool that managers and staff develop and use to assist them to manage and improve organizational performance" (Plant et al., 2005, p. 10). It is up to the system's designers to ensure that the proper philosophy is understood by all members of the organization.

Performance measurement systems must never be "implemented unilaterally by top management" (p. 10). Its main purpose is to "enable staff at all levels to identify and remove the barriers to performance, not to exercise top-down control over staff action" (p. 12).

> Performance measurement, particularly in local government, presents many measurement challenges with respect to what should be measured and how, and what standards should be used for assessing performance. These challenges include measuring the wrong thing . . . , measuring at the wrong time [and] generating data that are too general to be useful. (p. 10)

Conclusion

For decades, authentic learning was a relatively rare occurrence in policing in the United States. Organizational culture and hierarchical structure reinforced the notions of control, conformity, routinization, reduction of variance, and risk aversion. Police organizations suffered from a form of inertia that prevented them from recognizing and reacting to the dynamic nature of policing.

Fortunately, this traditional hierarchical management approach to policing has become a thing of the past. In its place, a far more responsive, reflective, and effective model has emerged that, if embraced, will increase organizational efficiency, facilitate the delivery of effective services, and increase the overall level of public safety. This new model recognizes the unpredictability of police work as well as the value of thoughtful and creative responses solicited from all levels of the department that anticipate and address new challenges. Effective police managers now continually challenge themselves by asking whether they possess sufficient data to accurately describe the changing organizational landscape. They ask themselves, "What is it that we *do know*?" and "What do we still *need to know*?" Accurate and timely information is collected, maintained, analyzed and actively used to inform and support management decisions.

In many respects, developing this capacity is as much a business process issue as it is a technology issue. Many police agencies currently possess the requisite information technology capability yet lack a complete understanding of its true potential as a decision support mechanism. PBM systems can and should be used to assemble and analyze accurate performance data that can help an organization identify efficient and effective practices and discard ineffective ones. They also perform a training function, as the information is shared and discussed, as well as an auditing and inspections function.

Obviously, the more timely the data, the more useful it becomes. As data approach "real-time," then can provide a stream of continuous feedback that fosters real-time decisions and enables the organization to maximize effectiveness, minimize mistakes, and make "on the fly" adjustments as necessary (such as resource allocation, new training, etc.) Such a system can help an organization discover hidden patterns and relationships among data, increase overall effectiveness, and capitalize on unexpected opportunities. It provides needed decision support, sustains problem-solving efforts and facilitates true organizational learning (Hendry, 1996).

All public agencies, particularly police departments, need the ability to link their organizational mission to their strategic plan, which in turn should be linked to both short and long-term organizational goals and operations. These goals should not exist in a vacuum. They must be specific, clearly stated, derived from the mission and linked to a particular strategy for achieving "success." Organizational goals should also not be stated as dichotomous variables (that is, simply determining whether or not they have been achieved). They should be expressed as a continuum, on a scale, whereby incremental progress can be measured providing evidence of achievement as the organization moves forward. Perhaps this is most easily understood in relation to the use of fuel gauges in automobiles. These devices would be entirely useless if they only had two possible readings, "full" or "empty." Motorists would run out of gas before they would ever realize that they had a problem. Similarly, when planning a trip, it's important to be able to calculate whether there is enough fuel in the tank to allow you to reach and return from your destination. Police managers need a similar ability to plan. They need to see incremental change in organizational performance (both positive and negative) and ask themselves how and why it occurs. That measurement occurs by means of accurate performance indicators and an effectively functioning PBM system.

Police leaders cannot hold on to outdated management techniques and principles. They must embrace a management philosophy and techniques that have radically changed the private sector and other public agencies. Police leaders must frame every discussion and every decision in terms of the results they are trying to achieve. Framing the discussion this way lets everyone know—both the community and department insiders—what is most important. It also reinforces a culture of accountability throughout the organization (Osborne & Hutchinson, 2004).

Although PBM systems have proliferated quickly through U.S. policing, it has been observed that they have been adopted at somewhat of a slower pace by smaller departments at the town level. As previously mentioned, there can always be some concern about airing sensitive or confidential issues (such as ongoing investigations) in a small agency within a reactively tight-knit community. It also appears that some small departments experience a great deal of difficulty in assembling the necessary parties for a Compstat-like meeting. Paradoxically, it seems that larger agencies are better able to assemble the necessary parties, while still maintaining minimum staffing levels on patrol and within other units. Small agencies (which, one would assume, can easily convene and transmit information) are less likely to have sufficient personnel and resources to meet without seriously reducing staffing and/or incurring unwanted overtime costs.

Although such a challenge might exist, it certainly is no reason to abandon the concept of a PBM system. PBM systems do not require the formalized meeting processes that developed under the Compstat model. They can also be created with a relatively small expenditure of resources. Small-town police managers might rightly choose to forgo formalized crime analysis meetings, but they certainly should not consider themselves immune from the light of inquiry into the quantity and quality of their police operations. They need to demonstrate not merely that they are personally aware of all information that is necessary to their department's operations but also that they are monitoring organizational performance and using that information as a basis for ongoing business decisions. As repeated often, capturing information is not enough; it must be analyzed and *used* effectively.

Perhaps most importantly, departments must recognize that anecdotal assessments of performance are no longer acceptable in response to legitimate inquiries by key stakeholders, such as politicians and taxpayers. A PBM system can be incredibly useful in this regard. It can be used as a personal management tool for the chief as a basis for ongoing business decisions and periodic disclosures to third parties as necessary.

A leader of a smaller police agency might conclude that he/she has no need for a PBM system, since the incidence of crime within the jurisdiction is so low. Because PBM systems measure far more than reported crime rates, this reasoning overlooks potential valuable input. For example, if the total number of reported crimes (such as auto larceny) for a particular month is zero, that number has meaning and should be recorded and tracked. If the number remains unchanged for an extended period, this information should be communicated to public officials and shared with residents. If the number unexpectedly increases, it would require prompt attention.

Leaders of police agencies of any size need timely and accurate data to communicate effectively with stakeholders. While public officials do not routinely need to be made aware of where and when all summonses for moving violations are issued, there are times when such information is vitally important, such as in the aftermath of a fatal motor vehicle accident where a speeding motorist struck a child in a school zone. Senior police officials regularly meet with public officials and discuss such matters as part of their normal duties and responsibilities. Neither the police nor the public officials should arrive at these meetings armed only with a blank legal pad. Both parties should have access to a subset of meaningful performance measures that can be discussed and used as the common basis of future decisions and planning.

In order for a PBM system to be truly effective in any police organization, a sea change must take place, reflecting an entirely new organizational mind-set, a change in organizational values, and an "appeal for new concepts and categories of thinking about [policing]" (DiIulio, 1993, p. 5). Individual commanders must be: given the authority and flexibility to address crime problems, encouraged to become risk takers, and urged to try new approaches for reducing crime. They must be empowered to act decisively and creatively to combat crime and be rewarded for their successes and held accountable for their failures (Ward, 2005). They must believe and be committed to the fact that the *police can make a difference* in reducing crime.

The performance-based management model has proven to be an effective choice for improving police operations and achieving organizational goals. Performance management requires a true commitment by an agency's senior leadership. Performance-based management systems must be fully integrated and must serve as the organization's primary command and control system. Most importantly, this system must be understood, trusted, and embraced by employees throughout the organization. If it is not, it will undoubtedly fail, as the inertia associated with a dysfunctional organizational culture or faulty organizational structure will undermine reforms and succeed in restoring the status quo.

In its simplest form, policing is all about information. The better you manage and use information, the better your agency will perform. Ideally, every manager would like to see the advancing iceberg on the horizon and avoid it. At the very least, however, once you have struck, you need to know immediately how badly you have been damaged. A PBM system can provide this vital information.

PBM systems perform both a predictive and a reflective function that are an absolute necessity in this modern era of policing. This is our present reality.

We should reflect on the following: hammers are potentially very useful tools, but only when wielded by a skilled craftsman. Similarly, PBM systems have great promise, assuming that they are utilized by capable and thoughtful managers. Any management system will certainly fail if it is viewed and understood merely as a passing fad or fashionable management trend. In order to be effective, PBM systems should be used by true believers.

Note

[1] This material was derived from research that was funded by the IBM Center for the Business of Government (O'Connell, 2001b).

APPENDIX
COMPSTAT REPORT, WHITE PLAINS, NY

The pages that follow present the Compstat reports for the City of White Plains Department of Public Safety for the week of January 2, 2007. Use the key below for all the summary reports.

*The 7 Day Comparison is Sunday, December 24th through Saturday, December 30th, 2006, compared to Sunday, December 17th through Saturday, December 23rd, 2006.

**The 28 Day comparison is December 3rd through December 30th compared to November 5th through December 2nd, 2006.

***The year to date comparison is January 1st through December 30th, 2006, compared to January 1st through December 30th, 2005.

Note: Compstat figures are preliminary and subject to futher analysis and revision.

COMPSTAT
POLICE SUMMARY REPORT

The City of White Plains Department of Public Safety.

Presented: January 2nd, 2007

Frank G. Straub Ph.D.
Commissioner

WHITE PLAINS, N.Y. PUBLIC SAFETY

CRIME COMPLAINTS

	Crime Type	7 Day Comparison *			28 Day Comparison **			Year to Date ***		
		Cur	Pri	% Chng	Cur	Pri	% Chng	Cur	Pri	% Chng
PART 1 — Person	Murder	0	0	0.0%	0	0	0.0%	2	2	0.0%
	Rape	0	0	0.0%	0	1	-100.0%	4	5	-20.0%
	Robbery	0	0	0.0%	1	4	-75.0%	45	45	0.0%
	Agg Assault - Dom	0	0	0.0%	0	2	-100.0%	15	16	-6.3%
	Agg Assault N/Dom	1	1	0.0%	3	2	50.0%	44	40	10.0%
PART 1 — Prop.	Burglary	0	1	-100.0%	4	7	-42.9%	69	70	-1.4%
	Larcenies	23	29	-20.7%	91	80	13.8%	1019	1,075	-5.2%
	Auto Theft	1	1	0.0%	2	3	-33.3%	40	53	-24.5%
	TOTAL	**25**	**32**	**-21.9%**	**101**	**99**	**2.0%**	**1,238**	**1,306**	**-5.2%**

ARRESTS

	Crime Type	Cur	Pri	% Chng	Cur	Pri	% Chng	Cur	Pri	% Chng
Other	Assault - Domestic	1	0	0.0%	2	5	-60.0%	74	80	-7.5%
	Assault - N/Domestic	2	3	-33.3%	7	6	16.7%	96	97	-1.0%
	Crim Mischief	6	8	-25.0%	33	34	-2.9%	403	378	6.6%
	Arrests (Highest Charge)	70	83	-15.7%	341	400	-14.8%	4,214	4,729	-10.9%

SPECIAL INCIDENTS

Domestic Incidents	20	19	5.3%	66	64	3.1%	943	995	-5.2%
Total Calls for Service	894	909	-1.7%	3,626	3,519	3.0%	50,034	49,348	1.4%

TRAFFIC ENFORCEMENT

UTT Productivity	194	419	-53.7%	1,449	1,782	-18.7%	22,996	26,159	-12.1%
208 Summonses	503	676	-34.4%	2,693	2,818	-4.6%	35,789	38,768	-7.7%
Auto Accidents	62	65	-4.6%	254	209	21.5%	2540	2592	-2.0%

RESPONSE TIME

Response Time	N/A		4:26	4:22	1.6%	4:10	4:17	-2.8%

OVERTIME / SICK TIME

				FYTD Spent	Budget	% Spent
Operational Overtime	$26,680	$29,223	-8.7%	$416,060	$434,500	95.8%
Sick Time	342	377.25	-9.3%	N/A N/A	16,261	14,131	15.1%

PART 1 CRIME
Year Comparison Cumulative

COMPSTAT FIRE SUMMARY REPORT

The City of White Plains Department of Public Safety.

Presented: January 2nd, 2007

Frank G. Straub Ph.D.
Commissioner

CALLS FOR SERVICE

Call Type	7 Day Comparison *			28 Day Comparison **			Year to Date ***		
	Cur	Pri	% Chng	Cur	Pri	% Chng	Cur	Pri	% Chng
Structure Fire	2	1	100.0%	4	3	33.3%	37	34	8.8%
Compactor/Incinerator	0	0	0.0%	0	1	-100.0%	4	5	-20.0%
Other Inside Fire	2	0	0.0%	3	6	-50.0%	43	49	-12.2%
Vehicle/Mobile Property	0	0	0.0%	0	0	0.0%	22	35	-37.1%
Brush/Grass/Outdoor Fire	0	1	-100.0%	3	3	0.0%	73	75	-2.7%
Overpressure, Ruptur, Explo	0	0	0.0%	0	0	0.0%	5	9	-44.4%
EMS Assist, Rescue	3	4	-25.0%	10	14	-28.6%	124	139	-10.8%
Stuck Elevator	6	3	100.0%	20	10	100.0%	191	143	33.6%
MVA	7	3	133.3%	18	14	28.6%	154	131	17.6%
Hazrdous Cond, Bomb Scare	9	7	28.6%	38	37	2.7%	610	430	41.9%
Service Call	12	5	140.0%	29	37	-21.6%	344	424	-18.9%
Good Intent	13	5	160.0%	30	29	3.4%	420	344	22.1%
False Alarm, Malicious	2	2	0.0%	5	7	-28.6%	91	103	-11.7%
False Alarm, Malfunction	7	15	-53.3%	45	40	12.5%	776	771	0.6%
False Alarm, Other	26	18	44.4%	87	89	-2.2%	1117	1102	1.4%
Other	0	0	0.0%	0	0	0.0%	6	15	-60.0%
Code Complaint/PA Checks	6	6	0.0%	25	24	4.2%	311	313	-0.6%
TOTAL	95	70	35.7%	317	314	1.0%	4,328	4,122	5.0%

INSPECTIONS / TESTS

Fire Code Inspection	3	35	-91.4%	88	79	11.4%	1,796	1,489	20.6%
Safe Housing	0	0	0.0%	0	2	-100.0%	24	38	-36.8%
Alarm Violations	8	4	100.0%	22	25	-12.0%	392	410	-4.4%
Fire Alarm Test	2	11	-81.8%	25	13	92.3%	192	195	-1.5%
Smoke Purge Test	1	1	0.0%	2	2	0.0%	29	35	-17.1%
Public Education Detail	0	0	0.0%	14	8	75.0%	126	86	46.5%
Fire Drill	0	0	0.0%	1	1	0.0%	29	33	-12.1%
City Court	0	0	0.0%	5	8	-37.5%	60	49	22.4%
Re-Inspection	12	20	-40.0%	100	97	3.1%	1,240	1,019	21.7%
Consultation	0	2	-100.0%	7	1	600.0%	93	341	-72.7%
10 Day Letter Issued	0	0	0.0%	11	17	-35.3%	133	71	87.3%
Complaints	1	2	-50.0%	5	3	66.7%	61	33	84.8%
Others	0	14	-100.0%	30	32	-6.3%	367	401	-8.5%
TOTAL	**27**	**89**	**-69.7%**	**310**	**288**	**7.6%**	**4,542**	**4,200**	**8.1%**

VIOLATIONS

Violations Issued	16	11	45.5%	73	196	-62.8%	3,342	2,753	21.4%

PREVENTION PERSONNEL ASSIGNED TO SUPPRESSION

# of Days	3	1	66.7%	9	3	66.7%	173	260	-33.5%

RESPONSE TIME

Response Time	N/A			4:18	4:33	-5.3%	4:32	4:22	3.9%

OVERTIME / SICK TIME

				FYTD Spent	Budget	% Spent
Operational Overtime	$5,948	$2,955	101.3%	$213,299	$253,000	84.3%
Sick Time	408	558	-26.9%	6,744	5,032	34.0%

COMPSTAT CRIME COMPLAINTS

The City of White Plains Department of Public Safety.

Presented: January 2nd, 2007

Frank G. Straub Ph.D.
Commissioner

Crime Type	28 Day Comparison			Year To Date Comparison		
	Current	Prior	Change	Current	Prior	Change
HOMICIDE	*0*	*0*	*0.0%*	*2*	*2*	*0.0%*
RAPE	*0*	*1*	*-100.0%*	*4*	*5*	*-20.0%*
ROBBERY	*1*	*4*	*-75.0%*	*45*	*45*	*0.0%*
HANDGUN	0	0	0.0%	5	3	66.7%
OTHER FIREARM	0	0	0.0%	0	0	0.0%
KNIFE, CUTTING INSTRUMENT	0	0	0.0%	3	10	-70.0%
OTHER DANGEROUS WEAPONS	0	1	-100.0%	1	5	-80.0%
HANDS, FIST, FEET	1	3	-66.7%	36	27	33.3%
AGGRAVATED ASSAULT	*3*	*4*	*-25.0%*	*59*	*56*	*5.4%*
DOMESTIC	0	2	-100.0%	15	16	-6.3%
NON DOMESTIC	3	2	50.0%	44	40	10.0%
TOTAL CRIMES - PERSON	*4*	*9*	*-55.6%*	*110*	*108*	*1.9%*
BURGLARY	*4*	*7*	*-42.9%*	*69*	*70*	*-1.4%*
SINGLE FAMILY HOME	2	2	0.0%	18	18	0.0%
MULTIPLE DWELLING (APARTMENT)	1	1	0.0%	30	32	-6.3%
OTHER RESIDENTIAL	0	0	0.0%	0	2	-100.0%
PUBLIC ACCESS BUILDING	0	0	0.0%	1	2	-50.0%
COMMERCIAL LOCATIONS	1	4	-75.0%	20	16	25.0%

AGAINST PERSON

AGAINST PROPERTY						
LARCENY	*91*	*80*	*13.8%*	*1019*	*1075*	*-5.2%*
POCKET PICKING	1	1	0.0%	4	3	33.3%
PURSE-SNATCHING	0	4	-100.0%	8	1	700.0%
SHOPLIFTING	55	47	17.0%	550	516	6.6%
THEFT FROM BUILDING	21	19	10.5%	294	342	-14.0%
THEFT FROM COIN MACH	0	0	0.0%	0	3	-100.0%
FROM MV	6	6	0.0%	81	77	5.2%
THEFT OF MV PARTS OR ACCESS	2	0	0.0%	26	30	-13.3%
THEFT FROM MAILBOX	0	0	0.0%	0	0	0.0%
ALL OTHERS	6	3	100.0%	56	103	-45.6%
MOTOR VEHICLE THEFT	*2*	*3*	*-33.3%*	*40*	*53*	*-24.5%*
AUTOS	2	2	0.0%	33	50	-34.0%
TRUCKS, BUSES	0	0	0.0%	1	0	0.0%
OTHER VEHICLES	0	1	-100.0%	6	3	100.0%
TOTAL CRIMES - PROPERTY	*97*	*90*	*7.8%*	*1128*	*1198*	*-5.8%*
TOTAL INDEX CRIMES	**101**	**99**	**2.0%**	**1238**	**1306**	**-5.2%**
OTHER CRIMES						
ARSON	*0*	*1*	*-100.0%*	*4*	*0*	*0.0%*
SIMPLE ASSAULT	*9*	*11*	*-18.2%*	*170*	*177*	*-4.0%*
DOMESTIC	2	5	-60.0%	74	80	-7.5%
NON DOMESTIC	7	6	16.7%	96	97	-1.0%
CRIMINAL MISCHIEF	*33*	*34*	*-2.9%*	*403*	*378*	*6.6%*
VEHICLES	17	15	13.3%	189	197	-4.1%
SCHOOLS	3	0	0.0%	13	4	225.0%
PARKING DEPARTMENT	0	1	-100.0%	3	5	-40.0%
ALL OTHERS	12	13	-7.7%	146	129	13.2%
GRAFFITI	1	5	-80.0%	52	43	20.9%
OTHER SEX OFFENSES	*1*	*1*	*0.0%*	*28*	*38*	*-26.3%*
NO FORCE RAPE	0	0	0.0%	7	10	-30.0%
SODOMY, AGG SEX ABUSE	0	0	0.0%	0	3	-100.0%
SEX ABUSE / TOUCHING MISC	1	1	0.0%	20	25	-20.0%
OTHER SEX OFFENSES	0	0	0.0%	1	0	0.0%

COMPSTAT

TRAFFIC ENFORCEMENT

The City of White Plains Department of Public Safety.

Presented: January 2nd, 2007

WHITE PLAINS, N.Y.
PUBLIC SAFETY

Frank G. Straub Ph.D.
Commissioner

U.T.T. PRODUCTIVITY

Statute		7 Day Comparison			28 Day Comparison			Year to Date Comparison		
		Current	Prior	% Change	Current	Prior	% Change	Current	Prior	% Change
VTL1180	Speed	64	140	-54.3%	420	377	11.4%	5,312	6,554	-19.0%
VTL1225C	Cell Phone	22	28	-21.4%	143	215	-33.5%	3,583	4,216	-15.0%
VTL1229C	Seatbelt	6	23	-73.9%	81	245	-66.9%	1,860	2,420	-23.1%
	Others	102	228	-55.3%	805	945	-14.8%	12,241	12,969	-5.6%
	TOTAL	194	419	-53.7%	1,449	1,782	-18.7%	22,996	26,159	-12.1%

208 ENFORCEMENT

	Current	Prior	% Change	Current	Prior	% Change	Current	Prior	% Change
208 Parking Summonses	503	676	-34.4%	2,693	2,818	-4.6%	35,789	38,768	-7.7%

TRAFFIC ACCIDENTS

	Current	Prior	% Change	Current	Prior	% Change	Current	Prior	% Change
Auto Accident / MV104	62	65	-4.6%	254	209	21.5%	2,540	2,592	-2.0%
Accident / UF-6	2	4	-50.0%	11	14	-21.4%	154	149	3.4%
TOTAL	64	69	-7.2%	265	223	18.8%	2,694	2,741	-1.7%

NOTE: The Year to Date comparison for 208 reflects through December 27th for the current Year, compared to the Prior Year which reflects through December 31st of 2005 as supplied by Parking Violations.

AUTO ACCIDENTS - Hot Spots - Past 28 Days

	Intersection	# of Accidents	Rank Last Week
1	Mamaroneck & Maple Ave	7	1
2	Main St & MLK	5	10
3	North St & Bryant Ave	4	2
4	Westchester Ave & So Kensico	4	3
5	Central Ave & Aqueduct Rd	4	5
6	Mamaroneck Ave & Quaropas	4	12
7	Hamilton Ave & Broadway	4	N/A
8	Main St & Bank St	3	4
9	Mamaroneck Ave & Bryant	3	6
10	MLK & E Post Rd	3	8
11	Main St & Court St	3	9
12	Martine Ave & So Broadway	3	13
13	Hamilton Ave & Lexington	3	N/A
14	Mamaroneck Ave & Martine	3	N/A
15	So Broadway & Mitchell Pl	3	N/A
16	So Broadway & Maple	3	N/A

	Address	# of Accidents	Rank Last Week
1	129 Westchester Ave	5	1
2	100 Main St	4	N/A
3	154 Westchester Ave	3	2

COMPSTAT OVERTIME / SICK TIME

The City of White Plains Department of Public Safety.

Presented: January 2nd, 2007

Frank G. Straub Ph.D.
Commissioner

POLICE BUREAU

	7 Day Comparison*			Year to Date (Fiscal)		
	Current	Prior	% Change	Current	Budget	% Used
REIMBURSEABLE OVERTIME						
Contracted	$6,131	$11,583	-47.1%	$419,422		
Housing	$0	$0	0.0%	$0		
Buckle Up New York	$0	$0	0.0%	$8,149		
DWI	$0	$0	0.0%	$3,597		
STEP	$0	$0	0.0%	$9,935		
IMPACT III Grant	$990	$1,326	-25%	$25,000		
TOTAL	$7,121	$12,909	-44.8%	$466,103	$825,000	56.5%
PARKING DEPARTMENT						
Parking Department	$1,813	$3,039	-40.3%	$53,557	$50,000	107.1%
OPERATIONAL OVERTIME						
Administration	$261	$0	0%	$2,825		
Anti-Crime	$0	$0	0%	$8,842		
Communications Dispatch	$0	$436	-100%	$4,309		
Community Advocacy	$54	$0	0%	$2,183		
Crime Prevention	$0	$0	0%	$466		
Crime Scene Processing	$0	$0	0%	$5,014		
Domestic Violence	$0	$0	0%	$136		

Emergency Service Unit	$819	$414	98%	$14,551		
General Investigations	$218	$385	-43%	$57,142		
Jail Operations	$258	$215	20%	$5,356		
MIS	$0	$0	0%	$218		
Mounted	$2,915	$440	563%	$12,276		
Narcotics	$787	$4,286	-82%	$11,180		
Patrol	$19,521	$18,565	5%	$270,011		
POP's	$0	$0	0%	$1,484		
Prisoner Transportation	$0	$217	-100%	$2,320		
Profesional Standards	$0	$0	0%	$555		
Security Investigations	$0	$0	0%	$218		
Special Operations Administration	$0	$0	0%	$503		
Special Victims	$926	$0	0%	$2,225		
School Resource Officer	$0	$0	0%	$999		
Special Response Team	$545	$3,601	-85%	$6,386		
Traffic	$376	$664	-43%	$2,949		
Training / Special Projects	$0	$0	0%	$3,806		
Warrants	$0	$0	0%	$106		
TOTAL	$26,680	$29,223	-9%	$416,060	$434,500	95.8%

SICK TIME

# of Hours						
Regular	298.00	322.00	-7.5%	13,124.75	10,137.75	29.5%
Duty Injury	44.00	55.25	-20.4%	3,136.00	3,993.00	-21.5%
TOTAL	342.00	377.25	-9.3%	16,260.75	14,130.75	15.1%
Public Safety Aides - Comm	4.00	29.00	-86.2%	613.00	370.50	65.5%
TOTAL	4.00	29.00	-86.2%	613.00	370.50	65.5%

COMPSTAT
OVERTIME / SICK TIME

The City of White Plains Department of Public Safety,

Frank G. Straub Ph.D.,
Commissioner

Presented: January 2nd, 2007

FIRE BUREAU

OPERATIONAL OVERTIME

	7 Day Comparison *			Year to Date (Fiscal)		
	Current	Prior	% Change	Current	Budget	% Used
Firefighter	$5,948	$2,596	-164.3%	$190,934		
Lieutenant	$0	$359	-500.0%	$15,999		
Deputy Chief	$0	$0	-380.0%	$6,366		
TOTAL	**$5,948**	**$2,955**	**101.3%**	**$213,299**	**$253,000**	**84.3%**

SICK TIME

Days / Hours	28 Day Comparison ****			Year to Date Comparison *****		
	Current	Prior	% Change	Current	Prior	% Change
# Sick Day	24	32	-33.3%	337	275	22.5%
# Sick Night	12	17	-41.7%	241	163	47.9%
Long Term Sick	20	22	-10.0%	326	305	6.9%
Total hours	568	734	-22.6%	9,352	7,472	25.2%
Sick Time Hours	**408**	**558**	**-26.9%**	**6,744**	**5,032**	**34.0%**

COMPSTAT ARRESTS SUMMARY

The City of White Plains Department of Public Safety.

Presented: January 2nd, 2007

Frank G. Straub Ph.D.
Commissioner

ARRESTS

Summmary (Top Charge)	7 Day Comparison			28 Day Comparison			Year to Date Comparison		
	Current	Prior	% Change	Current	Prior	% Change	Current	Prior	% Change
Felony	7	17	-58.8%	56	59	-5.1%	640	795	-19.5%
Misdemeanor	40	45	-11.1%	178	168	6.0%	2,102	2,385	-11.9%
Violation	23	21	9.5%	107	173	-38.2%	1,472	1,549	-5.0%
Total	70	83	-15.7%	341	400	-14.8%	4,214	4,729	-10.9%

BY DIVISION / UNIT

	Current	Prior	% Change	Current	Prior	% Change			
Patrol	34	35	-2.9%	138	169	-18.3%			
NCU	27	21	28.6%	100	123	-18.7%			
Dets	3	15	-80.0%	56	51	9.8%		N/A	
Warrants	3	6	-50.0%	19	8	137.5%			
USOC	0	1	-100.0%	8	23	-65.2%			
Comm Policing	2	5	-60.0%	18	23	-21.7%			
Traffic	1	0	0.0%	2	3	-33.3%			
Other	0	0	0.0%	0	0	0.0%			
Total	70	83	-15.7%	341	400	-14.8%			

BY SHIFT

	Current	Prior	% Change	Current	Prior	% Change			
12-8	21	18	16.7%	65	142	-54.2%			
8-4	9	10	-10.0%	66	75	-12.0%		N/A	
4-12	40	55	-27.3%	210	183	14.8%			
Total	70	83	-15.7%	341	400	-14.8%			

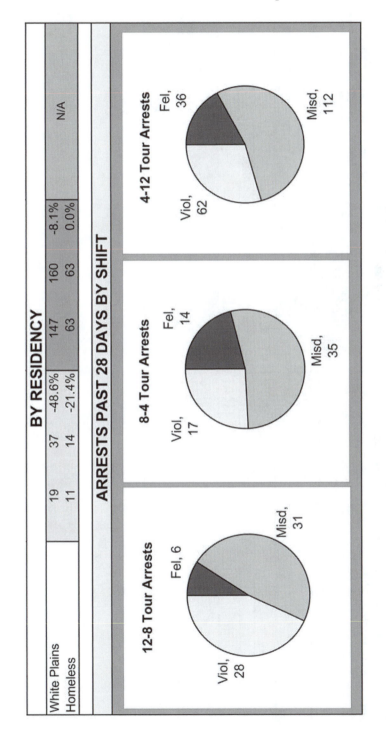

BY RESIDENCY					
White Plains	19	37	-48.6%	147	160	-8.1%	N/A
Homeless	11	14	-21.4%	63	63	0.0%

ARRESTS PAST 28 DAYS BY SHIFT

12-8 Tour Arrests

Fel, 6

Misd, 31

Viol, 28

8-4 Tour Arrests

Fel, 14

Misd, 35

Viol, 17

4-12 Tour Arrests

Fel, 36

Misd, 112

Viol, 62

COMPSTAT SPECIAL INCIDENT REVIEW

The City of White Plains Department of Public Safety.

Presented: January 2nd, 2007

Frank G. Straub Ph.D.
Commissioner

Incident Type	7 Day Comparison			28 Day Comparison			Year to Date Comparison		
	Current	Prior	% Change	Current	Prior	% Change	Current	Prior	% Change
DOMESTIC INCIDENTS									
Domestic Incidents	20	19	5.3%	66	64	3.1%	943	995	-5.2%
FIELD INTERVIEWS									
Field Interviews	77	53	45.3%	309	94	228.7%	1,262	1,004	25.7%
VEHICLE & TRAFFIC ARRESTS									
DWI - Alcohol	0	0	0.0%	3	5	-40.0%	66	127	-48.0%
DWI - Drugs	0	0	0.0%	0	0	0.0%	0	2	-100.0%
Suspended License	2	1	100.0%	9	16	-43.8%	223	245	-9.0%
All Other	0	0	0.0%	0	0	0.0%	2	53	-96.2%
TOTAL	2	1	100.0%	12	21	-42.9%	291	427	-31.9%

DISTURBANCES

Domestic	17	16	6.3%	51	44	15.9%	671	747	-10.2%
Landlord/Tenant Disputes	0	1	-100.0%	4	5	-20.0%	94	78	20.5%
Labor (Pickets)	0	0	0.0%	0	0	0.0%	0	2	-100.0%
Labor (Demonstrations)	0	0	0.0%	0	0	0.0%	1	2	-50.0%
Fights	0	0	0.0%	0	5	-100.0%	65	206	-68.4%
Disorderly Persons	0	0	0.0%	0	2	-100.0%	26	32	-18.8%
Employee/Employer	0	0	0.0%	1	2	-50.0%	37	21	76.2%
Customer/Business	2	7	-71.4%	21	28	-25.0%	410	363	12.9%
Neighbor Disputes	0	0	0.0%	2	2	0.0%	53	52	1.9%
Miscellaneous	9	19	-52.6%	66	76	-13.2%	965	732	31.8%
All Other	0	0	0.0%	6	28	-78.6%	161	179	-10.1%
TOTAL	28	43	-34.9%	151	192	-21.4%	2,483	2,414	2.9%

DETAILS

Finance	4	6	-33.3%	20	16	25.0%	241	236	2.1%
Violations	2	0	0.0%	3	11	-72.7%	218	248	-12.1%
County Jail Escort	3	6	-50.0%	18	18	0.0%	205	235	-12.8%
Funeral Escort	0	3	-100.0%	5	8	-37.5%	121	116	4.3%
Council Letter Delivery	0	1	-100.0%	5	3	66.7%	44	25	76.0%
Subpoena Service	6	2	200.0%	26	10	160.0%	280	280	0.0%
Special Traffic Details	4	22	-81.8%	65	81	-19.8%	1,421	1,948	-27.1%
Special School Crossings	1	0	0.0%	3	0	0.0%	82	155	-47.1%
Miscellaneous	1	4	-75.0%	8	28	-71.4%	443	281	57.7%
Vacant House	3	2	50.0%	21	9	133.3%	567	481	17.9%
Directed Patrol	70	133	-47.4%	366	421	-13.1%	8,044	7,177	12.1%
Bar Checks	3	0	0.0%	23	60	-61.7%	238	211	12.8%
Domestic Preparedness	0	0	0.0%	0	2	-100.0%	19	279	-93.2%
TOTAL	97	179	-45.8%	563	667	-15.6%	11,923	11,672	2.2%

TOTAL CALLS FOR SERVICE

Calls for Service	894	909	-1.7%	3,626	3,519	3.0%	50,034	49,348	1.4%

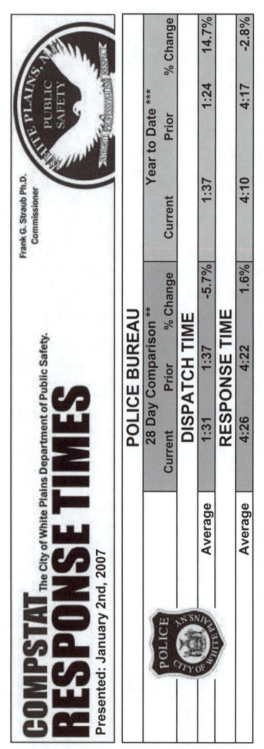

COMPSTAT RESPONSE TIMES

The City of White Plains Department of Public Safety.

Presented: January 2nd, 2007

Frank G. Straub Ph.D.
Commissioner

PUBLIC SAFETY
WHITE PLAINS, N.Y.

POLICE BUREAU

| | 28 Day Comparison ** | | | Year to Date *** | | |
	Current	Prior	% Change	Current	Prior	% Change
DISPATCH TIME						
Average	1:31	1:37	-5.7%	1:37	1:24	14.7%
RESPONSE TIME						
Average	4:26	4:22	1.6%	4:10	4:17	-2.8%

Notes: Time Analysis only involves calls for service with a priority 1 or 2 and does not include cancelled calls for service, duplicate calls, FOA arrests, Bench warrant arrests, 33's or serving TOP's.

FIRE BUREAU

	28 Day Comparison **			Year to Date ***		
	Current	Prior	% Change	Current	Prior	% Change
DISPATCH TIME						
Average	:10	:10	5.1%	:13	:13	-2.3%
RESPONSE TIME						
Average	4:18	4:33	-5.3%	4:32	4:22	3.9%

AMBULANCE RESPONSE

	7 Day Comparison *			Year to Date ***		
	Current	Prior	% Change	Current	Prior	% Change
# of Calls	131	114	13.0%		N/A	
7 minutes and under	127	111	12.6%			
% of 7 min and under	97%	97%				
over 7 minutes	4	3	25.0%			
excluded times	2	2	0.0%			

REFERENCES

Almgren, G. (2004). Statistics for human service workers. In A. R. Roberts & K. R. Yeager (Eds.), *Evidence-based practice manual: Research and outcome measures in health and human services* (pp. 101–112). New York: Oxford University Press.

Ammons, D. N. (1995). Overcoming the inadequacies of performance measurement in local government: The case of libraries and leisure services. *Public Administration Review, 55*(1), 37–47.

Anderson, J. L. (2004). Managing professional relationships: Considerations for the FTO and probationary officer. *Law and Order, 52*(6), 56–59.

Anechiarico, F., & Jacobs, J. B. (1996). *The pursuit of absolute integrity: How corruption control makes government ineffective.* Chicago: Chicago University Press.

Argyris, C. (1957). *Personality and organization.* New York: Blackwell Business.

Argyris, C. (1993). *Knowledge for action: A guide to overcoming barriers to organizational change.* San Francisco: Jossey-Bass.

Argyris, C. (1999). *On organizational learning.* New York: Blackwell Business.

Argyris, C., & Schon, D. (1974). *Theory in practice.* San Francisco: Jossey-Bass.

Artley, W., Ellison, D. J., & Kennedy, B. (2001). Establishing and maintaining a performance-based management program. In *The performance-based management handbook: A six-volume compilation of techniques and tools for implementing the Government Performance and Results Act of 1993 (GPRA),* Vol. 1. Washington, DC: Performance-Based Management Special Interest Group.

Baltazar, H. (2001). Knowledge management has a human side. *eWeek, 18*(15), 74.

Battalino, J., Beutler, L., & Shani, A.B. (1996). Large system change initiative: Transformation in progress at the California Department of Correction. *Public Productivity and Management Review, 20*(1), 22–44.

Bayer, R. (1995). *The dependent center: The first decade of the AIDS epidemic in New York City.* New Brunswick, NJ: Rutgers University Press.

Bazerman, M. H., & Chugh, D. (2006). Decisions without blunders. *Harvard Business Review, 84*(1), 88–97.

167

Behn, R. D. (2004). *Performance leadership: 11 better practices that can ratchet up performance*. IBM Center for the Business of Government. Retrieved December 22, 2006, from http://www.businessofgovernment.org/pdfs/BehnReport2.pdf

Bennett, E. (2006). Safety in numbers: Serious crime in Los Angeles is down. A big reason for the drop: The LAPD's use of an analytics system to tailor its enforcement strategies. *Baseline, 1*(55), 1–4.

Bennett, W. W., & Hess, K. (2001). *Management and supervision in law enforcement*. New York: Wadsworth.

Bennis, W. (1978). *Changing organizations: Essays on the development and evolution of human organization*. New York: McGraw-Hill.

Bernstein, D. J. (1999). Comments on Perrin's "Effective use and misuse of performance measurement." *American Journal of Evaluation, 20*(1), 85–94.

Bierne, P. (1993). *Inventing criminology: Essays on the rise of homocriminalis*. Albany: State University of New York Press.

Boba, R. L. (2005). *Crime analysis and crime mapping*. Thousand Oaks, CA: Sage.

Bolman, L. G., & Deal, T. E. (2003). *Reframing organizations: Artistry, choice and leadership*. San Francisco: Jossey-Bass.

Bossidy, L., & Charan, R. (2002). *Execution: The discipline of getting things done*. New York: Crown Business.

Boyne, G. A., Gould-Williams, J. S., Law, J., &. Walker, R. M. (2004). Toward the self-evaluating organization? An empirical test of the Wildavsky model. *Public Administration Review, 64*(4), 463–473.

Bozeman, B. (2000). *Bureaucracy and red tape*. Upper Saddle River, NJ: Prentice-Hall.

Bratton, W. J. (1994, May 12). *Reengineering teams*. Internal Departmental Memorandum, New York City Police Department, New York.

Bratton, W. J. (1996a, April 5). How to win the war against crime. *The New York Times*, p. A27.

Bratton, W. J. (1996b, October 15.). *Cutting crime and restoring order: What America can learn from New York's finest*. A paper delivered to the Heritage Foundation, Washington, DC.

Bratton, W. J. (1995, November 28). Great expectations: How higher expectations for police departments can lead to a decrease in crime. Paper presented at the National Institute of Justice Policing Research Institute Conference, Washington, DC.

Bratton, W., & Knobler, P. (1998). *Turnaround: How America's top cop reversed the crime epidemic*. New York: Random House.

Brickley, J. A., Smith, C. W., Jr., & Zimmerman, J. L. (1997). Management fads and organizational architecture. *The Bank of America Journal of Applied Corporate Finance, 10*(2) 24–39.

Brown, M. M., & Brudney, J. L. (2003). Learning organizations in the public sector?: A study of police agencies employing information and technology to advance knowledge. *Public Administration Review, 63*(1), 43.

Bruns, B. (1989). *Operation bootstrap: Opening corporate classrooms to police managers*. Washington, DC: United States Department of Justice, National Institute of Justice.

Buckmaster, N. (2000). The performance measurement panacea. *Accounting Forum, 24*(3), 264–277.

Buntin, J. (2005, September). Battle of the badges. *Governing*, 46–52.

Burns, T., & Stalker, G. M. (1961). *The management of innovation*. London: Tavistock.

Bushe, G R. & Shani, A. B. (1988). A review of the literature on the use of parallel learning structure interventions in bureaucratic organizations. *Academy of Management Proceedings*, 258–262.

Butterfield, F. (2003, January 17). Rise in killings spurs new steps to fight gangs. *The New York Times*, p. A1.

Byrd, J. S. (2006). Confirmation bias, ethics, and mistakes in forensics. *Journal of Forensic Identification, 56*(4), 511–526.

Camasso, M. J. (2004). Treatment evidence in a non-experimenting practice environment: Some recommendations for increasing supply and demand. In A. R. Roberts & K. R. Yeager (Eds.), *Evidence-based practice manual: Research and outcome measures in health and human services* (pp. 233–246). New York: Oxford University Press.

Carter, J. R. (1984). *Computer mapping: Progress in the 1980's*. Washington, DC: Resource Publications in Geography.

Case, P. (1999). Remember re-engineering?: The rhetorical appeal of a managerial salvation device. *Journal of Management Studies, 36*, 419–445.

Cawley, D. M. (1966). The police and the computer. In *Electronic computer: A weapon for law enforcement*. New York: New York City Police Department.

Chaiklin, H. (2004). Problem formulation, conceptualization, and theory development. In A. R. Roberts & K. R. Yeager (Eds.), *Evidence-based practice manual: Research and outcome measures in health and human services* (pp. 95–101). New York: Oxford University Press.

Chan, K. W. & Mauborgne, R. (2003). Tipping point leadership. *Harvard Business Review, 81*(4), 60–69.

Chang, S. K., Simms, W. H., Makres, C. M., & Bodnar, A. (1979). *Crime analysis system support: Descriptive report of manual and automated crime analysis functions*. Gaithersburg, MD: International Association of Chiefs of Police.

Chapel, T. (2004). Constructing and using logic models in program evaluation. In A. R. Roberts & K. R. Yeager (Eds.), *Evidence-based practice manual: Research and outcome measures in health and human services* (pp. 636–647). New York: Oxford University Press.

Charan, R. (2006). Home Depot's blueprint for culture change. *Harvard Business Review, 84*(4), 61–70.

Charles, S. K. (2002). Knowledge management lessons. *Online, 26*(1), 22 –28.

Choo, C. W. (1998). *The knowing organization*. New York: Oxford University Press.

Clarke, R. V., & Felson, M. (1993). *Routine activity and rational choice: Advances in criminological theory*. New Jersey: Transaction.

Coe, B. A. (1997). How structural conflicts stymie reinvention. *Public Administration Review, 57*(2), 168–173.

Coe, C. (1999). Local government benchmarking: Lessons learned from two major multi-government efforts. *Public Administration Review, 59*(2), 110–130.

Collier, P. M. (2001, July/September). Police performance measurement and human rights. *Public Money and Management, 35*–39.

Collier, P. M., Edwards, J. S. & Shaw, D. (2004). Communicating knowledge about police performance. 53 *International Journal of Productivity and Performance Management 53*(5), 458–467.

Comptroller General of United States (2006). *Government auditing standards, exposure draft*. Retrieved January 5, 2007, from http://www.gao.gov/govaud/d06729g.pdf

Cook, S. D. N., & Brown, J. S. (1999). Bridging epistemologies: The generative dance between organizational knowledge and organizational knowing. *Organization Science, 10*(4), 381–400.

Corsianos, M. (2006). Discretion in detectives' decision making and "high profile" cases. In V. E. Kappeler (Ed.), *The police and society: Touchstone readings* (pp. 258–276). Long Grove, IL: Waveland Press.

Craglia, M., Haining, R., & Wiles, P. (2000). A comparative evaluation of approaches to urban crime pattern analysis. *Urban Studies, 37*(4), 711–730.

Crank, J. P. (1997). *Understanding police culture.* Cincinnati, OH: Anderson.

Crime in a free society: President's commission on law enforcement and the administration of justice. (1967). Washington, DC: Government Printing Office.

Davenport, T. H. (1993). *Process innovation: Re-engineering work through information technology.* Boston: Harvard Business School Press.

Davenport, T. H. (2006). Competing on analytics. *Harvard Business Review,* January, 99–107.

Davies, A., & Thomas, R. (2003). Talking cop: Discourses of change and policing identities. *Public Administration, 81*(4), 681–699.

Davis, R. C., Henderson, N. J., & Ortiz, C. W. (2005). *Can federal intervention bring lasting improvement in local policing?: The Pittsburgh consent decree.* New York: Vera Institute of Justice.

Dawes, S. S., & Pardo, T. A. (2004). *Critical issues and practical challenges of IT tools for policy analysis and program evaluation.* Paper presented at the annual meeting of the Association for Public Policy Analysis and Management, Atlanta.

de Lancer Julnes, P., & Holzer, M. (2001). Promoting the utilization of performance measures in public organizations: An empirical study of factors affecting adoption and implementation. *Public Administration Review, 61*(6), 693–708.

deHaven-Smith, L., & Jenne, K. C. (2006). Management by inquiry: A discursive accountability system for large organizations. *Public Administration Review, 66*(1), 64–76.

DiIulio, J. J. (1993). Rethinking the criminal justice system: Toward a new paradigm. In *Performance measures for the criminal justice system* (pp. 1–18). Washington, DC: Bureau of Justice Statistics.

Dineley, D. (2001). Knowledge management with human smarts. *InfoWorld, 23*(6), 50.

Dodenhoff, P. C. (1996, December 31). *Law Enforcement News* salutes its 1996 people of the year: The N.Y.P.D. and its Compstat process. *Law Enforcement News,* 28.

Downes, B. T. (1998). Recent literature on leading and managing change in public service organizations. *Social Science Journal, 35*(4), 657–673.

Drake, L. M., & Simper, R. (2004). The economics of managerialism and the drive for efficiency in policing. *Managerial and Decision Economics, 25,* 509–523.

Drake, L. M., & Simper, R. (2005). The measurement of police force efficiency: An assessment of U.K. home office policy. *Contemporary Economic Policy, 23*(4), 465–482.

Drucker, P. F. (1995). *Managing in a time of great change.* New York: Truman Talley Books.

Duffy, J. (2001). Knowledge management finally becomes mainstream. *Information Management Journal, 35*(4), 62–66.

Dziegielewski, S. F., & Roberts, A. R. (2004). Health care evidence-based practice. In A. R. Roberts & K. R. Yeager (Eds.), *Evidence-based practice manual: Research and outcome measures in health and human services* (pp. 200–205). New York: Oxford University Press.

Eck, J., & Spelman, W. (1987). *Problem-solving: Problem-oriented policing in Newport News*. Washington, DC: Police Executive Research Forum.

Editorial (2007, January 13). White Plains citizens, police, others deserve kudos for crime gains. *The Journal News*, p. 6B. Retrieved January 19, 2007, from http://www.thejournalnews.com/apps/pbcs.dll/article?AID=/20070113/OPINION/701130323/1015/OPINION01.

Edwards, D., & Thomas, J. C. (2005). Developing a municipal performance-measurement system: Reflections on the Atlanta dashboard. *Public Administration Review, 65*(3), 369–376.

Eggers, J., & Brown, R. M. (2000). NIC's performance measurement system. *Corrections Today, 62*(2), 181.

Elliot, P. J., Cuzick, D. E., & Stern, R. (1996). *Geographical and environmental epidemiology: Methods for small-area studies*. Oxford: Oxford University Press.

Epstein, I., & Blumenfeld, S. (Eds.). (2001). *Clinical data-mining in practice-based research: Social work in hospital settings*. New York: The Haworth Social Work Practice Press.

Eskildsen, J. K., Dahlgaard, J. J., & Norgaard, A. (1999). The impact of creativity and learning on business excellence. *Total Quality Management, 10*(4), 523–531.

Etzioni, A. (1964). *Modern organizations*. Englewood Cliffs, NJ: Prentice-Hall.

Fazalollah, M., McCoy, C., & Moran, R. (2000, March 21). Timoney to allow sex-case oversight. Retrieved December 22, 2006, from http://inquirer.philly.com/packages/crime/html/032100coders.asp

Figlio, R. M., Hakim, S., & Rengert, G. (Eds.). (1986). *Metropolitan crime patterns*. New York: Willow Tree.

Foldy, S. L., Biedrzycki, P. A., Baker, B. K., Swain, G. R., Howe, D. S., Gieryn, D., et al. (2004). The public health dashboard: A surveillance model for bioterrorism preparedness. *Journal of Public Health, Management and Practice, 3,* 234–240.

French, W. L., & Bell, C. H., Jr. (1990). *Organization development: Behavioral science interventions for organizational improvement*. Englewood Cliffs, NJ: Prentice-Hall.

Fritz, R. (1996). *Corporate tides*. San Francisco: Berrett-Koehler.

Fulmer, R. M., Gibbs, P., & Keys, J. B. (1998). The second generation learning organizations: New tools for sustaining competitive advantage. *Organizational Dynamics, 27*(2), 7–19.

Fulmer, R. M., & Keys, J. B. (1998). A conversation with Peter Senge: New developments in organizational learning. *Organizational Dynamics, 27*(2), 33–42.

Furterer, S., & Elshennawy, A. K. (2005). Implementation of TQM and lean six sigma tools in local government: A framework and a case study. *Total Quality Management, 16*(10), 1179–1191.

Galaskiewicz, J., & Wasserman, S. (1989). Mimetic processes within an organizational field. *Administrative Science Quarterly, 34*(3), 454–480.

Galbraith, J. R. (1973). *Designing complex organizations*. Reading, MA: Addison-Wesley.

Gascon, G. (2005). Compstat plus. *The Police Chief, 72*(5), 34.

Gaskell, S. (2005, July 15). Bytes out of crime: Cops' $11m data center. *The New York Post*, p. 25.

Gawthrop, L. C. (1971). *Administrative politics and social change*. New York: St. Martin's Press.

Geller, W. A. (1997). Suppose we were really serious about police departments becoming "learning organizations"? *National Institute of Justice Journal, 234,* 2–8.

Gendar, A., & Katz, C. (2005, July 15). Do a crime, cops know in real time. *Daily News (New York)*, p. 26.

Gephart, M. A., & Marsick, V. J. (1996). Learning organizations come alive. *Training and Development, 50*(12), 34–45.

German, E. (2006, March 27). Citistat has big apple roots. *Knight Ridder Tribune Business News*, p. 1.

Gilmour, J. B. (2006). *Implementing OMB's program assessment rating tool (PART): Meeting the challenges of integrating budget and performance*. IBM Center for the Business of Government, Managing for Performance and Results Series. Retrieved December 22, 2006, from http://www.businessofgovernment.org/pdfs/GilmourReport.pdf

Ginsberg, L. (2004). Budgeting and fiscal management in program evaluations. In A. R. Roberts & K. R. Yeager (Eds.), *Evidence-based practice manual: Research and outcome measures in health and human services* (pp. 628–635). New York: Oxford University Press.

Giuliani, R. W. (1997, March 13). *Testimony before the House Committee on Government Reform*. Retrieved December 22, 2006, from http://www.nyc.gov/html/rwg/html/97a/reform.html

Giuliani, R. W. (2002). *Leadership*. New York: Hyperion.

Gluckstein, N., & Packard, R. (1977). The internal external change agent team: Bringing change to a "closed" institution. *Journal of Applied Behavioral Science, 13*, 41–52.

Goldstein, H. (1990). *Problem-oriented policing*. Philadelphia: Temple University Press.

Goodridge, E. (2001, December 3). Intelligence agency bets on knowledge management. *Information Week, 866,* 16.

Gore, A. (1993). *Creating a government that works better and costs less: Gore report on reinventing government*. New York: Random House.

Gorgol, G. F. (1966). Other police electronic processing applications. In *The electronic computer: A weapon for law enforcement*. New York: New York City Police Department.

Gorta, W. (1998, Winter). Zero-tolerance—The real story, or hidden lessons, of New York. *Police Research and Management, 34–43.*

Government Accounting Office. (2003). *Government auditing standards*, 2.09, GAO-03-673G.

Grassie, R. G., Macsas, C. J., & Wallace, W. D. (1977). *Integrated criminal apprehension program: Crime analysis manual*. Washington, DC: United States Department of Justice, Law Enforcement Assistance Administration.

Green, A. A. (2006, March 3). Measure seeks protection for police whistleblowers: Bill would affect officers who refuse orders to underreport crimes. *Knight Ridder Tribune News*, p. 1.

Greene, E., Pratt, G. K., Davies, S. P., & Branham, V. C. (1929). *A survey of mental hygiene facilities and resources in New York City*. New York: New York City Committee on Mental Hygiene of the State Charities Aid Association.

Groff, E. R., & LaVigne, N. G. (2001). Mapping an opportunity surface of residential burglary. *Journal of Research in Crime and Delinquency, 38*(3), 257–278.

Guyot, D. (1978). *Bending granite: Attempts to change the rank structure of American police departments*. A paper presented to the annual meeting of the Academy of Criminal Justice Sciences, New Orleans, LA.

Hafner, K. (2004, November 11). Wanted by police: A good interface. *The New York Times*. Retrieved December 22, 2006, from http://www.nytimes.com/2004/11/11/technology/circuits/11cops.html

Hahn, J. K., Cunningham, D. S. III, & Bratton, W. J. (2004). *LAPD state of the department: Plan of action for the Los Angeles that is and the Los Angeles that could be.* Los Angeles: Los Angeles Police Department.

Hammond, J. S., Keeney, R. L., & Raiffa, H. (2006). The hidden traps in decision making. *Harvard Business Review, 84*(1), 118–126.

Hansen, M. T. (1999). The search-transfer problem: The role of weak ties in sharing knowledge across organization subunits. *Administrative Science Quarterly, 44*(1), 82–111.

Harries, K. (1999). *Mapping crime: Principle and practice.* Washington, DC: United States Department of Justice, National Institute of Justice.

Harris, K. J. (2002). *Law enforcement tech guide How to plan, purchase and manage technology (successfully).* Washington, DC: United States Department of Justice, Office of Community Oriented Policing Services. Retrieved January 6, 2007, from http://www.cops.usdoj.gov/Default.asp?Item=512

Hatry, H. P., Morley, E., Rossman, S. B., & Wholey, J. S. (2003). How federal programs use outcome information: Opportunities for federal managers. IBM Endowment for the Business of Government. Retrieved December 22, 2006, from http://www.businessofgovernment.org/pdfs/HatryReport.pdf

Hayward, R. (2004). Informing health choices: Reflections on knowledge integration strategies for electronic health records. In A. R. Roberts & K. R. Yeager (Eds.), *Evidence-based practice manual: Research and outcome measures in health and human services* (pp. 29–46). New York: Oxford University Press.

Heinrich, C. (2002). Outcomes-based performance management in the public sector: Implications for government accountability and effectiveness. *Public Administration Review, 62*(6), 712–725.

Hendry, C. (1996). Understanding and creating whole organizational change through learning theory. *Human Relations 49*(5), 621–642.

Horowitz, C. (1995, August 14). The suddenly safer city. *New York Magazine,* 21–27, 82.

Hughes, V. and Love, P. E. D. (2004). Toward cyber-centric management of policing: Back to the future with information and communication technology. *Industrial Management and Data Systems, 104*(7), 604–612.

Huselid, M. A., Beatty, R. W., & Becker, B. E. (2005, December). A players or A positions?: The strategic logic of workforce management. *Harvard Business Review,* 110–117.

Illich, I. (1973). *Tools for conviviality.* New York: Harper and Row.

Bates, S. (1987). *Spatial and temporal analysis of crime,* Chicago: Illinois Criminal Justice Information Authority.

International Association of Chiefs of Police. (1975). *Geographic base files for law enforcement: Descriptive report.* Gaithersburg, MD: Author.

Jaggi, R. (2003, December 13). Pledge to "reverse tide" of target setting in public sector. *Financial Times,* p. 5.

Janis, I. L., & Mann, L. (1977). *Decision making: A psychological analysis of conflict, choice, and commitment.* New York: The Free Press.

Jensen, A. J., & Sage, A. P. (2000). A systems management approach for improvement of organizational performance measurement systems. *Knowledge Systems Management, 2*(1), 33–61.

Jones, B. D. (2003). Bounded rationality and political science: Lessons from public administration. *Journal of Public Administration Research and Theory, 13*(4), 395–412.

Junod, T. (2000, June). The last cop in Camelot. *Esquire*, 112–119, 154, 156–157.

Kamarck, E. C. (2005). Transforming the intelligence community: Improving the collection and management of information. IBM Center for the Business of Government. Retrieved December 22, 2006, from http://www.businessofgovernment.org/pdfs/KamarckReport2.pdf

Kamensky, J. (2006, December). Apple state creates core measures. *Public Administration Times*, pp. 9–10.

Kanji, G. K. (2002). Business excellence: Make it happen. *Total Quality Management, 13*(8), 1115–1125.

Kelling, G. L. (1974). *The Kansas City Preventive Patrol Experiment: A summary report*. Washington, DC: The Police Foundation.

Kelling, G. L., & Bratton, W. J. (1993). *Implementing community policing: The administrative problem*. Washington, DC: National Institute of Justice.

Kelling, G. L., & Bratton, W. J. (2006). Policing terrorism. *Civic Bulletin, 43*. Retrieved December 22, 2006, from http://www.manhattan-institute.org/html/cb_43.htm

Kelling, G. L., & Sousa, W., Jr. (2001). Do police matter: An analysis of the impact of New York City's police reforms. *Civic Report, 22*. Retrieved December 22, 2006, from http://www.manhattan-institute.org/html/cr_22.htm

Kettl, D. F. (2005). The next government of the United States: Challenges for performance in the 21st century. IBM Center for the Business of Government. Retrieved December 22, 2006, from http://www.businessofgovernment.org/pdfs/KettlReport.pdf

Kiel, L. D., & Seldon, B. J. (1998). Measuring temporal complexity in the external environment: Nonlinearity and the bounds of rational action. *American Review of Public Administration, 28*(3), 246–266.

Kissler, G. R., Fore, K. N., Jacobson, W. S., Kittredge, W. P., & Stewart, S. L. (1998). State strategic planning: Suggestions from the Oregon experience. *Public Administration Review, 58*(4), 353–359.

Kling, R., & Dutton, W. H. (1982). The computer package, dynamic complexity. In J. N. Danziger, W. H, Dutton, R. Kling, & K. L. Kraemer (Eds.), *Computers and politics: High technology in American local governments* (pp. 22–50). New York: Columbia University Press.

Kling, R., & Scacchi, W. (1982). The web of computing: Computer technology as social organizations. *Advanced Computing, 21*, 1–90.

Knox, K. S. (2004). Evidence-based practice with eye movement desensitizing and reprocessing. In A. R. Roberts & K. R. Yeager (Eds.), *Evidence-based practice manual: Research and outcome measures in health and human services* (pp. 324–331). New York: Oxford University Press.

Kohler, J. (2005, August 28). Abused by the system. *St. Louis Post-Dispatch*, p. A1.

Kotter, J. P. (2007). Leading change: why transformation efforts fail. 85 *Harvard Business Review 85*(1), 96–103.

Kowalewski, R. (1996). *Using outcome information to redirect programs: A case study of the Coast Guard's pilot project under the Government Performance and Results Act*. Washington, DC: United States Coast Guard, Office of Marine Safety, Security and Environmental Protection.

Kravchuk, R. S., & Schack, R. W. (1996). Designing effective performance measurement systems under the Government Performance and Results Act of 1993. *Public Administration Review, 56*(4), 348–358.

Kueng, P. (2000). Process performance measurement system: A tool to support process-based organizations. *Total Quality Management, 11*(1), 67–85.

Kuhn, R. (Ed.). (1993). *Generating creativity and innovation in large bureaucracies.* Westport, CT: Quorum Books.

Kuhn, T. S. (1996). *The structure of scientific revolutions.* Chicago: University of Chicago Press.

Langan-Fox, J., & Tan, P. (1997). Images of a culture in transition: Personal constructs of organizational stability and change. *Journal of Occupational and Organizational Psychology, 70*(3), 273–294.

Lawson, A., Biggere, A., Bohning, D., Lesarrre, E., Viel, J.-F. and Bertollini, R. (Eds.). (1999). *Disease mapping and risk assessment for public health.* Chichester, England: John Wiley and Sons.

Lee, J. (2000). Knowledge management: The intellectual revolution. *IIE Solutions, 32*(10), 34–37.

Lefkowitz, M. (2006, March 24). New stats for ACS: In continuing overhaul, child-aid agency will implement statistical system to track cases, ID trends. *Knight Ridder Tribune Business News*, p. 1.

Leigh, D. (2004). Needs assessments: A step-by-step approach. In A. R. Roberts & K. R. Yeager (Eds.), *Evidence-based practice manual: Research and outcome measures in health and human services* (pp. 622–627). New York: Oxford University Press.

Levinson, H. (1994, May). Why the behemoths fell: Psychological roots of corporate failure. *American Psychologist,* 428–436.

Levinthal, D. A., & March, J. G. (1993). The myopia of learning. *Strategic Management Journal, 14*(3), 95–112.

Liebson, R. (1999, July 14). Police leave county's cities for more pay and less work. *The Journal News*, p. 1A.

Liebson, R. (2001, December 30). Public safety chief retires after 36 years. *The Journal News*, p. 3B.

Liebson, R. (2002, January 7). Search for new safety chief irks union. *The Journal News*, p. 1B.

Lindblom, C. E. (1997). Initiating change: Modes of social inquiry. *American Behavioral Scientist, 40*(3), 264–277.

Lipman-Blumen, J., & Leavitt, H. J. (1999). *Hot groups: Seeding them, feeding them and using them to ignite your organization.* New York: Oxford University Press.

Loshin, P. (2001). Knowledge management. *Computerworld, 35*(43), 56.

Luthans, F. (2005). *Organizational behavior.* Boston: McGraw-Hill Irwin.

MacBride, S. A. (2006, November). Government restructuring: merging two organizations into one. *Public Administration Times*, pp. 5, 7.

MacDonald, S. (1995). Learning to change: An information perspective on learning in the organization. *Organization Science, 6*(5), 557–568.

Maguire, E. R. (2004, August). Police departments as learning laboratories. Washington, DC: The Police Foundation, Retrieved January 15, 2007, from http://www.policefoundation.org/pdf/Ideas-Maguire.pdf.

Maltz, M. D., Gordon, A. C., & Friedman, W. (1991). *Mapping crime in its community setting: Event geography analysis.* New York: Springer Verlag.

Mankins, M. C., & Steele, R. (2006). Stop making plans start making decisions. *Harvard Business Review, 84*(1), 76–84.

Maple, J., & Mitchell, C. (1999). *The crime fighter: Putting bad guys out of business.* New York: Doubleday.

Marshall, M. (1996). *Development and use of outcome information in government, Prince William County, Virginia.* Washington, DC: ASPA, Center for Accountability and Performance.

Martensen, K. R. (1966). Law enforcement applications in California. In *Electronic computer: A weapon for law enforcement*. New York City: New York City Police Department.

Marzulli, J. (1998, July 19). Cops tackle road perils: Computer helping them to identify hot spots. *Daily News*, p. 4.

McClendon, B. W. (2001). Working smarter by using performance audits. Retrieved October 14, 2005, from http://www.gao.gov/govaud/yb2003/html/chap 25.html

McClintock, C. (2004). Integrating program evaluation and organization development. In A. R. Roberts & K. R. Yeager (Eds.), *Evidence-based practice manual: Research and outcome measures in health and human services* (pp. 598–606). New York: Oxford University Press.

McDonald, P. (2002). *Managing police operations: NYPD crime control model COMPSTAT.* New York: Wadsworth.

McGuire, P. G. (1999). The New York Police Department Compstat process: Mapping for analysis, evaluation, and accountability. In V. Goldsmith, P. G. McGuire, J. H. Mollenkopf, & T. A. Ross (Eds.), *Analyzing crime patterns: Frontiers of practice* (pp. 134–141). Newbury Park, CA: Sage.

Medina, W. A. (1982). *Changing bureaucracies: Understanding the organization before selecting the approach.* New York: Marcel Dekker.

Melkers, J., & Willoughby, K. (2004). *Staying the course: The use of performance measurement in state governments.* IBM Center for the Business of Government. Retrieved December 22, 2006, from http://www.businessofgovernment.org/pdfs/MelkersReport.pdf

Melkers, J., & Willoughby, K. (2005). Models of performance-measurement use in local governments: Understanding budgeting, communication, and lasting effects. *Public Administration Review, 65*(2), 180–190.

Merjanian, A. (1996). *Strategic budgeting in Texas: A systems approach to planning, budgeting, and performance measurement.* Washington, DC: ASPA, Center for Accountability and Performance.

Metzenbaum, S. H. (2006). *Performance accountability: The five building blocks and six essential practices.* IBM Center for the Business of Government, Managing for Performance and Results Series. Retrieved December 22, 2006, from http://www.businessofgovernment.org/pdfs/MetzenbaumReport2.pdf

Meyerson, D. E. (2001). Radical change, the quiet way. *Harvard Business Review, 79*(9), 92–100.

Moore, M. H. (1995). *Creating public value: Strategic management in government.* Cambridge, MA: Harvard University Press.

Moore, M. H. (2003). Sizing up Compstat: An important administrative innovation in policing. *Criminology and Public Policy, 2*(3), 469–494.

Moore, M. H., & Braga, A. (2003). The "bottom line" of policing: What citizens should value (and measure!). In *Police Performance*. Washington, DC: Police Executive Research Forum.

Moore, M. H., & Braga, A. A. (2004). Police performance measurement: A normative framework. *Criminal Justice Ethics, 23*(1), 3–19.

Moore, M. H., & Trojanowicz, R. C. (1988). Corporate strategies for policing. *Perspectives on Policing, 6.* Washington, DC: National Institute of Justice.

Morris, J. (1982). *Crime analysis charting: An introduction to visual investigative analysis.* Orangevale, CA: Palmer.

Morris, M. H., & Jones, F. F. (1999). Entrepreneurship in established organizations: The case of the public sector." *Entrepreneurship: Theory and Practice, 24,* 71–91.

Moynihan, D. P. (2006). Managing for results in state government: Evaluating a decade of reform. *Public Administration Review, 66*(1), 77–89.

National Commission on Terrorist Attacks Upon the United States. (2004). *Final report of The National Commission on Terrorist Attacks Upon The United States,* New York: W.W. Norton and Company.

Neidorf, R. (2002). Knowledge management: Changing cultures, changing attitudes. *Online, 26*(5), 60–62.

New York City Police Department. (1966). *The electronic computer: A weapon for law enforcement.* New York: Author.

New York City Police Department. (1980). *Procedures for the performance of precinct crime analysis.* New York: Office of Management Analysis, Crime Analysis Section.

New York City Police Department. (1996). *Compstat: Leadership in action.* New York.

New York City Police Department. (1996). *Managing for results: Building a police organization that can dramatically reduce crime, disorder and fear.* New York.

New York City Police Department. (1998). *The Compstat process.* New York: Office of Management Analysis and Planning.

Newman, O. (1972). *Defensible space: Crime prevention through urban design.* New York: Macmillan.

Nicholson-Crotty, S., Theobald, N. A., & Nicholson-Crotty, J. (2006). Disparate measures: Public managers and performance-measurement strategies. *Public Administration Review, 66*(1), 101–113.

Niederhoffer, A., & Blumberg, A. (1976). *The ambivalent force: Perspectives on police.* Hinsdale, IL: Dryden Press.

Nunn, S. (2001). Police information technology: Assessing the effects of computerization on urban police functions. *Public Administration Review, 61*(2), 221–234.

O'Connell, P. E. (2001a). *An intellectual history of the Compstat model of police management.* Dissertation, City University of New York.

O'Connell, P. E. (2001b). *Using performance data for accountability: The New York City Police Department's Compstat model of police management.* The Pricewaterhouse-Coopers Endowment for the Business of Government. Retrieved December 22, 2006, from http://www.businessofgovernment.org/pdfs/Oconnell_Report.pdf

O'Dell, C., & Grayson, C. J. (1998). If only we knew what we know: Identification and transfer of internal best practices. *California Management Review, 40*(3), 154–163.

O'Hara, P. (2005). *Why law enforcement organizations fail.* Durham, NC: Carolina Academic Press.

O'Rourke, H., & O'Connell, P. E. (2001). Training as performance. *American Jails, 14*(6), 23–26.

Oakes, K., & Rengarajan, R. (2002). The hitchhiker's guide to knowledge management. *T + D, 56*(6), 75–78.

Orlikowski, W. J., & Iacono, C. S. (2001). Research commentary: Desperately seeking the "IT" in IT research—A call to theorizing the IT artifact. *Information Systems Research, 12*(2), 121–134.

Osborne, D., & Gaebler, T. (1992). *Reinventing government: How the entrepreneurial spirit is transforming the public sector.* Reading, MA: Addison Wesley.

Osborne, D., & Hutchinson, P. (2004). Budgeting for outcomes. *Government Finance Review, 20*(5), 5–15.

Osborne, D., & Plastrik, P. (1997). *Banishing bureaucracy: The five strategies for reinventing government*. New York: Plume.

Ostroff, F. (2006). Change management in government. *Harvard Business Review, 84*(5), 141.

Ottaway, T. A., & Burns, J. R. (1997). Adaptive, agile approaches to organizational architecture utilizing agent technology. *Decision Sciences, 28*(3), 483–511.

Page, S. (2005). What's new about the new public management? Administrative change in the human services. *Public Administration Review, 65*(6), 713–727.

Pandey, S. K., & Garnett, J. L. (2006). Exploring public sector communication performance: Testing a model and drawing implications. *Public Administration Review, 66*(1), 37–52.

Pane, N. (2004). The data whisperer: Strategies for motivating raw-data providers. In A. R. Roberts & K. R. Yeager (Eds.), *Evidence-based practice manual: Research and outcome measures in health and human services* (pp. 615–621). New York: Oxford University Press.

Paoline, E. A. (2001). *Rethinking police culture: Officers' occupational attitudes*. New York: LFB Publishing.

Parry, M. (2006, December 28). Wal-Mart gives police little to smile about. *Albany Times Union*. Retrieved January 3, 2007, from http://timesunion.com/AspStories/story.asp?storyID=548619&category=ALBANY&BCCode=&newsdate=12/28/2006

Pascale, R. T., & Sternin, J. (2005). Your company's secret change agents. *Harvard Business Review, 83*(5), 72–81.

Pascale, R., Millemann, M., & Gioja L. (1997, November/December). Changing the way we change. *Harvard Business Review*, 127–139.

Patton, M. Q. (1978). *Utilization-focused evaluation*. Beverly Hills, CA: Sage.

Pauly, G. A., McEwen, J. T., & Finch, S. (1967). Computer mapping—A new technique in crime analysis." In S. A. Yefsky (Ed.), *Law Enforcement Science and Technology, vol. 1*. New York: Thompson Book Company.

Peak, M. H. (1997). Training: No longer for the fainthearted: Training directors in learning organizations are remaking their departments to meet rigorous goals set in the boardroom. *Management Review, 86*(2), 23–28.

Perrin, B. (1999). Performance measurement: Does the reality match the rhetoric?; a rejoinder to Bernstein and Winston. *American Journal of Evaluation, 20*(1), 101–112.

Perrin, B. (2006). Moving from outputs to outcomes: Practical advice from governments around the world. IBM Center for the Business of Government. Retrieved December 22, 2006, from http://www.businessofgovernment.org/pdfs/PerrinReport.pdf

Perrow, C. (1970). *Organizational analysis: A sociological view*. London: Tavistock.

Perrow, C. (1972). *Complex organizations: A critical essay*. Glenview, IL: Scott, Foresman and Company.

Peters, T., & Waterman, R., Jr. (1982). *In search of excellence*. New York: Harper and Row.

Pfeffer, J., & Sutton, R. I. (2006). Evidence-based management. *Harvard Business Review, 84*(1), 62–74.

Plant, T., Agocs, C., Brunet-Jailly, E., & Douglas, J. (2005). *From measuring to managing performance: Recent trends in the development of municipal public sector accountability*. Toronto, Ontario: The Institute of Public Administration of Canada.

Presthus, R. (1965). *The organizational society: An analysis and a theory*. New York: Vintage Books.

Proctor, E. K., & Rosen, A. (2004). Concise standards for developing evidence-based practice guidelines. In A. R. Roberts & K. R. Yeager (Eds.), *Evidence-based practice manual: Research and outcome measures in health and human services* (pp. 193–199). New York: Oxford University Press.

Punch, M. (1983). *Control in police organizations.* Cambridge, MA: MIT Press.

Pyle, G. F. (1974). *The spatial dynamics of crime.* Chicago: University of Chicago Press.

Quinn, R. E., & Rohrbaugh, J. (1981). A competing values approach to organizational effectiveness. *Public Productivity Review, 5,* 122–140.

Quinn, R. E., & Rohrbaugh, J. (1983). A spatial model of effectiveness criteria: Towards a competing values approach to organizational analysis. *Management Science, 29*(3), 363–378.

Rainey, H. G., & Steinbauer, P. (1999). Galloping elephants: Developing elements of a theory of effective government organizations. *Journal of Public Administration Research and Theory, 9*(9), 1–29.

Reed, C. N., III. (1980). *An information system approach to the spatial display and analysis of urban crime data.* Dissertation, State University of New York at Buffalo.

Reinier, G. H., Sweeney, T. J., Waymire, R. V., Newton, F. A., III, Grassie, R. G., White, S. M., et al. (1977). *Integrated criminal apprehension program: Crime analysis operations manual.* Washington, DC: United States Department of Justice, Law Enforcement Assistance Administration.

Reiss, A. J. (1992). Police organization in the twentieth century. In M. H. Tonry & N. Morris (Eds.), *Modern Policing* (pp 51–98). Chicago: University of Chicago Press.

Reuland, M. M. (Ed.). (1995). *Information management and crime analysis: Practitioners' recipes for success.* Washington, DC: Police Executive Research Forum.

Reuss-Ianni, E. (1983). *Two cultures of policing: Street cops and management cops.* New Brunswick, NJ: Transaction.

Rich, T. (1995). The use of computerized mapping in crime control and prevention programs. *Research in Action.* Washington, DC: National Institute of Justice.

Richardson, J. B., & Stout, R. K. (1975, April). Incident prediction model for police placement. *The Police Chief,* 24–26.

Roberts, A. R., & Yeager, K. R. (2004). *Evidence-based practice manual: Research and outcome measures in health and human services.* New York: Oxford University Press.

Robertson, P. J., & Seneviratne, S. J. (1995). Outcomes of planned organizational change in the private sector: A meta-analytic comparison to the private sector. *Public Administration Review, 55*(6), 547–558.

Saldarini, K. (2000). Agencies' performance plans get mixed reviews. Retrieved December 29, 2006, from http://www.govexec.com/dailyfed/0800/080300k1.htm

Sampson, R. J. (2004). The community. In J. Q. Wilson & J. Petersilia (Eds.), *Crime: Public policies for crime control* (pp. 225–252). Oakland, CA: Institute for Contemporary Studies.

Schaffer, R. H., & Thomson, H. A. (1992, January–February). Successful change programs begin with results. *Harvard Business Review,* 80–89.

Schein, E. H. (1997). *Organizational culture and leadership.* San Francisco: Jossey-Bass.

Schiesel, S. (2004, October 21). In the ER, learning to love the PC. *The New York Times,* pp. G1–G7.

Senge, P (1994). *The fifth discipline: The art and practice of the learning organization.* New York: Currency Doubleday.

Senge, P. (1996). Leading learning organizations. *Training and Development, 50*(12), 36–38.

Serieyx, H. (1993). *Le big bang des organizations*. Paris: Calman-Levy.

Shaw, C. R. (1966). *The jack-roller*. Chicago: University of Chicago Press.

Sherman, L. W. (1998). *Evidence-based policing*. Washington, DC: Police Foundation.

Sherman, L., Gartin, P., & Buerger, M. (1989). Hot spots of predatory crime: Routine activities and the criminology of place. *Criminology, 27, 27*–52.

Sherman, L. W., Milton, C. H., & Kelly, T. V. (1973). *Team policing: Seven case studies*. Washington, DC: The Police Foundation.

Sherman, L. W., & Rogan, D. P. (1995). Effects of gun seizures on gun violence: "Hot spots" patrol in Kansas City. *Justice Quarterly, 12*(4), 673–693.

Silverman, E. (1999). *NYPD battles crime: Innovative strategies in policing*. Boston: Northeastern University Press.

Silverman, E., & O'Connell, P. E. (1999). Changing decision-making in the New York City Police Department. *International Journal of Public Administration, 22*(2), 217–259.

Simeone, R., Carnevale, J., & Millar, A. (2005). A systems approach to performance-based management: The national drug control strategy. *Public Administration Review, 65*(2), 191–202.

Simmons, J., & Kenney, D. J. (1995). *Information management and crime analysis: Practitioners' recipes for success*. Washington, DC: Police Executive Research Forum.

Sirkin, H. L., Keenan, P., & Jackson, A. (2005, October). The hard side of change management. *Harvard Business Review*, 109–118.

Skogan, W. G., & Maxfield, M. (1981). *Coping with crime*. Beverly Hills, CA: Sage.

Skolnick, J. H., and Bayley, D. H. (1986). *The new blue line: Police innovation in six American cities*. New York: The Free Press.

Smith, D. C., & Grinker, W. J. (2005). The transformation of social services management in New York City: "Compstating" welfare. New York: Seedco. Retrieved January 15, 2007, from http://www.seedco.org/publications/publications/compstating_welfare.pdf

Snyder, W. M. and Cummings, T. G. (1998). Organization learning disorders: Conceptual model and intervention hypotheses." *Human Relations, 51*(7), 873–896.

Sparrow, M. K., Moore, M. H., & Kennedy, D. (1992). *Beyond 911: A new era for policing*. New York: Basic Books.

Spelman, W. (1998). *Beyond bean counting: New approaches for managing crime data*. Washington, DC: Police Executive Research Forum.

Stamp, L. D. (1965). *The geography of life and death*. Ithaca, NY: Cornell University Press.

Stowers, G. N. (2004). *Measuring the performance of e-government*. IBM Center for the Business of Government. Retrieved December 22, 2006, from http://www.businessofgovernment.org/pdfs/8493_Stowers_Report.pdf

Strati, A. (1998). Organizational symbolism as a social construction: A perspective from the sociology of knowledge. *Human Relations, 51*(11), pp. 1379–1408.

Straub, F. & O'Connell, P. E. (1999). Why the jails didn't explode. *City Journal, 9*(2), 28-37. Retrieved January 15, 2007, from http://www.city-journal.org/html/9_2_why_the_jails.html.

Stromquist, N., & Samoff, J. (2000). Knowledge management systems: On the promise and actual forms of information technologies." *Compare: A Journal of Comparative Education, 30*(3), 323–332.

Swanson, C. R., Territo, L., & Taylor, R. W. (2005). *Police administration: Structures, processes, and behavior*. Upper Saddle River, NJ: Pearson–Prentice Hall.

Swiss, J. E. (2005). A framework for assessing incentives in results-based management. 65 *Public Administration Review, 65*(5), 592–603.

Taaffe, E. J., & Gauthier, H. L. (1973). *Geography of transportation*. Englewood Cliffs, NJ: Prentice-Hall.

Taylor, R. B., & Harrell, A. V. (1996). *Physical environment and crime. A final summary research report presented to the National Institute of Justice*. Washington, DC: United States Department of Justice, National Institute of Justice.

Taylor, R. B., & Covington, J. (1988). Neighborhood changes in ecology and violence. *Criminology, 26,* 553–589.

Teague, G. B., Trabin, T., & Ray, C. (2004). Toward common performance indicators and measures for accountability in behavioral health care. In A. R. Roberts & K. R. Yeager (Eds.), *Evidence-based practice manual: Research and outcome measures in health and human services* (pp. 46–60). New York: Oxford University Press.

Theurer, J. (1998). Seven pitfalls to avoid when establishing performance measures. *Public Management, 80*(7), 21–25.

Thomas, J. C., Kellogg, W. A., & Erickson, T. (2001). The knowledge management puzzle: Human and social factors in knowledge management. *IBM Systems Journal, 40*(4). http://www.research.ibm.com/journal/sj/404/thomas.html

Toch, H., & Grant, J. D. (1982). *Reforming human services: Change through participation*. Beverly Hills, CA: Sage.

Tran, A., Gardon, J., & Polidori, L. (2004). Application of remote sensing for disease surveillance in urban and suburban areas. In A. R. Roberts & K. R. Yeager (Eds.), *Evidence-based practice manual: Research and outcome measures in health and human services* (pp. 368–378). New York: Oxford University Press.

Tyworth, M., & Sawyer, S. (2006). Organic development: A top-down and bottom-up approach to design of public sector information systems. Paper delivered at the Seventh Annual International Conference on Digital Government Research, San Diego.

Van Wart, M. (1998). *Changing public sector values*. New York, NY: Garland.

Van Wart, M. (1995). The first step in the reinvention process: Assessment. *Public Administration Review, 55*(5), 429–438.

Verton, D. (2003). FBI begins knowledge management face-lift. *Computerworld, 37*(16), 10.

Vollmer, A. (1971). *The police and modern society*. Montclair, NJ: Patterson Smith.

Walker, S. (2003). New approaches to ensuring the legitimacy of police conduct: The new paradigm of police accountability: The U.S. Justice Department "pattern or practice" suits in context. 22 *St. Louis U. Pub. L. Rev., 22*(3), 3–52.

Walker, S., Milligan, S. O., & Berke, A. (2005). *Supervision and intervention within early intervention systems: A guide for law enforcement chief executives*. Washington, DC: Police Executive Research Forum.

Ward, T. J. (2000). Commissioners, chiefs and Compstat. *Law & Order, 48*(7), 133–138.

Ward, T. J. (2005). Beating the numbers: A commentary on the dark side of NYPD's famed Compstat system." *St. John's University, Professional Studies Review, 2*(1), 99–104.

Weisburd, D., Mastrofski, S. D., McNally, A. M., Greenspan, R., & Willis, J. J. (2003, July). Reforming to preserve: Compstat and strategic problem solving in American policing. *Criminology & Public Policy,* 421–456.

Weisburd, D., Mastrofski, S. D., Greenspan, R., & Willis, J. J. (2004, April). The growth of Compstat in American policing." *Police Foundation Reports*. Retrieved November 29, 2006, from http://www.policefoundation.org/pdf/growthofcompstat.pdf

Whisenand, P. M., & Ferguson, R. F. (2005). *The managing of police organizations*. Upper Saddle River, NJ: Pearson-Prentice Hall.

Wholey, J. S. and Hatry, H. P. (1992). The case for performance monitoring. *Public Administration Review, 52*(6), 604–610.

Willis, J. J., Mastrofski, S. D., & Weisburd, D. (2003). *Compstat in practice: An in-depth analysis of three cities*. Washington, DC: The Police Foundation. Retrieved November 29, 2006, from http://www.policefoundation.org/pdf/compstatinpractice.pdf

Willis, J. J., Mastrofski, S. D., Weisburd, D., & Greenspan, R. (2003). *Compstat and organizational change in the Lowell Police Department*. Washington, DC: Police Foundation. Retrieved November 29, 2006, from http://www.policefoundation.org/pdf/compstat.pdf

Wilson, J. Q. (1989). *Bureaucracy: What government agencies do and why they do it*. New York: Basic Books.

Wilson, J. Q., & Kelling, G. L. (1982, March). Broken windows: The police and neighborhood safety. *The Atlantic Monthly*, 29–38.

Wincelowicz, V. C. (2004). *The police culture and the marginally performing employee*. Lewiston, NY: Edwin Mellen Press.

Wright, K. N. (2003). Developing a national performance measurement system. *Federal Probation, 67*(1), 37–41.

Wuestewald, T., & Steinheider, B. (2006). Can empowerment work in police organizations? *The Police Chief, 73*(1), 48–55.

Wulczyn, F., Kogan, J., & Dilts, J. (2001). The effect of population dynamics on performance measurement. *Social Service Review, 75*(2), 292–317.

Yohe, J. P. (1997). *Management and organizational change within the NYPD: Two contrasting approaches*. Unpublished paper submitted to City University of New York, John Jay College.

INDEX